The Credential Society
**AN HISTORICAL SOCIOLOGY OF
EDUCATION AND STRATIFICATION**

The Credential Society

AN HISTORICAL SOCIOLOGY OF EDUCATION AND STRATIFICATION

Randall Collins
Department of Sociology
University of Virginia
Charlottesville, Virginia

ACADEMIC PRESS
New York   San Francisco   London
A Subsidiary of Harcourt Brace Jovanovich, Publishers

ACADEMIC PRESS, INC.
111 Fifth Avenue, New York, New York 10003

United Kingdom Edition published by
ACADEMIC PRESS, INC. (LONDON) LTD.
24/28 Oval Road, London NW1 7DX

Library of Congress Cataloging in Publication Data

Main entry under title:

The Credential society.

  Bibliography: p.
  1. Educational sociology--History.
2. Educational anthropology. I. Collins, Randall,
Date   II. Title.
LC189.C7   370.19'3   78-20042
ISBN 0-12-181360-6

Contents

The role played in former days by the "proof of ancestry" as prerequisite for equality of birth, access to noble prebends and endowments, and wherever the nobility retained social power, for the qualifications to state offices, is nowadays taken by the patent of education. The elaboration of the diplomas from universities, business and engineering colleges and the universal clamor for the creation of further educational certificates in all fields serve the formation of the privileged stratum in bureaus and in offices. Such certificates support their holders' claims for connubium with the notables (in business offices too they raise hopes for preferment with the boss's daughter), claims to be admitted into the circles that adhere to "codes of honor", claims for a "status-appropriate" salary instead of a wage according to performance, claims for assured advancement and old age insurance, and above all, claims to the monopolization of socially and economically advantageous positions.

If we hear from all sides demands for the introduction of regulated curricula culminating in special examinations the reason for this is, of course, not a suddenly awakened "thirst for education", but rather the desire to limit the supply of candidates for these positions and to monopolize them for the holders of educational patents. For such monopolization, the "examination" is today the universal instrument—hence its irresistable advance. As the curriculum required for the acquisition of the patent of education requires considerable expenses and a long period of gestation, this striving implies a repression of talent (of the "charisma") in favor of property, for the intellectual costs of the educational patent are always low and decrease, rather than increase, with increasing volume. The old requirements of a knightly style of life, the prerequisite for capacity to hold a fief, is nowadays in Germany replaced by the necessity of participating in its surviving remnants, the dueling fraternities of the universities which grant the patents of education; in the Anglo-Saxon countries the athletic and social clubs fulfill the same function.

MAX WEBER (1968:1000)

1

The Myth of Technocracy

There is a naive conception of social history that is extremely popular. People with different viewpoints give it different slants, but the basic story is much the same. The leading character is called Technology, or sometimes Science; very sophisticated storytellers have twin leads called Science and Technology. They are the active agents in the drama. In some versions, they are the heroes; in others, the villains. In all, they are endowed with overwhelming power.

There are some other characters, too. One of them is called Modern Society, who is more or less the dutiful wife, following where Technology leads her. In some accounts she drags her feet; in others she eggs him on. But it does not make very much difference one way or the other because they are married, for better or for worse. There is one other character, a kind of stepchild called the Individual. His job is to fit into the family as best he can. This requires him to be diligent and skillful. Since the family is changing, getting more scientific, technological, and complex all the time, this can be a hard job.

There are a lot of dramatic possibilities here, and our writers have exploited them all.

If it's a success story, one dwells on how the good boy works hard in school and gets his rewards and how the bad boy gets his deserts.[1] This is sometimes attached to a historical yarn about the bad old days before Society met Technology, when the good boys didn't get their rewards because somebody else had already inherited them. Academic storytellers call this the shift from "ascription" to "achievement."

If it's to be a lament, we hear all about how lonely, cruel, and alienating it is to live in this household full of modern hardware.

For do-gooders and alarmists, there is the disturbing tale with the hopeful ending: how some of the stepchildren don't really have a chance to show that they are good boys because they weren't brought up right, didn't have a good school in their neighborhood, or for some reason didn't learn what society required of them. This has been an especially popular story, since it gave people something to rush out and correct when they got through listening to it.

On the other hand, some observers have noticed that opportunities are not becoming more equal, and that the children of the same social classes and racial groups get more or less the same relative rewards as their parents got, regardless of how many efforts people make to give everyone more schooling. This has led to a resurgence of a new "scientific" racism and hereditism, for if the system is just and meritocratic, failure must be the fault of the genes.

For more way-out types, there is the twist in the story in which Technology gets so advanced that it can carry on Society all by itself and the stepchildren don't have to come in from their play after all. This hasn't happened quite yet, of course. Some writers say that all we need is a revolution, others that we just have to wait for our longhaired children to grow up and take command.

For power seekers who feel unduly neglected, there is the pronouncement that Society can no longer be managed by old-fashioned politicians and business executives because it is time for the technical experts to emerge from their laboratories and faculty clubs to take command. Why they haven't done so already is a bit of a mystery, if the story of how things happen in the modern world is otherwise true.

From the point of view of literature, Technocracy isn't a very good story. It has been repeated so many times since it was invented in the eighteenth century by Condorcet and the French *philosophes* that it's gotten to be a bore. Its popularity is obviously owing to something besides entertainment value. One reason might be that the Technocracy story is true. The problem is that it isn't. As we shall see, the sociological evidence is heavily against it, and so are the sociological theories that attempt any sophisticated view of stratifi-

---

[1]Somehow, the story never talks about the *girl* who works hard in school and gets *her* rewards. May this, although sexist, be a concession to empirical reality?

cation. So it's not truth that upholds the Technocracy story, but rather the appeals of myths.

Yet the Technocracy story does have some facts in its favor, and it is important to see just what they mean. One such fact is that existence of a very considerable amount of technological change over the last two centuries (indeed, even further back) with especially visible effects in the twentieth century on economic productivity and the organization of work. The other fact is the increasing prominence of education in our lives. American sociologists concerned with stratification have concentrated on social mobility, and one main fact has emerged from their research: Education is the most important determinant yet discovered of how far one will go in today's world. Moreover, it has been growing steadily more important in the sense that each new generation of Americans has spent more and more time in school and taken jobs with higher and higher educational requirements. And since schooling has been defined as an agency for meritocratic selection, the rising prominence of education has been the strongest argument for the existence of Technocracy.

Of all those variables that are easily measurable, education (usually indicated simply by the number of years in school) has been found to be the most important predictor of occupational success, along with parents' occupation itself, and much of the effect of parents' occupational level appears to operate through its effect on children's education. The most thorough national survey found a correlation of .60 between occupational level and years of education, as compared to a correlation of .40 between father's occupation and son's occupation, and a correlation of .44 between father's occupation and son's education (Blau and Duncan, 1967:202). This study was able to explain 42% of the variance in occupational attainment; of this, 24% was attributable to education alone, with 18% attributable to father's position, both directly and by its effect on son's educational opportunity. Another methodologically thorough study, a 7-year follow-up of all the 1957 high school graduates in Wisconsin, found education was correlated .62 with job level, whereas father's occupational job level was correlated .33 with son's job level (Sewell *et al.,* 1970). Numerous other studies support this result (Lipset and Bendix, 1959: 189–192; Eckland, 1965; Sewell and Hauser, 1975).

Studies of more specialized occupational groups, such as lawyers (Smigel, 1964: 39, 73–74; Ladinsky, 1967) and scientists (Hargens and Hagstrom, 1967), also show that education is more important than the background influence of father's occupation. Because of such findings, mobility researchers have come to focus primarily on factors determining educational attainment. Much evidence has been amassed to show how class and ethnic advantages and disadvantages operate and to show what are the relative effects of contemporary pressures, such as peer groups, teachers' practices, and the organization of educational bureaucracies (Coleman, 1966; Boudon,

1973; Cicourel *et al.*, 1974; Useem and Miller, 1975). Moreover, these patterns have existed for a long time. The expansion of educational opportunities in twentieth-century America has not much affected the way in which different social classes take advantage of these opportunities; educational attainment has maintained the same degree of correlation with father's occupation and education throughout the last 50 years (B. Duncan, 1967). In view of this failure to overcome class and racial differences, some researchers have raised again the question of innate differences in ability in affecting educational attainment (Block and Dworkin, 1976).

Historical trends show the rising importance of education in people's lives. Table 1.1 shows the rates of educational enrollment for school age groups through the last century. In 1870, 2% of the age group graduated from high school and 1.7% attended college; in 1920, 17% graduated from high school and 9% attended college; by 1970, this had risen to 77% graduating

Table 1.1
Educational Attainment in the United States, 1870–1970[a]

Year	High school students/ population 14–17 years old (%)	High school graduates/ population 17 years old (%)	College students/ population 18–21 years old (%)	B.A.s or first/ professional degree/ population 21 years old (%)	M.A.s or second/ professional degree/ population 25 years old (%)	Ph.D.s/ population 30 years old (%)	Median years of school completed/ population 25 years and older (%)
1870	2.1	2.0	1.7				
1880	2.4	2.5	2.7				
1890	3.6	3.5	3.0				
1900	7.9	6.4	4.0	1.7	.12	.03	
1910	11.4	8.8	5.1	1.9	.13	.02	
1920	26.4	16.8	8.9	2.3	.24	.03	
1930	44.3	29.0	12.4	4.9	.78	.12	
1940	62.4	50.8	15.6	7.0	1.24	.15	8.6
1950	66.0	59.0	29.6	14.8 (1949)	2.43	.27	9.3
1960	87.8	65.1	34.9	14.3	3.25	.42	10.5
1970	92.9	76.5	52.8	21.1	7.83	1.04	12.2

Sources: *Historical Statistics of the United States*, Series A28–29, H223–233, H327–338; *Statistical Abstract of the United States, 1971*, Tables 6, 24, 149, 151, 153, 164, 192, and 205.

[a]All figures involve some degree of estimation from available data, especially for the years before 1900. Note also that these are the ratios of enrollments or degrees awarded in each particular year to the size of the age group in that same year (with the exception of the last column); these are not tabulations of the members of that age group who are enrolled or achieve a degree that year. Hamilton and Wright (1975) present some data that suggest that the college attendance figures are overestimates.

from high school and 53% attending college, with 21% acquiring college degrees. The rising level of educational attainment is typically explained as follows: Industrial society develops through the application of scientific advances to new forms of technology (e.g., Kerr *et al.,* 1960; Clark, 1962; Galbraith, 1967; Bell, 1973). As a result, the school requirements of jobs change. Unskilled positions are greatly reduced, first with the decline of agriculture, then of heavy manual labor; skilled positions become proportionately more common with the rising demand for skilled technicians, clerical workers, and professional specialists. The requirements for administrative leadership positions are upgraded too, in the larger, more complex, and technically more innovative modern organizations. According to this explanation, elites must come to depend on skill rather than on family background or political connections. In general, modern societies move away from ascription to achievement, from a system of privilege to a technical meritocracy.

One implication of this analysis is that educational requirements for jobs change over time. The point is not often documented wi;h systematic evidence, however, and hence certain ambiguities remain as to just what changes in "requirements" mean. As we shall see, the evidence as to what education is *actually necessary* for jobs does not necessarily support this thesis. However, it is possible to show what requirements *employers* have set for jobs at different periods (see Table 1.2). A somewhat diverse set of samples makes precise numerical estimates unreliable, but the general trends are clear. In 1937–1938, 11% of employers required high school diplomas or more for skilled laborers; in the 1945–1946 period, this had risen to 19%; and in 1967 to 32%. For clerical jobs, the percentage requiring high school or more rose more slowly: 57% in 1937–1938; 56–72% in 1945–1946; 72% in 1967. For managers there is a dramatic postwar rise, from 12% of employers requiring college degrees in 1937–1938 (68% in the 1945–1946 sample), to 44% in 1967.

For earlier periods we must use estimates. It seems that formal schooling was of little importance through the mid-nineteenth century. This was true even for the professions, where apprenticeship training prevailed. Toward the latter part of the century, college training became necessary for the major professions; high school degrees became common among major businessmen and among minor professionals such as teachers. After World War I, professions had established firm requirements of higher education; college education in any field became the norm among major businessmen, and high school degrees began to become the criterion for clerical work. Secondary and elementary teaching now required a college degree. The Depression saw a great expansion of the school system, and after World War II these standards became less preferential and more rigorously required. Postcollege training became required by the traditional elite professions and began to

Table 1.2

Percentage of Employers Requiring Various Minimum Educational Levels of Employees, by Occupational Level, 1937–1938, 1945–1946, and 1967

Education required	Unskilled	Semiskilled	Skilled	Clerical	Managerial	Professional
National survey, 1937–1938[a]						
Less than high school	99	97	89	33	32	9
High school diploma	1	3	11	63	54	16
Some college				1	2	23
College degree				3	12	52
Total (%)	100	100	100	100	100	100
New Haven, 1945–1946[b]						
Less than high school	96	96	81		44	43
High school diploma	4	4	17		50	40
Vocational training beyond high school			2		4	1
Some college					2	10
College degree						6
Total (%)	100	100	100		100	100
Number surveyed	62	74	78		123	107
Charlotte, N. C., 1945–1946[c]						
Less than high school	100	86	81		28	30
High school diploma		14	18		65	50
Vocational training beyond high school					4	3
Some college			1		3	9
College degree						8
Total (%)	100	100	100		100	100
Number surveyed	67	91	99		104	104
San Francisco Bay area, 1967[d]						
Less than high school	83	76	62	29	27	10
High school diploma	16	24	28	68	14	4
Vocational training beyond high school	1	1	10	2	2	4
Some college				2	12	7
College degree					41	70
Graduate degree					3	5
Total (%)	100	101	100	101	99	100
Number surveyed	244	237	245	306	288	240

[a]Source: Bell (1940: 264), as analyzed in Thomas (1956: 346). Bell does not report the number of employers in the sample but it was apparently large. Totals differing from 100% are due to rounding.

[b]Source: Computed from Noland and Bakke (1949: 194–195).

[c]Ibid.

[d]Source: Survey conducted by the Institute of Industrial Relations, University of California at Berkeley, 1967.

become common among engineers and business managers. The college degree became required for managers in major business and government organizations. Clerical work, becoming confined largely to females, still remained around the norm of a high school degree, although the educational level of such workers began to move beyond this. High school graduation, and sometimes vocational training after high school, began to become required for manual positions, most commonly at skilled levels but occasionally at lower job levels as well. For example, high school degrees were required by 17% of employers of unskilled laborers in 1967, and the figure is probably higher today.

At the same time, educational requirements have become more specialized. Business administration training for managers was virtually unknown in 1900 and put in only a scattered appearance in the 1920s. With the advance of college enrollments and employers' educational requirements after World War II, however, business administration has taken on a new importance; in a 1967 survey done by the Institute for Industrial Relations at the University of California, Berkeley (see Table 1.2) researchers found that 38% of those employers who required college degrees preferred business administration students and another 15% preferred engineers. More recent data, if it were available, would probably show even more emphasis on specialization.

The explanation for these trends has commonly been treated as obvious: Education prepares students in the skills necessary for work, and skills are the main determinant of occupational success. That is, the hierarchy of educational attainment is assumed to be a hierarchy of skills, and the hierarchy of jobs is assumed to be another such skill hierarchy. Hence education determines success, and all the more so as the modern economy allegedly shifts toward an increasing predominance of highly skilled positions.

In this chapter and in the one that follows, I will break down this theory into its component parts and examine them against the relevant empirical evidence. This has rarely been done, although the evidence on most points is plentiful enough; it has only to be drawn together from disparate and perhaps overspecialized academic studies. When one does so, the technocratic model crumbles at virtually every point where one can test it against empirical evidence in a more detailed fashion. The educationocracy, which is its backbone, is mostly bureaucratic hot air rather than a producer of real technical skills. Whichever way we look at it—comparing the performance of more educated and less educated people at work, finding out where vocational skills are actually learned, examining what students pick up in the classroom and how long they remember it, examining the relationship between grades and success—the technocratic interpretation of education hardly receives any support. The same is true if we test the functional theory of stratification, of which the technological theory is a particular application.

We are left in the position of looking for an explanatory theory that will work. How do we account for the fact that modern America has come to be stratified around an educational credential system with a stranglehold on occupational opportunities and a technocratic ideology that cannot stand close examination?

In the last few years, there has been an undercurrent of radical questioning of the dominant technocratic model. But those who raise this criticism have not displaced the technocratic model because they do not really disprove it. They present plausible alternative interpretations of some of the same facts upon which technocratic theory bases itself, and in some cases add useful new evidence and new theoretical schemes. These radical critiques are not conclusive for another reason as well: They do not agree among themselves upon the particular mechanisms of an alternative explanation of educational stratification.

The most limited critique is that of Jencks *et al.* (1972). Based upon the analysis of aggregate census and survey data, they show that a good deal of career stratification is produced other than by education (some 60% of the variance is left unexplained and might just as well be attributed to chance, they argue). Examining historical trends and hypothetical projections, they claim that changes in the distribution of education do not produce changes in the distribution of rewards, and hence that educational reform is not the answer to reducing economic inequality but a diversion from that task.

The main results seem to be accurate. But the analysis leaves some central questions unanswered: Why is it that *some* stratification is correlated with, and presumably produced by, educational attainment? And why is it that this overall stratification structure exists in which increasing numbers of people have sought increasing amounts of education, even if their relative stratification positions on the whole have not changed? These are not trivial questions, for if one can understand how education contributes to stratification, even if it explains only part of the pattern, it may give us the paradigm for a more general model that explains most of stratification rather than leaving most career outcomes to an unexplicated concept of "chance."

Illich (1970), on the other hand, claims that education is indeed central to economic stratification. Education, he asserts, is not the basis of technical skills, but it does serve as a means by which opportunities to practice particular forms of work are monopolized, and hence a basis for restricting access to the actual on-job acquisition of skills. For him, the highly credentialized professions are the epitome of modern stratification. His solution for creating greater equality, then, is deschooling: to eliminate formal, compulsory education as it now stands and substitute opportunities for on-job experience in any desired occupation. The argument that education is an artificial device for monopolizing access to lucrative occupations is plausible, and it may well be that deschooling would produce an actual change in economic inequality. In both respects, the theory makes stronger claims than Jencks *et al.* But it leaves open the explanatory question: If education is technically irrelevant, by what means has it proven possible for it to monopolize job opportunities? Why do employers accept it? What general mechanism is involved?

The most systematic explanations have come from Marxian-oriented sociologists and economists. Unfortunately, these tend toward two opposing versions of the mechanism of educational stratification.[2]

On one side, there is the position found among French thinkers who argue that education serves to reproduce the class relations of capitalism. Althusser (1971) gives a very abstract argument that education serves to reproduce the social relations of production (as opposed to the material means of production), especially by providing ideological legitimation for class domination.[3] Bourdieu and his colleagues (Bourdieu and Passeron, 1964, 1977; Bourdieu *et al.*, 1974) give an empirical version of the class reproduction argument. By presenting data on the educational careers of children of different social classes, they are able to describe how class advantages are passed along through the meritocratic educational system itself. The key concept is "cultural capital," a set of cultural outlooks and predispositions that children receive from their home environment and invest in formal education. This capital determines their progress through the schools and is cumulatively enhanced or diminished, according to the previous accumulation of cultural capital, at any transition point among different levels and types of schooling within the system. Thus the older system of direct inheritance of material property has been supplanted by a system of indirect material inheritance through the direct inheritance and investment of cultural property.

The specifics of Bourdieu's reproduction argument are quite plausible. But the model does not actually disprove a technocratic interpretation of education-based work skills or even a biological-hereditist explanation of the transmissions of class advantages. In fact, Bourdieu *et al.* present the same kind of data from which American sociologists have traditionally argued

---

[2]Not all Marxian and left-oriented theories have rejected the technocratic model, however. O'Connor (1973) accepts the technocratic interpretation of education; the skills education allegedly provides are one of the infrastructural supports that the modern state provides for capitalists, and hence one of the costs contributing to the fiscal crisis. Giddens' (1973) eclectic approach includes education-based work skills as one basis of stratification.

[3]Similarly, Habermas (1970), Althusser's German counterpart in Marxist philosophical sociology, asserts that science and technology are *ideologies* by which modern stratification is legitimated and the real bases of class interest are hidden. The argument is not an empirical one, but is based on analysis of the ideas of science and technology in themselves.

technocratic claims or mildly reformist interpretations of the need to expand educational access, as well as racist-hereditist interpretations. Direct evidence to disprove the empirical contentions of the technocratic theory is needed to show that an alternative explanation is superior. Also, the larger mechanism explaining the macro pattern of educational stratification and its historical development is obscure in Bourdieu's model. To claim that this form of self-perpetuating "cultural capitalism" comes into being to protect modern industrial capitalism is formally similar to the functional model of a self-equilibrating system; only the moral tone changes from adulation of the system, in the case of American functionalists, to condemnation of it, in the case of the French. To provide an explanation of why structures develop as they have historically, one needs to compare divergent structural cases, and these raise a question as to whether capitalism per se is a sufficient explanation—as an even more exclusive reliance on stratification by culture (education) can be found in most of the communist countries today.

Another alternative that is not ruled out by the cultural capital model is contained in the claims made on behalf of black, Chicano, and other minorities that education is a form of cultural imperialism (Valentine, 1971; Carnoy, 1974). Minority members are kept in inferior class positions because they compete in a school system in terms of a culture that is alien to their own, and hence they compete at a disadvantage. The argument is most plausible for the United States and seems hardly applicable to the more ethnically homogeneous countries of Europe and elsewhere. But it cannot be ruled out as at least a partial explanation of one possible case, as the United States has a much more highly developed educational system than any other country in the world. The argument does illustrate the general difficulty of definitively accepting or rejecting plausible explanations based on showing the *results* of education for stratifying people, rather than by giving a causal explanation of how a stratification system works under particular conditions to produce various organizational structures and distributional outcomes.

The most novel and best documented work in an explicitly Marxian vein is that of Bowles and Gintis (1976). But their results and interpretations give a mechanism of educational stratification the obverse of that presented by Bourdieu's cultural capital argument (and implicitly by the ethnic minority critics as well). Bowles and Gintis present evidence that education produces compliant, disciplined workers; historically, it has been imposed on workers from above. But this contradicts the conception of Bourdieu that education is a *possession,* valued above all by the higher classes for their own benefit.[4] If

⁴Bernstein's (1971, 1973, 1975) interpretation of education tends to bolster, and give a specific interpretation of, Bourdieu's concept of education as cultural capital. Bernstein sees education as selecting and rewarding the cognitive and linguistic traits of the white-collar class, as

education is an imposition of control upon others, why is it that people compete to attain education, thereby expanding the educational system in the United States far beyond any other in the world? Why is it that the upper class and the independent, professional, upper middle class have the most education, while the order-taking working class has the least? Yet Bowles and Gintis's evidence of the psychological effects of education are strong. The contradiction is not on the level of their data but on their interpretation of it.

In sum, there are two difficulties with the critical theories of education:

1. If education leads to stratification, how does it do this? Is it a weapon or resource in the hands of those who possess it, and if so, of what nature? Is it technical skills (which most such theorists reject) or cultural capital? If the latter, how does this operate? Is it Bernstein's linguistic skills (themselves very close to functional work skills), or sheer prestige (ethnic or otherwise), or an arbitrary bureaucratic credential? Or, on the contrary, is education not a possession but an imposition, a mark of socialization into subservience?

2. These are questions of process *within* a system of educational stratification. The question also arises, Why does the *structure* take that particular form—why do educational requirements arise at particular times in history, and why do the structures of the educational systems and of the organization of occupational careers vary as they do among different countries of the modern (and premodern) world?

In what follows, I shall systematically review the evidence regarding the place of education in the economy generally and in individual careers specifically. The evidence comes from a variety of approaches. In this chapter, I review aggregate data on shifting educational levels, job skill levels, and economic development; I also review here correlations of education with on-job productivity, the sources of vocational training, and studies of what is actually learned in school. Chapter 2 will deal with studies of organizations, where work actually takes place. This will show what we know of technology's effects on work, of the struggles for control and advancement within organizations, and how education fits into these processes.

In all this, two themes become steadily more prominent: (*a*) the place of education as a cultural basis of group formation, especially for groups strug-

---

against the different cognitive—linguistic traits of the working class. Bernstein's interpretation, though, is not far from a technocratic one; these cognitive—linguistic traits are regarded as work-relevant skills based on the demands of jobs in industrialism (and increasingly, in late industrialism); the only difference from the usual meritocratic interpretation is that Bernstein sees these as directly transmitted via the family and only reinforced in the school system. Bourdieu's concept of cultural capital, on the other hand, seems to represent more of the qualities of a leisure "high culture."

gling to shape their occupational positions and careers; and (*b*) the role of technology in setting the problems and material rewards around which these struggles hinge. In Chapter 3, I will outline a general theory of the interrelations between the two realms of material production and cultural domination, within which educational stratification finds its place. The second half of the book then goes on to apply this perspective to the historical development of educational stratification in the United States. A more complete analysis would be more comparative and would show the conditions that have produced different sorts of educational structures in various parts of the world.[5] But even with a more limited historical focus, it should be possible to see how successful this approach is in accounting for the macro-structural patterns as well as the micro processes of educational stratification in America.

THE TECHNOLOGICAL RELEVANCE OF EDUCATION

The technological function theory of education may be stated in terms of the following propositions:

1. The school requirements of jobs in industrial society constantly increase because of technological change. Two processes are involved:
   a. The proportion of jobs requiring low skill decreases and the proportion requiring high skill increases.
   b. The same jobs are upgraded in skill requirements.
2. Formal education provides the training, either in specific skills or in general capacities, necessary for the more highly skilled jobs.
3. Therefore, educational requirements for employment constantly rise and increasingly larger proportions of the populace are required to spend longer and longer periods in school.

Proposition 1a. *Educational requirements of jobs in industrial society increase because the proportion of jobs requiring low skill decreases and the proportion requiring high skill increases.*

Available evidence suggests that this process accounts for only a minor part of educational upgrading, at least in a society that has passed the point of initial industrialization. Folger and Nam (1964) found that 15% of the increase in education of the U.S. labor force during the twentieth century may be attributed to shifts in the occupational structure: a decrease in the proportion of jobs with low skill requirements (unskilled laboring and service positions)

---

⁵I have outlined some part of this elsewhere, especially for historical cases prior to the twentieth century, in Collins (1977).

and an increase in jobs with high skill requirements (skilled manual, professional, technical, and managerial positions). The bulk of the educational upgrading (85%) has occurred within job categories.

Proposition 1b. *Educational requirements of jobs in industrial society rise because the same jobs are upgraded in skill requirements.*

The only available evidence on this point is Berg's study of data collected by the U.S. Department of Labor in 1950 and 1960, which judges the amount of change in skill requirements of specific jobs (1970: 38–60). Berg compares these shifts in skill requirements with overall changes in educational levels in the labor force. For several reasons, the results are not entirely clear-cut. Berg's analysis does not separate changes in the proportions of different kinds of jobs from changes in skill requirements of the same jobs. If we use Folger and Nam's figure of 15% as an estimate of changes in *kinds of jobs,* then most of Berg's evidence on skill levels shift must refer to changes *within* jobs, although the overall shifts in his data attributable to such internal job changes must be curtailed somewhat. Another ambiguous point is how much skill particular levels of education must be regarded as providing. Berg gives a number of alternative models embodying different assumptions. Under the most plausible ones, it appears that the educational level of the labor force changed somewhat in excess of that necessary to keep up with the skill requirements of jobs between 1950 and 1960. Overeducation for available jobs was found particularly among males who had graduated from college and females with high school degrees or some college, and overeducation appears to have increased during the decade 1950–1960. Whether this decade was a typical one, of course, remains to be seen. In any case, just how much the education "necessary" for employment has changed due to changes in skill levels as against other causes cannot yet be settled by quantitative measures until we know just how much skill is embodied in education and whether skills can be acquired in any other way. Evidence on this point will be taken up below.

Proposition 2: *Formal education provides required job skills.*

This proposition may be tested in two ways: (a) Are better educated employees more productive than less educated employees?; and (b) Are vocational skills learned in school or elsewhere?

Are Better Educated Employees More Productive?

The evidence most often cited for the productive effects of education is indirect, consisting of relationships between *aggregate* levels of education within a society and its overall economic activity. These are of three sorts.

1. The national growth approach involves calculating the proportion of the growth in the U.S. gross national product attributable to conventional inputs of capital and labor (Schultz, 1961: 1–16; Denison, 1965: 328–340). These inputs leave a large residual that is attributed to improvements in skill of the labor force based on increased education. This approach suffers from the difficulty in distinguishing among technological change affecting productive arrangements, changes in the abilities of workers acquired by the experience of working with new technologies, changes in skills due to formal education, and motivational factors associated with a competitive or achievement-oriented society. To assign a large proportion of the residual category to education is basically arbitrary. Denison makes this attribution because persons with higher levels of education have proportionately higher incomes, which he interprets as rewards for their contributions to productivity. Yet, although it is a common assumption in economic argument that wage returns reflect output value, wage returns cannot be used to prove the productive contribution of education without circular reasoning.

2. International correlations of levels of education and level of economic development show that the higher the level of economic development of a country, the higher the proportions of its populations in elementary, secondary, and higher education. Harbison and Myers (1964) divided countries into four groups:

> Level I comprises 17 countries (almost all in Africa) with an average per capita GNP of $84.
> Level II comprises 21 countries (all in Asia and Latin America) with average per capita income of $182.
> Level III includes 21 countries (mostly in southern and eastern Europe, plus the richest Asian and Latin American countries) with an average per capita GNP of $380.
> Level IV includes 16 countries (Europe plus the English-speaking countries) with average per capita GNP of $1,100.

These four groups correlate .89 with a composite index of enrollment in schools of all grades.

But *within* each of these four economic levels, there is no significant correlation between economic development and education. Within Level IV, for example, Denmark and Sweden have the lowest education enrollment indices (77 and 79 respectively, as compared to a median of 105 for the whole group and a high of 261 for the United States) but have per capita GNPs well above the median; conversely, France, Japan, and the Netherlands have educational indices above the median (108, 111, and 134) but per capita GNPs below the median. Many of these variations are explicable in terms of political demands for access to education (Kotschnig, 1937; Ben-

David, 1963–1964: 247–330; Hoselitz, 1965: 541–565). Even the overall correlations of educational enrollment with levels of economic development do not settle the question of causality: Which causes which? Education may be a luxury that richer countries can afford or that more democratic governments are made to provide by the people. The overproduction of educational personnel in countries whose level of economic development cannot absorb them suggests that the demand for education need not come directly from the economy and may run counter to economic needs.

3. Time lags of education and economic development can help settle the question of the direction of causality. Such correlations show that increases in the proportion of the population in elementary school precede increases in economic development (Peaslee, 1969: 293–318). The take-off point occurs once 30–50% of the 7- to 14-year-old group is in school. Peaslee suggests similar anticipations of economic development for increases in secondary and higher educational enrollment, but the data do not support this conclusion. The pattern of advances in secondary school enrollments preceding advances in economic development is found in only a small number of cases (12 of 37 examined by Peaslee). The pattern in which growth in university enrollments is followed by subsequent economic development is found in 21 of 37 cases, but the exceptions (including the United States, France, Sweden, Russia, and Japan) are of such importance as to cause serious doubt on any *necessary* contribution of higher education to economic development. The main contribution of education to economic productivity, then, appears to occur at the level of the transition to mass literacy and not significantly beyond this level.

Direct evidence of the contribution of education to *individual* productivity is summarized by Berg (1970: 85–104, 143–176). It indicates that better educated employees are not generally more productive and in some cases are less productive than others among samples of American workers at various levels. The levels of education being compared, of course, are relative to a particular range. Among factory workers (both male and female), maintenance men, and department store clerks, comparisons are between various levels of education at or below the high school degree. Among bank tellers, secretaries, factory technicians, insurance salesmen, airport controllers, and military technical personnel, comparisons centered on high school versus some college training or college degrees; in these cases, where differences did exist, workers with high school training were found to be more productive than persons with more education, but they were also more productive than persons with less education. In a number of these samples, education was not related to performance at all. Berg also includes a study of engineers and research scientists in major electrical manufacturing industries; this contrasted educational qualifications from below the B.A. level through the Ph.D., and found the average performance evaluation of Ph.D.s to be the highest, but no differences among below-B.A., B.A., and M.A. levels.

This evidence does not show that persons with no schooling at all are better employees than those with college or advanced degrees; since virtually no such totally uneducated employees are available today, the comparisons are simply not made. Most plausibly, given the necessity for literacy and certain cognitive skills in these jobs, certain minimal educational qualifications do exist. What Berg's data do show is that job skill cannot be assumed to be related to educational levels in a simple linear fashion, and that beyond certain plateaus the relationships may well be reversed. Berg also shows that better educated employees are more likely to be dissatisfied with jobs and to change jobs more often than less educated persons—evidence that education may be primarily regarded as a matter of status by those who possess it.

Are Vocational Skills Learned in School or Elsewhere?

There are a number of ways to approach this question. For some specific manual skills, there are studies of on-the-job and vocational school training. There is also evidence of how retraining is carried out in organizations experiencing technological changes. For higher level jobs, evidence is less direct. As we shall see, it is plausible that many of the skills for the learned professions, as well as for other high-level posts, are acquired on the job, but the existence of legal requirements for degrees (e.g., in medicine, law, or pharmacy) makes a comparison group of noneducated practitioners unavailable, at least in the modern era. As a substitute, we may examine evidence on what is learned in schools and what bearing school grades have on subsequent occupational performance.

Vocational Education

Vocational education in the schools for manual positions is virtually irrelevant to job fate. A 1963 study showed that most skilled workers in the United States acquired their skills on the job or casually (Clark and Sloan, 1966: 73). Of those (41% of the total) who did have some formal training, over half (52%) received this in the armed forces, in apprenticeship programs, or in company training rather than in public schools, commercial schools, or correspondence courses. Persons who do have formal vocational education do not generally fare better than those without it; graduates of vocational education programs are no less likely to be unemployed than high school dropouts (Plunkett, 1960: 22–27; Duncan, 1964: 121–134). A major reason for the failure of vocational schooling is probably that vocational high schools are known as places where youthful troublemakers are sent to remove them from the regular schools. The warfare between teachers and students at a regular high school is considered mild compared with the real gang-type violence (often with ethnic or racial overtones) that is reputed to occur at "Tech." Even if a vocational student happens to learn some usable skills, his or her attendance at a vocational high school is likely to be taken by the discerning employer as a sign of bad character.

Retraining

A 1967 survey of 309 employing organizations in the San Francisco Bay area provides information on retraining in response to technological change.[6] Retraining for technological change appears to be surprisingly easy. The vast majority of organizations (84% in this survey) were able to retrain their own labor force informally on the job in a period of not more than 3 months. Formal education was used little in retraining, and when it was used, 90% of the organizations completed it in less than 3 months. In one very modern and highly innovative chemical plant, a major technical change—the building of a new type of power plant—required only that one man be sent out for 2 months of technical training. This plant seemed to be on a technological plateau. It already had relatively high educational requirements and had been undergoing technological changes constantly for many years. As a result, changes were handled internally without changes in educational requirements for employment; the only trend reported by the industrial relations manager was the promotion of semiskilled workers to maintenance jobs. Such technological plateaus may have been reached by many (or most) organizations in this sample. Previous studies have shown similar patterns: relatively easy retraining for technological change, although sometimes accompanied by decreases in employment for less skilled workers (Bright, 1958: 85–97).

What Is Learned in School?

There has been little study of what is actually learned in school and how long it is retained. What evidence is available, though, suggests that schools are very inefficient places of learning. Many of the skills used in managerial and professional positions are learned on the job, and the lengthy courses of study required by business and professional schools exist in good part to raise the status of the profession and to form the barrier of socialization between practitioners and laymen. The degree to which education provides mainly

---

[6]Organizations employing 100 or more persons were sampled from all industry groups. Further information on this survey is provided in Collins (1969) and Gordon and Thal-Larsen (1969).

these status and socialization functions varies among occupations. It seems to
be great in pharmacy, where the 4-year university course is felt by the practitioners to be "good for the profession," but in which a few months' training
is sufficient for work competence (Weinstein, 1943: 89). Schools of education
are often criticized as requiring courses of little value to the actual practice of
teaching. Schools of medicine and law include many requirements that practitioners admit are forgotten in later practice and do not include many of the
essentials that are learned through experience and coaching on the job. Business schools are increasingly used as a recruitment channel for managers, but
their level of instruction is not generally high. Most business schools prepare
their students for a particular first job rather than teaching skills that may be
useful throughout the career. Moreover, the particular kind of training taken
often turns out to be irrelevant, as most graduates find jobs outside of their
own specialty (Pierson, 1959: 9, 55–85, 140; Gordon and Howell, 1959:
1–18, 40, 88, 324–337).

There are also indications that most students, at least in the United
States, do not learn very much in school. Learned and Wood, testing college
students at 2-year intervals in the 1930s, found very small increments in their
performance on standardized tests in their areas of study, suggesting that very
little of what is learned in particular courses remains even through the next
few years (1938: 28). More recent applications of achievement tests to high
school students found that average levels of proficiency in reading, science,
and mathematics are far below what is considered the norm for such levels.
International comparisons of mathematics proficiency scores of high school
seniors found American students the lowest of 12 countries, with an average
score of 13, as compared to scores of 22 to 37 for the other 11 countries.[7]

These results should be seen in the context of studies of what happens in
American schools. From the 1920s through the 1960s, observational and
survey research has shown that the primary focus of attention in schools has
been on nonacademic concerns (Waller, 1932; Coleman, 1961; Holt, 1964;
Becker *et al.*, 1968).[8] Teachers have been mainly concerned with maintaining authority in an ongoing struggle with the students. Athletics and other
extracurricular activities are stressed by teachers and administrators as well as
by students, especially for their ritual functions in maintaining school order. At
college as well as at secondary levels, close studies of what actually happens
find students preoccupied with strategies for achieving grades with a

---

[7]*National Assessment of Educational Progress* (1970); Husen *et al.* (1967). It is claimed that
the top American students are comparable to those elsewhere. But this is beside the point.
Clearly the massive American educational system does not provide *widespread* scientific skills
"demanded" by a high stage of technological development exemplified in America.

[8]See Bidwell (1965: 972–1022) for a summary of organizational studies.

minimum of learning. As in other formal organizations, there is a struggle in schools over standards of evaulation and much goal displacement away from official aims in the direction of meeting the informal exigencies of keeping the institution running.

The content of public school education has consisted especially of middle-class culture rather than academic skills per se. The nineteenth-century schools emphasized more than anything else strict obedience to old-fashioned standards of religious propriety. The Progressive reforms resulting from the influx of working-class children through compulsory attendance laws substituted milder forms of socialization, such as student government and supervised activities. Studies from the 1920s through the 1960s have indi-cated the general success of such programs in involving at least the middle-class students, plus an upwardly mobile minority of others, into these adult-controlled imitations of middle-class adult sociability (Waller, 1932: 15–131; Becker, 1961: 96). Their success is also indicated by the widespread inculca-tion of nonpartisan but highly idealized beliefs about the political system among American school children (De Charms and Moeller, 1962: 136–142; Hess and Torney, 1967). In sum, what is learned in school has much more to do with conventional standards of sociability and propriety than with instru-mental and cognitive skills.

Grades and Success

Such observations are relevant to interpreting the data on the relation-ships between grades and subsequent occupational performance. Evidence on this point is mixed. A 20-year follow-up of high school graduates in several cities found that grades in high school were not related to subsequent income, unless the student went on to graduate from college (Wolfle and Smith, 1956: 201–232). A study of living college graduates in 1947–1948 found that men who reported mostly A grades in college had higher incomes than others, but that the differences among B, C, and D students were negligible (Havemann and West, 1952, Charts 37–38). Among women, however, there were few differences by grades even at the A level, except that women in nonteaching professions who had A records earned somewhat more than others. A study of Dartmouth College alumni from the class of 1926, followed up 30 years later, used college records rather than personal recollections of grades; it also reported that students with the highest grades reported the highest incomes (Husband, 1957: 157–158). This result was confined to a contrast between the very best students (those with grade point averages of 3.10 and over on a scale of 0–4.00) and all the others; among the remaining (with grade point averages from 1.7 to 3.09), there were no differences in income. Even sharper differences in income were found between those with high and low participation in extracurricular activities, especially in campus politics; intercollegiate athletics were also important for later success. A 1951 study of Fresno State College graduates, on the other hand, found no relationships between grades and income (Jepsen, 1951: 616–628). Similarly, a 1963 follow-up of a national sample of a 1958 college graduating class found little relationship between grades and subsequent occupational success (Sharp, 1970: 110).

Other studies show very low correlations between college grades and success for students trained in business, engineering, medicine, school teaching, and scientific research (Goslin, 1966: 153–167; Jencks and Riesman, 1968: 205). Medical school grades bear no relationships to success in various kinds of medical practice (Price *et al.*, 1963). For officers graduating from military academies, academic record makes little or no difference to subsequent evaluation or promotion; instead, participation in intercollegiate athletics has been the best predictor of success (Janowitz, 1960: 134–135). Among business students as well, participation in extracurricular activities has been generally more important than grades (Gordon and Howell, 1959: 79–80). A 5-year follow-up of 1963 business school graduates found no correlations between occupational success and either grades, instructors' ratings, or school achievement tests (Cox, 1968). For engineers, high college grades and degree levels generally predict high levels of technical responsibility and high participation in professional activities, but not high salary or supervisory responsibility (Perrucci and Perrucci, 1970: 451–463).

The most reliable finding is that grades are good predictors of subsequent *academic* performance. Thus high school grades predict college grades, and college grades predict admission to graduate school (Holland and Nichols, 1964: 55–65; Wegner, 1969: 154–169). It is probably for this reason that grades bear some relation to occupational success, especially in the Haveman and West 1948 study of college students (1952) and among the Dartmouth students (Husband, 1957); grades are particularly important in providing access to the advanced training required for the high-paying professions. Thus a follow-up study of students entering the University of Illinois in 1952 found that high school grade rank had a small effect on occupational attainment, mainly because the better students went on to professional training (Eckland, 1965).

It appears, then, that grades are tied to occupational success primarily because of the certification value of educational degrees rather than for the skill (often negligible) that they themselves may indicate. It is known that employers generally do not select employees on the basis of their school grades; rather, they look for the completion of a degree in particular subjects and especially for diffuse "personality" characteristics (Thomas, 1956: 356–357; Drake *et al.*, 1972: 47–51). Grades, and the capacity to get them, operate as specialized forms of control within the school system itself, reflecting the teacher's judgment on students' compliance with instruction. The sheer amount of school work done seems to be the best predictor of high grades, with the highest grades reserved for work done in amounts beyond what is asked for (Sexton, 1961: 279–280). It is also known that grades are not related to measures of creativity and possibly bear some inverse relation to creativity. Teachers prefer and reward the hardworking, compliant students and tend to dislike the more innovative ones, especially if they do not respect routine discipline (Getzels and Jackson, 1962; Torrance, 1964).[9]

It is also known that grades are highly correlated to social class background (Sexton, 1961: 25–86). Strikingly enough, when class background factors are held constant by statistical analysis, differences in achievement scores among schools by quality of teaching, facilities, or by the amount of funds spent on them disappear (Coleman, 1966: 290–330). This suggests that schools have relatively little effect on learning, except insofar as they mold those disciplined cultural styles already prominent among the higher social classes; grades simply reward and certify displays of middle-class self-discipline.

In sum, shifts in the proportions of more skilled and less skilled jobs do not account for the observed increase in the educational level of the American labor force. Economic evidence indicates no clear contributions of education to economic development beyond the provision of mass literacy. Education is often irrelevant to on-the-job productivity, and is sometimes counterproductive. Specifically vocational training seems to be derived primarily from work experience rather than from formal school training. The actual performance of schools themselves, the nature of the grading system and its lack of relationship to occupational success, and the dominant ethos among students suggest that schooling is very inefficient as a means of training for work skills.

The evidence so far has focused on education. But it is also possible to investigate the nature of work itself and the organizational relationships within which it takes place. This is the subject of Chapter 2.

---

[9]Higher creativity scores are found among students in conflict-ridden urban schools than in conformist suburban and small-town schools. See Boyle (1969: 71–90).

2

Organizational Careers

Organizations and occupations by now have been thoroughly studied, and the general theoretical principles involved are relatively clear. It is striking how little the technological version of functionalist argument shows up in this area. For the major findings of organizational studies—from the industrial management tradition of Mayo, Barnard, and Simon; from the Chicago tradition of Hughes, Wilensky, Goffman, and Dalton; from the power-oriented analyses of Weber and Michels, Selznick, Gouldner, Etzioni, and Crozier—have been that organizations are sites of incessant maneuvers for autonomy and control. The main actors on the stage are informal groups, alike at the level of workers and managers, staff and line, professional and layman. Technology enters into the picture above all as it affects the resources for power struggles. In Weber and Michels, we see it as a resource for centralized control, especially as it allows for concentration of the channels of communication upon which organizational members depend. More recent studies (e.g., Simon *et al.,* 1954) have shown many instances of it operating with the reverse effect, providing areas of local autonomy down in the organizational structure where members control access to areas of uncertainty and hence shape the communications upon which their hierarchic superiors must act. Crozier (1964: 145–174) and Wilensky (1956, 1968) have raised this to a systematic principle, showing that the power of technical experts can be either high or low, depending on whether they can control exclusive access to an area of crucial uncertainty. Accordingly, technicians are motivated to shape their "skills" for maximal political effect on the organization, in some instances keeping them traditionalistic, in others innovative, depending on where the greatest threat to their autonomy is found. Technology is thus a resource whose use is shaped by its place in the more central organizational process: the struggle of informal groups for favorable power positions.

THE IMPORTANCE OF TECHNOLOGY IN ORGANIZATIONS

Theory and research on organizations has put technology in an important place. It is crucial in explaining organizational structure and organizational processes. Organizational structure is correlated with the type of task attempted and with the technology available to carry it out (Woodward, 1965; Collins, 1975: 315–329). Organization theory distinguishes four main types:

1. In **unit production,** a single unique item or a few items are produced at a time, as in skilled crafts or innovative engineering projects.
2. **Mass production** consists in the making (or procuring) and assembling of many separate parts, as in most manufacturing of machinery.
3. **Process production** is a continuous flow of materials from one stage of processing to the next, as in chemical plants or many kinds of food production.
4. In **pooled production,** a number of independent units or individuals all carry out similar operations, supplied and administered by a central staff, as in banking or many clerical agencies.

Each technology is associated with a distinctive type of organizational structure. It is relatively flat and unbureaucratic in unit production. Mass production organizations are the archetypal organizational pyramid, highly bureaucratic, with many specialized staff and line divisions, and with considerable divergence of informal and formal networks. Process production is organized as a relatively smoothly operating bureaucracy, with few lower-level workers and relatively routine administrative divisions above. Pooled production has a large base and a relatively small administrative component and tends to be bureaucratically rigid and static.

Does this mean that we can speak straightforwardly of technological determinism in organization? Not if we mean to imply that other variables do not remain important for our explanations. The question is: Into what *social* relations does technology fit? Production is not a simple issue of moving and combining materials, but of controlling, coordinating, and motivating the individual workers. Organizations are structures of power. Since power both leads to intrinsic rewards or pains and is the means for appropriating wealth and physical ease, any power structure generates an implicit struggle to gain, hold, or evade control. Different tasks attempted and different technologies to work with lead to differences in the organization's control problems.

The principal variable is: How standardized and easily inspectable are the outcomes of work? For example, unit production has a relatively undifferentiated organization because the innovative, highly unsettled work patterns result in difficulties in establishing any rigid hierarchic controls; power is more equally spread among the participants, resulting in a flatter, more informal structure. Mass production, however, results in a sharp differentiation of the lower-level workers with repetitive, highly controllable jobs from the higher-level workers involved in the activities of coordinating the various parts of the process, negotiating its schedules, and experiencing the unpredictable difficulties of this operation. The result is a very hierarchic, complex, and conflictual bureaucracy. Tasks and technologies also affect power struggles by establishing particular degrees of coordination problems. Pooled production involves relatively easy coordination, since administrators have only to provide resources and check up on personnel whose activities are essentially independent of each other. Process production also makes coordination easy, since machines do most of it, linking the various areas together automatically and reducing the worker's role in checking and troubleshooting. High coordination problems, on the other hand, exist in unit and mass production types, although they have different ways of structurally dealing with this because of their differences in the inspectability of the basic tasks and hence in the autonomy of the lower-level workers.

In other words, technology feeds resources and problems into an ongoing social struggle for control and autonomy and for the goods and rewards one may get from organizations. The correlation between technologies and types of organizational structure is explainable only because different kinds of problems and material resources lead to different sorts of distributions of power in these struggles. A complex technology does not necessarily result in increased skill demands of the workers; its effects can go in either direction. The greatest power within organizations does not necessarily go to those with the highest technical skills nor to those working directly with the most advanced machinery. Rather, the technology merely sets part of the stage for the whole environment of organizational power struggles. The crucial variable is the ease or difficulty of control. If highly productive machinery or highly technical skills are easily planned, their outcomes easily predictable and observable, then the power of their practitioners is low, since it can be routinely controlled by others.

e-level administrators, by passing along, withholding, and struc-
nation about one part of the organization for the view of other
ower analogous to (but more local than) those of the externally
ministrators at the top.

ne viewpoint, the "political" side of organizations—the uncertain-
rmation, finances, and external influences mediated by admin-
can be seen as control of a type of technology, the technology
nications. And indeed, historical differences among types of organi-
epend strongly upon the availability of different types of technology
1975: 315–413). The shift from patrimonial to bureaucratic forms
zation depended upon the introduction of massive communications
gies in the form of written reports and records. Modern communica-
transportation technologies—telephones, automobiles, duplicating
es, computers, etc.—have further shifted resources for control in the
strative arena. The tradition of analysis that most successfully explains
within political organizations, for example, within political parties, fo-
n control of the means of communications as the key resource. In one
then, we can see organizational control as highly affected by the crucial
rces of technology. But we must distinguish between **technologies of
uction** and **technologies of administration and communication.**
e latter that rules organizations in the sense of giving its controllers the
ions of highest prestige, material rewards, and of power in the long-run
e of major organization-shaping decisions.

If we push our analysis one step further, we may see that the crucial
ors in administrative power are fundamentally social and political. The key
nnological resources are the means of communication and administration,
these are the outer forms of the structure of domination. That structure
lf is a network of persons making bargains and threats and manipulating
pectancies and solidarities. It is a social network in which participants play
the ideas and emotions of the others in an effort to acquire their confi-
ence or awe, which in turn will result in the financial and political credit that
n be transmitted into internal organizational domination. It is through suc-
essful interpersonal politics of this sort that communications technology is
nade to pay off, and it is through this kind of success that further access to
communications technology is generated. The technology itself is thus appropriated by a political process.

The fundamentals of that process are essentially interpersonal, which is
to say cultural. The key resource of powerful individuals is their ability to
impress and manipulate a network of social contacts. This depends on their
easy understanding of the criteria of membership and prestige, and their
ability to use them—first, for social acceptance into the network itself and then
for prominence within it. These cultural styles may come from previous status
group traditions (such as class, ethnic, or educational cultures), or they may

Power depends instead on being i
is crucial for other organization member
levels of power as well as for the hig
production organization, maintenance n
cause they alone can deal with breakdow
does not mean that they dominate the org;
much informal deference, since they can l
others' work. The maintenance men, howe
policy in general, or hire and fire others; tl
resources whose provision has an element
different level of the organization. Top manag
advisors) have this power when they operate
the organization in which political and fin
(Wilensky, 1956). Some areas of uncertainty, i
damental than others. Maintenance men may c
uncertainties of machine breakdowns; top admin
cians control access to negotiations over crucia
influence that may keep the entire organization (
tirely.

Notice how these uncertainties relate to tecl
technology is *most* reliable that its practitioners h;
where it is *least* reliable, but where it is in a middle
effective, but not in a fashion absolutely predictable
technology is of the greatest advantage for power. Bι
must be astride the flow of production in such a way t.
dent upon it. Above all, it is how the particular task
structure of organizational coordination that is crucial. A
tions derive greater or lesser power to become autonom
highly prestigious, and remunerative professions, dependii
involve a task skill in this esoteric middle range of effectiven
is a skill crucial to the profession's clients (as we shall see i

The most crucial uncertainties, then, may not be clos
basic productive technology at all. The most fundamental ι
business organization is its finances; for any government (
nances are mediated by its environment of political support
Those who control the finances control the very presence of al
pants in the organization. However, this power is not absolute.
operations, once an organizational pattern has been set up, main
and other analogous controllers of local, intermediary, and intei
uncertainty have their moments of power when they cannot be o
a more complex view of an organization, we would recognize mai
modes of power at different moments; the internal communications

of the middl
turing infor
parts, has ι
oriented ac
From
ties of inf
istrators—
of commι
zations d
(Collins,
of organ
technolc
tion an
machin
admini
power
cuses (
sense,
resou
prod
It is t
posit
sens

fact
tecl
bu
itse
ex
oi
d
c

be to some extent created anew within the experiences of that organizational network. But it is ultimately this culture of "organizational politics" that is the crucial resource, one that can bring all the other resources into its orbit.

Technology, then, is an important aspect of organizations, and it is a variable that correlates with major differences in organizational structure and with differences in power position within organizations. It is not so much the productiveness of the technology that bestows power, however; it is the way that technology plays into the political process of organizations that makes it a variable determining organization structure. Ultimately, the political process rests upon social and cultural ground—the ground of human manipulation of communications into various kinds of interpersonal networks.

SKILL DEMANDS AND ORGANIZATIONAL PROCESSES

There is considerable evidence that the "demands" of any occupational position are not fixed, but represent whatever behavior is settled upon in bargaining between the persons who fill the positions and those who attempt to control them. Individuals want jobs primarily for the rewards to themselves in material goods, power, and prestige; the amount of productive skill they must demonstrate to hold their positions depends on how much clients, customers, or employers can successfully demand of them, and this in turn depends on the balance of power between workers and those who pay for their work.

Much evidence has shown that work groups have informal structures as well as formal ones. Typically, the informal group in a work place sets and enforces norms controlling the rate of work of its members. Such informal controls over output have been most widely studied among workers in manufacturing, but they have also been found among sales and clerical personnel (Roy, 1952: 427–442; Blau, 1955; Lombard, 1955). The rate of work is usually set at a comfortable level, considerably below maximum possible output.

Managers have some formal discretion to set their own work pace, and they put in a longer working day on the average than do other categories of workers (Wilensky, 1961: 33–56). Nevertheless, it does not seem likely that the average manager is forced to work at his or her highest possible level of skill and effort either. An informal organization exists among managers as among other workers, and the amount of work that administrators do depends at least as much on their initiative and cooperation as on formal authority (Barnard, 1938; Merton et al., 1952: 397–422; Dalton, 1959). The widespread existence of "bureaucratic pathologies," such as evasion of responsibility, empire building, and displacement of ends by means ("red tape"), indicates that administrators often use their discretion in ways that minimize rather than maximize efficient performance. Since administrative work is only indirectly related to the output of the organization, it is difficult for employers to judge very precisely what the performance of their administrators is. Indeed, the busy supervisor rarely checks up on many of his managers' activities, especially the activities of those in staff positions (Strauss and Sayles, 1960: 463; Dill *et al.*, 1962).

The employer's conception of the skill requirements of most jobs, then, tends to be rather imprecise. In March and Simon's terms, the strategy is usually to "satisfice" rather than to optimize—that is, to set average levels of performance as satisfactory and to make changes in procedures or personnel only when the performance falls noticeably below the minimum standards (1958: 140–141). At all levels, wherever informal organizations exist, it appears that standards of performance reflect the power of the groups involved.

Ability Tests

Efforts have been made to predict work performance by objective tests, but without great success at this time. Part of the difficulty has been the problem of directly measuring performance, except on specific mechanical tasks (such as those involved in piloting an airplane) or in tests of academic knowledge (Anastasi, 1967: 297–306; Wesman, 1968: 267–274). Many tests have been based on measurements of attitudes and interests of incumbent job holders, such as samples of current managers. These tests are used to select new recruits who reveal personality traits similar to those already employed. Research psychologists have pointed out that such tests generally lack validation. In order to check them, a control group of persons *lacking these traits* must also be hired so that the performance of the two groups might be compared. But this has not been done. Given the imprecise nature of job assessment, it seems likely that a wide variety of personnel can perform most jobs satisfactorily; those persons selected by the use of tests do well enough because of the self-fulfilling prophecy involved in the use of nonvalidated tests.

Evidence that the ability requirements of many jobs in modern society are not stringent is provided by a study of 109 retarded children with IQs near 60, followed up when they were over 50 years old (Baller *et al.*, 1967: 235–327). Few were in institutions. Most worked as unskilled or semiskilled laborers, but 18% held white-collar jobs, including positions as office and sales clerk, policeman, shop foreman, auto and real estate salesman, photographer, laboratory worker, and businessman. Occupational success was not related to intelligence differences within this group. Rather, the more successful workers were those who had the middle-class patterns of dress, speech, and personal behavior, and those who had worked throughout their careers in a single big business or who early attained some skill such as barbering. Other studies have found that there is a considerable range of measured intelligence within any occupational group so that although professionals have higher average intelligence than manual workers, there is a considerable degree of overlap among them (Thomas, 1956: 285–310).

It is possible to see why measures of ability, such as IQ, cannot be used as simple predictors of success. "Intelligence" operates primarily within the context of the school system, and its greatest utility is in predicting grades (Duncan, 1966a, 1966b, 1968; Bajema, 1968: 317–319). Moreover, motivation and the cumulative effects of past learning are deeply entwined with inherent differences in capacity in affecting performance on such tests. The IQ scores of children diverge as they grow older and are affected by different environments; these scores also diverge as children build up different styles of behavior (Turner, 1964; Rehberg *et al.*, 1970).[1] It is most likely for these reasons that both school grades and IQ scores are highly related to social class and to race insofar as it corresponds to class distinctions.

The whole subject of innate versus environmental effects on IQ, including recent controversy over racial differences, is given undue prominence as a cause of social inequality. If the utility of IQ tests is confined almost entirely to measuring capacity for academic success—which is not surprising in view of the fact that IQ tests were developed for use in schools and have received few other applications—then the major issue concerns how and why education is tied to occupational stratification. If the ability differences, whether inherent or acquired, that determine school success are only artificially linked to occupational success through the certification value of school degrees, then the psychological problems of individual adaptation to the school system become secondary to the structural problems of explaining the links among social institutions. In practical terms, selection through the schools rewards a particular sort of conforming behavior.

Career Processes

Detailed evidence on the processes of organizational careers shows the overwhelming importance of both informal ties and the struggle to control positions. Studies of promotion patterns show a prevailing pattern of personal

---

[1]Turner argues that IQ is an *effect* of school success rather than simply its cause, through a cumulative enhancement of motivation. It is probably for this reason that scores of IQ and of creativity are not correlated. They indicate different sorts of motivation: the first for disciplined, methodological, and hence *nonoriginal* work; the second, for a relatively self-sufficient, autonomous kind of behavior. It is small wonder, then, that teachers upholding school discipline prefer students with high IQs and dislike those with high creativity (Getzels and Jackson, 1962; Torrance, 1964).

sponsorship, whether within industrial organizations, medical careers, or trade union bureaucracies (Glaser, 1968: 191–257). It is because of the importance of personal acceptability to the sponsoring official and group that ethnic background, old school ties, and club memberships are important in careers. Ethnic distinctions among positions have been pervasive in American industry (Nosow, 1956). A study of a New England factory found that promotion to managerial positions went heavily to WASPs or Germans, Republicans, Masons, and local yacht club members (Dalton, 1951: 407–415). A similar study of industries and businesses in one metropolitan area of the South found that promotion depended on membership in civic organizations, family status, and personal friendships (Coates and Pelligrin, 1957: 200–215). Social origins affect one's career by making one acceptable in the informal culture of the organization, even when they do not directly give one a position by inheritance or family influence.

Even where there are formal tests and evaluations, as in military promotions, often combined with formal rules of "up or out" by certain ages or time in grade, informal connections are crucial in acquiring the kinds of assignments that bring an individual to the attention of superiors and provide the background considered appropriate for promotion (Janowitz, 1968: 211–215). In industrial organizations as well, informal connections are crucial in assignment to those positions that allow horizontal movement and in avoiding too specialized dead-end jobs (Martin and Strauss, 1968: 203–210). The key to success, in other words, has little to do with skilled performance per se, but rather with maneuvering to reach the sequence of positions that lead upward. Positions as assistant to plant manager are a first key; in big corporations, the final line to the top moves through the biggest divisions or plants.

Studies of organizational succession show the same pattern. As in the theory of vacancy chains (White, 1970) such evidence shows that individual success depends much less on the quality of performance than on being in the right place at the right time; insofar as individual cleverness or motivation pays off, it is by differentiating between persons who are aware of such contingencies and those who are not. The very fact that filling a given vacancy sets off a chain reaction of promotions helps to reinforce informal organization around cliques; a vertical group of leaders, protégés, and subprotégés attempts to capture an entire line of vacancies, and part of the "political" strategy of organizational leaders is the deliberate manipulation of vacancy prospects to ensure subordinates' loyalty (Glaser, 1968: 307–376).

Demotion fits the pattern again. The striking thing about evidence on demotions is that so much effort is spent on disguising demotions, by giving meaningless titles, transfers, and failing to promote; overt demotion into a lower position is very rare indeed for incumbents of white-collar or managerial positions (Glaser, 1968: 259–306). A ruthless application of criteria of efficient performance is rarely seen; instead, one gets the impression that white-collar careers are heavily ritualized and devoted to disconnecting as far as possible any direct connection between performance and reward. The causes cited for demotions do not mention merit judgments; rather, individuals are caught in impersonal conditions such as sharply fluctuating work loads, organizational crises caused by mergers or lack of profits, position obsolescence, or previous promotion to levels where rivalry for further movement becomes too great for the individual's resources (usually his or her informal connections relative to others') (More, 1968: 287–294).

One supposes that there must be *some* "merit" factor in organizational careers, but within any large organizational structure, it seems to be very difficult to measure the individual's contribution apart from the rest of the organization and the external contingencies of the time. Certainly organizations spend little effort on serious, comparative measures of individual efficiency (i.e., attempting to hold other factors constant). The overriding fact is that an organizational career is made in a political environment, and success goes to those individuals who recognize that fact and act on it most assiduously. The one who makes it to the top is the organizational politician, concerned above all with informal ties, maneuvering toward the crucial gatekeepers, avoiding the organizational contingencies that trap the less wary.

GATEKEEPERS AND CULTURAL CONTROLS

The basic problem of all organizational authorities is controlling members and gaining their active cooperation. Organization theorists have listed a number of means of control and have suggested that different controls may be substituted for one another (see especially Etzioni, 1961; Collins, 1975: 298–315). If an organization can exercise **normative control** (internalization of organizational goals and values by its participants), it can improve performance and avoid the disruptive consequences of relying on coercive authority or purely financial rewards. The expensiveness of labor turnover adds a direct economic incentive for selecting workers for their loyalty to the organization.

Organizational authorities may develop loyalty or normative control in several ways: by recruiting already committed persons; by indoctrinating new recruits within the organization; by exposing its members to the influence of informal work groups and isolating them from contacts with outside; by offering them possibilities for promotion; by offering pensions and fringe benefits tied to length of service; or by selecting individuals who have acquired the proper values and attitudes through education. The higher the organization's demand for loyalty, the more of these means of control it may be expected to use.

All jobs require some initiative and cooperation, but some require more than others. Managers have more autonomy and responsibility than production and clerical workers; hence it is most important to exercise normative control over managers. Moreover, the managerial tasks in some organizations require more loyalty than in others. In some organizations there is considerable emphasis on interpersonal coordination, especially through personal contacts; such coordination can be accomplished most easily if the people involved share common values and backgrounds. A manager's success often depends on his or her "personality" (i.e., social skills and values). According to the personnel managers in 90 large American corporations surveyed in the 1950s, motivation, interpersonal skill, and moral character are the most important qualities for business managers (Gordon and Howell, 1959: 79–80). Extremely high intellect is not considered necessary nor even desirable, and specialized or technical skills are considered to be of minor importance, at least above the level of lower supervisory jobs and specialized staff jobs such as accounting. The importance of common social standards for good managerial coordination is illustrated by the administrative difficulties of the early period in the United Nations, when there were great differences in cultural styles among staff members (Kehoe, 1949: 375–380). Managers often advance in an organization by becoming part of a team or clique, usually working closely as assistants to a sponsoring executive. Failure, too, depends heavily on social skills; a survey of 76 large corporations in 1952 reported that 90% of the managers dismissed from their jobs were reported to have been lacking in desirable personality traits, not in technical skills (Martin and Strauss, 1968: 203–210).

Evidence that education has been used as a means of cultural selection may be found in several sources. Hollingshead's study of midwestern school children, school dropouts, and community attitudes toward them suggests that employers used education as a means of selecting employees with middle-class attributes (1949: 360–388). School dropouts were largely from lower-class and working-class families, especially because of their conflict with middle-class values in the school. Although their expectation was to improve their economic position by finding immediately well-paying jobs, employment opportunities for them were limited to very menial positions, since employers regarded dropouts as untrustworthy and lacking in the qualities of desirable employees. Although high school graduates may also begin work at lower levels, their possession of education qualifies them in the eyes of employers (and in their own eyes) both for higher pay and promotion opportunities not open to dropouts. Similarly, a 1945–1946 survey of 240 employers in New Haven, Connecticut and Charlotte, North Carolina indicated that employers regarded education as a screening device for employees with desirable (i.e., middle-class) character and demeanor (Noland and Bakke, 1949: 20—63).

A more systematic test is provided by a 1967 survey of 309 California organizations.[2] The relative normative control emphasis of an organization was indicated in three ways:

1. It is indicated by the organization's relative emphasis on the absence of police record for job applicants; this proved to be significantly correlated ($\gamma = .25$) with an index of the organization's educational requirements.

2. It is indicated by the relative emphasis on a record of job loyalty among applications; reluctance to hire "job-hoppers" also proved correlated ($\tau - b = .18$) with educational requirements.

3. It is also indicated by a classification of organizational goals, deriving from Etzioni's comparative study of organizational control forms,[3] adapted to distinguish between "public trust" organizations, which emphasize a public image of service ideals, safeguards and/or confidentiality, and "market" organizations, which are primarily concerned with selling a product or service and making a profit, not with establishing a reputation of honor or trustworthiness. The public trust category includes financial, professional service (medical, legal, educational, engineering, accounting), government, public transport, communications, and utilities organizations. In the market category are included mining, manufacturing, business transportation, wholesale and retail trade, and other services.

Public trust organizations have considerably higher requirements than market organizations. Organizational control type is significantly associated with overall education ($\gamma = .40$, $p < .001$), with white-collar education

---

[2]Organizations employing 100 or more persons were sampled from all industry groups. Further information on this survey is provided in Collins (1969, 1974) and Gordon and Thal-Larsen (1969).

[3]Etzioni (1961) found that organizations with differing goals emphasize different types of controls over their employees: Organizations with narrowly profit-making goals emphasize remunerative (financial) controls; those with idealized goals of providing services or upholding standards emphasize normative controls (the internalization of organizational purposes through socialization); those with custodial goals emphasize coercive controls. Etzioni's classification derives from Max Weber's tripartite distinction of economic, status, and power realms. It also draws on Weber in that it is a set of analytical distinctions describing pure types, which are usually found mixed in particular cases and which may be used to characterize relative emphases. Thus remunerative controls are found especially in factories and stores; normative controls in churches, hospitals, religious institutions, research laboratories, professional firms, and public agencies; coercive controls in prisons, concentration camps, custodial mental hospitals, and peacetime armies. Etzioni's research summary deals primarily with the lower, nonmanagerial members of organizations and notes that all organizations at their higher ranks emphasize normative control, whatever controls are used below. Neverthelss, the scheme may be extended to all levels within organizations as a means of focusing on those in which there is a relative emphasis on normative control.

($\gamma = .33$, $p < .01$), and with manager's education ($\gamma = .31$, $p < .001$). There is no significant relationship between organizational control type and blue-collar educational requirements, however.

The three indicators of normative control are highly interrelated. Requirements for police records and reluctance to hire job-hoppers are significantly higher in public trust organizations than in market organizations. These interrelations tend to mutually validate the three indices as actually representing emphasis on normative control over employees. There appears to be a coherent group of organizations with relatively high educational requirements at white-collar and managerial levels, characterized by organizational goals emphasizing a public service image, carefully screening their employees for prior normative violations and for evidence of employee loyalty.

The 1967 survey of California organizations provides yet another piece of evidence to indicate the normative importance of educational requirements. Employers were asked what actions were taken to recruit for "hard-to-fill" vacancies in the organization. For every occupational group mentioned, one solution to recruitment difficulties was overwhelmingly popular: to increase the number of recruitment channels used. Only one organization in the sample indicated as its primary response that it lowered educational requirements. Apparently, organizations rarely lower their educational requirements except perhaps under conditions of severe labor shortage. Indeed, they almost never relax any of the specifications of the kind of employees they want, even such technically extraneous qualities as sex or appearance, nor do they often dilute the content of jobs or institute training programs in times of labor shortage if they do not have them already. We may term this tendency for educational requirements, once instituted, to change only in an upward direction, the "ratchet effect." It appears that there are strong normative and status reasons for organizations to keep up educational requirements, even when technical and economic pressures for doing so are absent or even contrary.

Business Administration Degrees

A more specialized use of education for normative control is business administration training. Surveys during the 1950s of employers in nationally prominent organizations indicated that they regarded college degrees as important in hiring potential managers, not because they were thought to ensure technical skills, but rather because they indicate "motivation" and "social experience" (Gordon and Howell, 1959: 121). Business school training is similarly regarded less as evidence of necessary training (as employers have been widely skeptical of the utility of this curriculum for most positions) than as an indication that the college student is committed to business attitudes.

Employers may want business values taught in special schools because liberal arts students are oriented toward the professions and their service ideals and are indifferent or even hostile to the profit-making interests of business. For example, liberal arts students are more dissatisfied with business jobs than business or engineering students (1959: 124; cf. Jacob, 1957). Furthermore, employers are more likely to refuse to hire liberal arts graduates if they come from a college that has a business school than if their college lacks a business school (Gordon and Howell, 1959: 84–87; see also, Pierson, 1959: 90–99). In the latter case, the students could be said not to have had a choice, but when both business and liberal arts courses are offered and the student chooses liberal arts, employers appear to take this as a rejection of business values.

The 1967 California survey also indicates that organizations concerned with normative control over their managers emphasize the selection of managers with business administration degrees. Overall, "public trust" organizations are more likely to require such degrees than "market" organizations. In a more detailed analysis, it appears that organizations desiring business administration students are concentrated in three industrial groupings: (*a*) an extremely marketing-conscious manufacturing group (food, fabricated metals, printing); (*b*) a public-relations-conscious transportation and utilities group (air and water transportation, gas and electric services); and (*c*) the administrators of large-scale service organizations (hospitals and schools). It is noteworthy that the latter are the service organizations in which administrators have the lowest status in relation to their professional staffs.[4]

The concern for business administration degrees, then, may be related to the status concerns of the managers themselves in organizations in which they are crucial but consider themselves underappreciated by the "production" personnel. The business administration degree also seems to be considered a loyalty test. As the personnel manager in the national headquarters of a food-processing company put it, his company wanted "business administration or other evidence that liberal arts graduates are interested in business."

STATUS LINKAGES BETWEEN EDUCATION AND OCCUPATION

The cultural membership model may also be tested by examining the cases in which it predicts that education will be relatively important in occupa-

---

[4]This pattern has also been found in Perrow (1965: 950).

tional attainment. Education should be most important where two conditions hold simultaneously: (*a*) where the type of education most closely reflects membership in a particular status group; and (*b*) where that status group controls employment in particular organizations. Thus education will be most important where the fit is greatest between the culture of the status groups emerging from schools and the status group doing the hiring; it will be least important where there is the greatest disparity between the culture of the school and that of the employers.

This fit between school group culture and employer's culture may be conceptualized as a continuum. The importance of elite education is highest where it is involved in selection of new members of organizational elites and should fade off where jobs are less elite (either lower-level jobs in these organizations or jobs in other organizations not controlled by the cultural elite). Similarly, schools that produce the most elite graduates will be most closely linked to elite occupations; schools whose graduates are less well socialized into elite culture are selected for jobs correspondingly less close to elite organizational levels.

In the United States, the schools that produce culturally elite groups, either by virtue of explicit training or by selection of students from elite backgrounds, or both, are the private prep schools at the secondary level and the elite colleges (the Ivy League and to a lesser extent the major state universities); at the professional training level, the schools that produce elite groups are those professional schools attached to the elite colleges and universities. At the secondary level, schools that produce respectively socialized, nonelite persons are the public high schools (especially those in middle-class residential areas); from the point of view of the culture of Anglo-Protestant employers, Catholic schools and all-black schools are less acceptable. At the level of higher education, Catholic and black colleges and professional schools are less elite, and commercial training schools are the least elite form of education.

In the United States, the organizations most clearly dominated by the Anglo-Protestant upper classes are the large, nationally organized business corporations and the largest firms (Domhoff, 1967: 38–62). Those organizations more likely to be dominated by members of minority ethnic cultures are the smaller, local businesses in manufacturing, construction, and retail trade; in legal practice, minoity ethnic cultures are more often found in solo than in firm employment. In government employment, local governments appear to be more heavily dominated by non-Anglo ethnic groups, whereas particular branches of the national government (notably the State Department and the Treasury) are dominated by WASP elites (Domhoff, 1967: 84–114, 132–137).

Education and Law Practice

Among lawyers, the predicted differences are clear: Graduates of law schools attached to elite colleges and universities are more likely to be employed in firms, whereas graduates of Catholic or commercial law schools are more likely to be found in solo practice (Ladinsky, 1967: 222–232). The elite Wall Street law firms have been most educationally selective in this regard, choosing not only from Ivy League law schools, but also from a group whose backgrounds include attendance at elite prep schools and colleges (Smigel, 1964: 39, 73–74, 117). These same firms have been selective in other ways as well. Membership in elite Wall Street law firms and promotion to partnership within them is greatly facilitated by having a Social Register background, and women, Catholics, Jews, and blacks have been almost automatically excluded. There are also indications that graduates of ethnically dominated professional schools are most likely to practice within the ethnic community: This is clearly the case among black professionals.

Education and the Business Elite

Studies based on both biographical and survey data give a consistent picture of the American business elite. The business elite has always been highly educated compared to the rest of the populace. For example, Newcomer found that 39.4% of the top executives in 1900 had some college education, as did 51.4% of the top executives in 1925, and 75.6% in 1950 (1955: 68–69). These figures may be compared with the total percentage of the male population of ages 18 through 21 enrolled in college in the census years (1870, 1890, 1910) nearest to the time that the median age of each executive group was 20: 4.6% in 1870; 4.7% in 1890; and 6.2% in 1910. Even in the early nineteenth century, the business elite was preponderantly drawn from the best educated section of the populace, as well as from the highest social classes. Those members of the elite from lower social origins also had less education than the businessmen of upper- and upper-middle-class origins.

Approximately 55–65% of the business leaders seem to have received significant assistance from relatives in their careers, the proportion remaining constant through the last century and a half. In the 1925 and 1950 cohorts of one study of executives, 14% had inherited their companies and another 7–14% had acquired them by financial investment; interestingly, the proportion inheriting their positions rises to 27% (1925) and 23% (1950) among those with college degrees (Newcomer, 1955: 80; cf. Lipset and Bendix, 1959: 138). To put a similar finding from another study in a different way,

72% of the more recent business leaders who inherited their positions attended college, as compared with 34% of those who achieved their positions by entrepreneurship (Bendix, 1956: 230). The business elite, then, is drawn from relatively high social origins, and such origins are important in business careers. The business elite has always been highly educated in relation to the American populace, but education seems to be a correlate of their social origins rather than the determinant of their success (Taussig and Joslyn, 1932: 200; Newcomer, 1955: 76; Mills, 1963: 128). In general, the evidence that graduates of black colleges and Catholic colleges (at least before very recent years) have attained lower occupational positions in business than graduates of white, Protestant schools also bolsters this interpretation (Jencks and Riesman, 1968: 357–366; Sharp, 1970: 64–67).[5]

Comparative Organizational Evidence

The 1967 California survey provides the most direct test of the effects of organizational status on educational requirements. Organizational status was indicated in two ways: (a) by a "national prominence" index, based on whether the organization's markets and its headquarters were local or national; and (b) by the size of the organization in terms of numbers of employees. Neither index is totally satisfactory as a pure indicator of organizational status, but size and national prominence are significantly associated and both relate to educational requirements in specific contexts in very similar fashion, suggesting that both indicate the same underlying variable. Size is significantly associated with overall educational requirements ($\gamma = .29$), as well as with white-collar educational requirements ($\gamma = .28$), blue-collar requirements ($\gamma = .25$), and manager's educational requirements ($\gamma = .26$). National prominence is significantly associated with the overall educational index ($\gamma = .23$), and approaches the .05 level of statistical significance in

---

[5]There is evidence that discrimination against a number of minority groups has dropped in the 1970s, with at least token integration into major businesses, law firms, and other organizations. Clearly, the source of this shift is political pressure, not a sudden rise in technological demand for skills selected on a nonascribed basis. Such trends do not affect the *analytical* significance of the earlier evidence, which is not cited for descriptive purposes, but rather to test the *relationship* among the factors by which employment patterns are being explained. Political factors are easily (in fact, quite centrally) within the scope of this model. But what would we expect, since shifting political pressures tend to prohibit overt discrimination by group background? The use of educational credentials as a more abstract kind of cultural current might be expected to rise. This has been demonstrated for France by Bourdieu *et al.* (1974). That it may be the case in the United States as well is suggested by the fact that in the California employer survey, the organizations that made the most efforts at racial integration were those with the highest educational requirements.

its association with white-collar education ($\gamma = .24$), blue-collar education ($\gamma = .17$), and manager's education ($\gamma = .20$). The 1946–1947 study of New Haven and Charlotte, N.C. (see Table 1.2) also reported higher educational requirements in the bigger, presumably more nationally organized firms (Noland and Bakke, 1949: 78).

It is possible to interpret this evidence according to the technical–functional theory of education, arguing that the elite schools provide the best technical training and that the major national organizations require the greatest degree of technical talent. What is necessary is to test simultaneously for technical and status conflict conditions. This is provided by the California

Table 2.1
Strength of Relationship between Organizational Type and Educational Requirements, with Controls for Technological Change and Size

	γ	$p<$	N
Organizational type			
and education index	.40	.001	307
Low technological change	.54	.001	144
High technological change	.21	.01	148
Less than 250 employees	.50	.001	130
250–999 employees	.24	.20	122
1000 or more employees	.26	.30	55
Organizational type and			
white-collar education index	.33	.01	306
Low technological change	.49	.001	144
High technological change	.14	.50	147
Less than 250 employees	.53	.01	130
250–999 employees	.16	.20	121
1000 or more employees	.06	.70	55
Organizational type and			
blue-collar education index	.04	.98	282
Low technological change	.15	.80	128
High technological change	−.07	.95	139
Less than 250 employees	−.46	.70	120
250–999 employees	−.26	.70	121
1000 or more employees	.32	.50	56
Organizational type and			
managers' education requirements	.31	.001	282
Low technological change	.51	.01	131
High technological change	.07	.05	136
Less than 250 employees	.53	.02	125
250–999 employees	.08	.01	114
1000 or more employees	.21	.70	48

Source: San Francisco Bay Area Employer Survey, 1967.

employers' study, which examines the effects of normative control emphasis and organizational prominence, while holding constant the organization's technological modernity as measured by the kinds of technological and organizational changes in the previous 6 years. Indeed, technological change was found to be significantly related to educational requirements at managerial ($\gamma = .13$) and blue-collar ($\gamma = .26$) levels (although not for overall or white-collar requirements), thus giving some support to the technical–functional theory of education.

It is possible that the relationships thus far reported are spurious. For example, large organizations may be those with higher rates of technical change, and hence their higher educational requirements may be the result of technological needs rather than organizational prominence per se. In order to control for such possibly spurious associations, each of the major variables—organizational size, technological change, and normative control emphasis—were introduced as controls into the analysis of educational requirements. The results shown in Tables 2.1 to 2.4 indicate that each variable has an independent effect on educational requirements, but each seems to

Table 2.2

Strength of Relationship between Size and Educational Requirements, with Controls for Technological Change and Organizational Type

	γ	$p<$	N
Size and education index	.29	.001	307
Market organizations	.34	.01	226
Public trust organizations	−.06	.20	81
Low technological change	.44	.01	144
High technological change	.10	.20	148
Size and white-collar education index	.28	.001	306
Market organizations	.37	.001	225
Public trust organizations	−.12	.70	81
Low technological change	.40	.01	144
High technological change	.14	.50	149
Size and blue-collar education index	.25	.05	282
Market organizations	.50	.10	217
Public trust organizations	.25	.20	65
Low technological change	.49	.10	127
High technological change	.05	.95	139
Size and managers' education	.26	.01	287
Market organizations	.33	.01	209
Public trust organizations	−.09	.10	78
Low technological change	.36	.10	137
High technological change	.16	.10	136

Source: San Francisco Bay Area Employer Survey, 1967.

Table 2.3

Strength of Relationships between National Prominence and Educational Requirements, with Controls for Organizational Type, Size, and Technological Change

	γ	$p<$	N
Prominence and education index	.23	.05	287
Market organizations	.39	.01	226
Public trust organizations	.14	.10	81
Less than 250 employees	.21	.20	130
250–999 employees	.27	.20	122
1000 or more employees	.19	.30	55
Low technological change	.33	.02	144
High technological change	.11	.70	148
Prominence and white-collar education index	.24	.10	306
Market organizations	.39	.01	225
Public trust organizations	.01	.80	81
Less than 250 employees	.23	.70	130
250–999 employees	.22	.70	121
1000 or more employees	.28	.50	55
Low technological change	.30	.10	144
High technological change	.17	.30	147
Prominence and blue-collar education index	.17	.10	282
Market organizations	.22	.10	217
Public trust organizations	−.06	.30	65
Less than 250 employees	.15	.20	120
250–999 employees	.24	.05	111
1000 or more employees	.02	.10	41
Low technological change	.28	.20	127
High technological change	.13	.20	139
Prominence and managers' education	.20	.10	282
Market organizations	.35	.05	209
Public trust organizations	−.09	.70	78
Less than 250 employees	.24	.30	125
250–999 employees	.27	.10	114
1000 or more employees	−.02	.30	47
Low technological change	.31	.20	137
High technological change	.09	.50	136

Source: San Francisco Bay Area Employer Survey, 1967.

operate most strongly in the organizational context where the other variables are weak. Technological change produces significantly higher educational requirements only in smaller, localistic organizations and in organizational sectors not emphasizing normative control. Organizational size and prominence produce significantly higher educational requirements in organizations

Table 2.4
*Strength of Relationships between Technological Change Index and Educational Requirements,
with Controls for Organizational Type and Size*

	γ	$p<$	N
Technological change index and education index	.12	.20	292
Market organizations	.23	.02	214
Public trust organizations	−.14	.30	78
Less than 250 employees	.21	.10	123
250−999 employees	−.01	.20	117
1000 or more employees	−.19	.50	52
Technological change index and white-collar education index	.12	.20	291
Market organizations	.22	.01	213
Public trust organizations	−.12	.50	78
Less than 250 employees	.20	.05	123
250−999 employees	.04	.50	116
1000 or more employees	−.16	.50	52
Technological change index and blue-collar education index	.26	.02	267
Market organizations	.30	.10	205
Public trust organizations	.14	.50	62
Less than 250 employees	.47	.10	113
250−999 employees	.14	.20	106
1000 or more employees	.03	.80	48
Technological change index and managers' educational requirements	.13	.001	272
Market organizations	.24	.001	198
Public trust organizations	−.14	.70	75
Less than 250 employees	.14	.01	118
250−999 employees	.11	.05	105
1000 or more employees	−.06	.50	46
Technological change index and professionals' educational requirements	.14	.98	225
Market organizations	.16	.70	157
Public trust organizations	.13	.98	70

Source: San Francisco Bay Area Employer Survey, 1967.

with low rates of technological change and in sectors de-emphasizing normative control. Normative control emphasis produces significantly higher educational requirements in organizations with low technological change and in
smaller and less prominent organizations. It appears that a ceiling effect is
operable: High educational requirements can be produced either by strong
normative control emphasis, organizational prominence, or a high rate of
technological change. Within contexts where one of these variables produces

high requirements, the introduction of other variables does not show significant differences.

The relative effects of normative control, organizational prominence, and technological change may be assessed by comparing the measures of association in the context in which each is strongest (i.e., within the realm where the other organizational variables are weak). At all levels except blue-collar requirements (which are especially influenced by organizational size and technology), the strongest determinant of educational requirements is organizational control type, followed by organizational prominence (measured either by organizational size or national prominence), with technological change producing the weakest effects.[6] The relative weakness of technological change in explaining upper-level educational requirements is in keeping with the findings of a study of top business executives in national business, which indicated that the most highly educated managers were found in the least economically vigorous firms rather than in the most rapidly developing ones (Warner and Abegglen, 1955: 141−143, 148).

CULTURAL CREDENTIALS AND MOBILITY BARRIERS

Finally, let us consider the nature of career channels within organizations. For although the prevailing rhetoric of meritocracy emphasizes the openness of career possibilities, the reality is closer to a castelike separation among major occupational blocs.

The California employers' survey is especially revealing on this score. Table 2.5 indicates the most generally used recruitment channels for the various occupational levels. Manual laborers are recruited primarily through

---

[6]For overall educational requirements, normative control emphasis produces γ of .54 and .50; size produces γ of .34 and .44; national prominence, .39 and .33; technological change produces γ of .23 and .21. For white-collar requirements, γ are: normative control emphasis, .49 and .53; size, .37 and .40; national prominence, .39 and .30; technological change, .22 and .20. For managers' educational requirements, γ are: normative control emphasis, .51 and .53; size, .33 and .36; national prominence, .35 and .31; technological change, .24 and .14. For blue-collar requirements, γ are: control emphasis, .15 and −.46; size, .50 and .49; national prominence, .22 and .28; technological change, .30 and .47. Another comparison of the relative strength of these variables in affecting educational requirements can be made by taking their uncontrolled measures of association, irrespective of interaction with other variables. For overall educational requirements, organizational control type is associated by a γ of .40; organizational size, .29; national prominence, .23; technological change, .12. For white-collar requirements, γ are: control type, .33; size, .28; prominence, .24; technological change, .12. For managerial requirements, γ are: control type, .31; size, .26; prominence, .20; technological change, .13. For blue-collar requirements we have: technological change, .26; size, .25; prominence, .17; control type, .04. However we look at it, the same rank order obtains.

Table 2.5
Percentage of Organizations Relying Primarily on Various Recruitment Channels, by Occupational Group

Recruitment channels	Professional	Managerial	Clerical	Sales	Skilled	Semiskilled	Unskilled	Service
Direct hiring	15	6	16	24	11	14	24	33
Employment agencies	20	6	56	18	12	10	20	21
Schools and colleges	15	2	1	2	1			
Unions	2		5	7	43	45	41	31
Newspaper advertisements	17	5	12	11	12	7	5	8
Promotion from within	10	73	2	22	11	13	4	
Personal referrals	9	4	2	15	5	2	3	3
Transfers	4	3	1	2				
Other channels	7	2	4		6	8	4	4
Total (%)	99	101	99	101	101	99	101	100
Number surveyed	261	302	304	166	247	239	244	207

Source: San Francisco Bay Area Employer Survey, 1967.

unions, clerical workers primarily through employment agencies. The only occupational group recruited in any numbers through schools and colleges is professionals. The highest concentration in one channel, however, is for managers: 73% of employers in this sample indicated that they ordinarily promote their managers from within.

There is a certain ideological tone about this claim. It is part of a general philosophy expressed by one personnel manager in a cliché delivered with ringing conviction: "There are no dead-end jobs, there are only dead-end people!" Numerous respondents commented in this vein. "There are no artificial barriers to advancement in this company. A man can go as far as his talents will take him." Like most ideologies, this kind of statement has some connection with reality; but like most ideologies, it also idealizes and over-generalizes that reality.

If an employer were seriously interested in promoting from within, one might expect that he would have low educational requirements for manage-rial positions. However, there is no statistically significant difference in educa-tional requirements for managers between organizations that recruit mana-gers primarily from within and those that do not. Even organizations recruiting primarily from within have educational requirements for managers that are a good deal higher than for any other occupational groups except professionals (see Table 1.2). Where, then, do they recruit their managers from? Higher managerial positions are no doubt filled from lower managerial positions, but where do the lower-level managers come from? Some personnel managers stated that they hired managers from within as a general policy, but they then added that the present managers were probably not replaceable from below. Like these organizations, numerous companies meet the problem by actually hiring from outside. Several personnel managers stated that college degrees were required of such outside recruits but not of managers promoted from below.

It can be inferred that managers rarely come from the manual level. When employers speak of every job as being "promotable," they mean that every entry job has some other job above it to which a worker may aspire. They do not usually mean to imply (except in the vaguest, most ideological sense) that there is a clear channel of promotion from the bottom to the top. There is almost always a promotion ladder from unskilled and service positions to skilled and sometimes foreman positions, and employers in interviews often volunteer comments about how much such upgrading occurred. Nevertheless, no prideful instances were ever cited about movement from manual into nonmanual positions, and some casual comments indicated that employers thought of manual and nonmanual (and clerical) categories as hermetically sealed off from each other, although the opportunities were wide open within each.

Somewhat more systemative evidence confirms this impression. When naming positions customarily filled by upgrading, employers mention managerial positions in relative frequency of rank (see Table 2.6). High-level managerial positions were most often mentioned, but the lowest-level managerial positions were mentioned relatively infrequently. Similarly, upper-level clerical jobs were the most mentioned as filled from within; lower-level clerical jobs the least; and the same pattern may be found within the skilled labor group.

If one compares the educational requirements for managers with those for skilled workers, it is clear that few skilled workers can hope to be promoted into the managerial ranks, at least not without quitting and getting an education before returning. One personnel manager epitomized this situation by stating, after emphasizing the virtues of promotion from within: "We never hire people for jobs who can't be upgraded. All our file clerks are trained to become secretaries."

It is also rarely the case that clerical workers are promoted to managerial positions. The caste system in this case is based on sex: Clerical workers are mostly women, and women are rarely made managers outside of supervisory positions in clerical sectors. There is a clear demarcation between the educa-

Table 2.6

Percentage of Jobs Customarily Filled by Promotion from Within

	Percentage mentioning particular classifications		
Managers and officials	54.7	Clerical jobs or office jobs	2.6
Managers, officials, administrators	21.6	Secretaries	1.3
Department managers or department heads	10.4	Stock clerks and shipping clerks	.3
Assistant department managers or assistant heads	2.9	Other clerical occupations	.7
Store managers	2.3	Skilled occupations	19.9
Assistant store managers	1.6	Foremen, leadmen	10.5
Supervisors or supervisory jobs	9.4	Dispatchers	1.3
First-line supervisors	4.9	Journeymen	2.9
Other managerial occupations	1.6	Other skilled occupations	5.2
		Semiskilled occupations	8.1
Professional and technical occupations	11.1	Truck drivers	.3
Instructors or teachers	.3	Apprentices in skilled trades	.3
Registered nurses	.7	Machine operators	2.0
Engineers, chemists	2.0	Assemblers	.3
Accountants	1.0	Pressmen, cutters, adjusters	.7
Draftsmen	.3	Inspectors	.3
Engineering technicians	.3	Other semiskilled occupations	4.2
Laboratory technicians and assistants	.7		
Other professional and technical	5.8	Unskilled occupations	1.0
		Lube and wash men (garage)	.3
Sales occupations	7.2	Other unskilled occupations	.7
Salesmen	6.9		
Junior salesmen	.3	Service occupations	5.9
		Head custodians	1.9
Clerical occupations	16.9	Policemen and firemen (above entry level)	.7
Upper-level clerical or top clerical jobs	12.0	Waiters and waitresses	.3
		Cooks	1.0
		Nurses' aides and orderlies	.3
		Gardeners and groundsmen	.7
		Busboys, etc.	.3
		Other service occupations	.7

All jobs customarily filled by upgrading	19.9
Almost all jobs customarily filled by upgrading	21.8
No jobs customarily filled by upgrading	2.6
Specific jobs or classifications mentioned	55.7
Total (%)	100
Number Surveyed	307

Source: Gordon and Thal-Larsen (1969, Table 8.11).

tional requirements for managers and clerical employees: High school is the modal requirement for the latter, college graduation for the former.[7]

The primary recruitment channels within organizations for managers are sales and professional positions. Several personnel managers stated that there were no entry jobs for managers and volunteered the information that managers were likely to come in as professionals. It is apparent that employers have a much broader view of "professional" jobs than professional associations do; 25% of employers indicated less than a college degree as the educational requirement for professionals and 10% indicated less than a high school degree (Table 2.2). Similarly, 10% of the employers indicated that they recruit their professionals from within (Table 2.5). It is likely that many employers consider any staff or technical job as "professional."[8] Many studies have shown that there is considerable movement back and forth between staff and line positions and, indeed, between professional and managerial positions.

When employers recruit managers from within, then they mean primarily that they recruit from other high-level positions in the organization and from professional positions. Moreover, it is for "professional" positions, whatever the actual content of the job, that the "recruitment from within" ideology is generally *not* held to apply. Organizations that recruit their managers from within (very likely from professional ranks) are just as likely as other organizations to have high educational requirements for professionals. Some 74% of the former require college degrees or higher of their managers, as compared to 78% of the latter, a difference that is not statistically significant.

Educational requirements act as a formidable barrier to promotion across the manual–nonmanual caste barrier in organizations (the clerical–managerial barrier seems less based on educational requirements, partly because it is so noncontroversial; rather, it is based quite blatantly on the ascriptive quality of sex). The "promotion from within" ideology is used to cover up this barrier, and the ideology is even carried out in practice, but within limits. Through such organizational subterfuges as promotion within the professional

---

[7]The survey indicates that there are relatively few organizations in which more than 5% of the managers are women, and these organizations are concentrated in a few industrial sectors: medical, educational, and personal services; government; finance; and certain types of trade (department stores, apparel, eating and drinking places). That is, women are found as managers: (*a*) in organizations that employ large numbers of women (schools, hospitals, department stores) or that have professional positions widely filled by women; (*b*) in organizations with very large clerical components (hence, creating large numbers of supervisory positions within clerical divisions); and (*c*) in organizations providing services relating to the traditional female domestic role (apparel trade, apparel manufacturing, restaurants). Women rarely become managers in proportion to their numbers as part of the white-collar section of organizations. See Collins (1971: 3–6).

[8]This is suggested by the fact that organizations with high rates of technological change have no higher educational requirements for these allegedly technical positions than organizations with low rates of change in any organizational context (Table 2.4).

group, educational requirements are kept as a major dividing line between managers and manual laborers. One personnel manager of a large, prominent bank commented rhetorically:

> The route up from janitor to Senior Vice President is now closed. To get anywhere, an education is now needed so we simply cannot hire out of high school any longer. This is serious for young men who will not continue on with their educations.

CONCLUSION

Looking back over this mass of evidence, what does it show? Clearly there is a substantially negative verdict on the meritocratic theory of modern society and on the technological–functional theory of education. We do find that within the manufacturing and related material-distribution sectors of the economy, there is some tendency for technological advance to be associated with higher educational requirements, especially for blue-collar jobs. But the bulk of the evidence is in the other direction. Education is not associated with employee productivity on the individual level, and job skills are learned mainly through opportunities to practice them, as retraining procedures for organizational innovations abundantly demonstrate. Social mobility surveys and observational studies of work both show that pressures for technical efficiency are submerged within the *social* struggles over positions, struggles in which membership in a cultural group is the crucial weapon.

It is not surprising, then, that educational credentials are most heavily emphasized within organizations stressing normative control—that is, cultural socialization—and in the large national bureaucracies; nor is it surprising that these are stronger determinants than technological change. This comparative organizational evidence has both a general theoretical significance and a historical one. For the variable—large national bureaucracy versus smaller local establishment—is essentially the distinction between the organizations controlled by the Anglo-Protestant upper class and those controlled by Catholic and other minorities. Crosscutting this is the second variable—"public trust" versus "market" organizations—which refers basically (if not altogether precisely) to the contrast between the tertiary and secondary sectors of the economy. The evidence here meshes with the historical analysis that we will find in subsequent chapters, which stresses the dual themes of the ethnic organization of the American economy and the effects of super-productive twentieth-century technology in creating a large "sinecure sector."

3

The Political Economy of Culture

Chapters 1 and 2 dealt with some general issues of stratification: how people get occupational positions, and from them, the financial and material rewards that make up the distribution of wealth. The question then arises, Who gets what out of this process? The technical—functional theory by which the prominence of education has been explained offers a general perspective on this process of occupational stratification: People obtain positions by competing on a market for skills, and they are paid in proportion to the marginal return upon the products of their labor. Those whose labor skills are relatively most productive of highly desired goods and services receive the greatest returns. Yet the evidence amassed in the previous chapters against the meritocratic interpretation of education in careers also casts strong doubts upon the more general formulation.

This same evidence suggests an alternative explanation. People are actively concerned with the process of gaining and controlling occupational power and income, not merely (or even primarily) with using skills to maximize production. This is not to say that no one is involved in productive work, but as we have seen, it is difficult to assess merit in most organizations, especially at white-collar levels, and the social organization of workers operates fairly deliberately to prevent accurate assessment. The workers with the greatest technical skills are not the best paid, but they are found mainly in the lower–middle levels of organizations (and side branches of the middle levels); the most important routes to power and income are through the realms of organizational politics and administration.

PRODUCTIVE LABOR AND POLITICAL LABOR

That is to say, there is not only **productive labor,** but there is also **political labor.** By the latter, I mean primarily efforts within the maneuverings of organizational politics. Productive labor is responsible for the material production of wealth, but political labor sets the conditions under which the wealth is appropriated. To the extent that one is paid for one's productive contribution, this does not happen automatically but because political labor has shaped the organizational structure and the labor market to make this possible. More generally, just how occupational incomes are distributed depends upon the political labor surrounding the work process.

Political labor is above all a matter of forming social alliances within and sometimes across organizations, and of influencing others' views of the realities of work. Both processes go on together, and via the same means: Social networks are formed by the process of communications, and the constructing of social realities is also a matter of communications. Both are crucially determined by cultural resources. The outcomes of organizational politics are the shaping of incomes, jobs, and the structures of organizations themselves.

This is done in three ways. First, as we have seen, there is the control of gatekeeping—the entry requirements into an occupation. Second, there is the structure of the career channel within the organization—whether it is a dead end, promotes in a self-contained branch, allows for transfers and rotations, allows potential promotion to the top level of authority, and so on. Third and most generally, there is the shaping of the "position" itself—what kinds of work are grouped together or separated off as distinct duties of an individual worker; how many people are deemed necessary at such positions; what degrees of tenure and what method of pay is adopted (piece rate, hourly, monthly, commission, etc.).

In all of these, the political process may involve several groups within the organization. Most obviously, there is the interest of the managers themselves in formulating entry requirements, career sequences, and positions. They do this not only with an eye for costs and productive efficiency, but also for the utility of various arrangements in controlling their subordinates.[1] Managers

---

[1]Historical analyses of the way in which work positions have been shaped, not from sheer technological necessity but by managers' efforts to maximize control over workers, may be found in Braverman (1974), Maglin (1974), and Stone (1975).

are concerned with shaping their own positions and careers as well. Since they are involved in a political process within the organization, managers must do this shaping in alliance with others, and often in opposition to rival individuals and groups. Hence much of position shaping may be complex and reactive, with results unlike what any particular party to the struggle intended.

This is all the more true when we consider that not only managers with line authority, but also other participants in organizations engage in shaping positions. Professional and technical specialists, even without explicit decision-making authority, have considerable influence by their ability to "expertly" define what technical problems exist or will be encountered, and hence what numbers of specialists with what qualifications are needed. Officially powerless manual workers demonstrate an even more potent weapon for position shaping: Their informal organization of the work group controls how hard they will work and hence their rate of output, thus indirectly determining how many workers of a given sort are "needed." Formally, unions and professional associations can demand certain entrance requirements and job descriptions, and sometimes even career channels; informally, workers can control selection by ostracizing or subverting members of particular groups, either influencing entry requirements or creating further subspecialties within the organization for undesirable workers.[2] And all these processes interact, so that the shape of an organization and the distribution of income it generates is the result of a complex of struggles.

This process is hidden if we view organizations and occupations through the lenses of the ideological categories used in struggles within them. Organizations are commonly defined as places where work is done; their structure is regarded as a way of dividing the labor, and occupations are considered to be work roles. But the work that is done and the way it is divided up are not the neutral bases of positions and structures; rather they are to be appropriated or shunted off to others as power resources permit.

Consider the blue collar–white collar distinction. This actually means the distinction between wage and salary modes of payment (as technicians and even "professionals" on the "white-collar" side may do most of their work with their hands), which is to say, a difference in degrees of job tenure. Wage positions are explicitly more short-term, salary positions more long-term, and they thus differ in lesser or greater protection from the vicissitudes of the employment market. The distinction also reflects different career channels; usually each is a separate employment sector with entry jobs at the bottom and no provision for promotion from one sector to the other. Given the existence of this organizational divide, subsequent maneuverings for advantage tend to reinforce the structure, as when long-term blue-collar employees

----

[2]Hughes (1958) thus describes the trend in American occupations to shunt off their "dirty work" to new subordinate subspecialties.

press for seniority rules governing promotion into protected jobs just below this line. The fact that certain organizations (such as U.S. police departments) promote from the bottom up shows that an alternative structure is possible (Skolnick, 1966) and that the particular kinds of power arrangements produce the prevailing dichotomous pattern. Similarly, the separate hierarchies for clerical workers in most modern organizations are based on little more than sexual segregation, usually with a separate pay scale; under different power conditions these could be organized into quite a different set of career channels and work responsibilities. In fact, before the introduction of female secretaries in the late nineteenth century, secretarial positions were not differentiated from other administrative jobs and had the promotional possibilities of the aide-de-camp or the apprentice.

The distinction between *productive* and *political labor,* then, is crucial for understanding how organizations are shaped and, as a result, how people are stratified. The distinction separates the two major social classes: the working class engaged in productive labor, and the dominant class engaged in political labor. Both classes expend energy, but it is the subordinated class that produces the wealth, whereas the dominant class determines its distribution.

Yet the division between productive labor and political labor is an abstract one; in empirical reality, the same person may do both. Consider the range of modern occupations. Some are almost completely devoted to material work, producing food, housing, clothes, and other essentials. Others are devoted entirely to activities of domination, exercising or threatening the use of force (the military, the police). Some concentrate on acting to gain and defend political offices and sinecures (which may exist widely in nongovernment organizations as well as in government ones) and others on producing cultural resources (as in the educational and communications industries). Other occupations are in an intermediate zone, for material production involves not only the physical labor of production, but also the labor of transportation and distribution, and the lighter talking-and-paperwork labor of planning both production and distribution. The people who carry out these activities, though—the white-collar sector in organizations—are not engaged in these activities alone. We must not be misled by our everyday definitions of what a job *is,* for the sole legitimate definitions are in terms of productive labor. In fact, many white-collar activities involve the political labor of attempting to control others and defending one's own autonomy from their control. Probably the greater part of clerical activities are devoted to communications of this sort—conferences, paperwork, reports, records—that bear little relation to material production but are part of the incessant political maneuvering, under the guise of planning and distributing (but also often called "personnel administration"), to take the initiative in the realm of domination, or simply to fill time with the appearance of working.

Thus we have an analytical distinction between the two kinds of activities, productive and political. Any job may be apportioned between the two in varying degrees. The "working-class" aspect (productive labor) and the "dominant-class" aspect (political labor) may both appear in the same job. It is the relative mixture of class conditions within each individual's daily life that produces various forms of class cultures and attitudes toward authority; as the evidence indicates (Collins, 1975: 61–87), individuals vary across the range of attitudinal mixtures according to their particular cases. Hence the actual population does not necessarily fall into clear-cut class-wide allegiances but rather into much smaller local interest groups. It should be borne in mind that even positions toward the core of the materially productive sector have their political elements. Important sectors of blue-collar workers (especially the upper working class) have cultural and organizational resources that they use to influence their situations, both formally through unions and even more importantly, informally in the social relations of the work place. As a result, they can introduce some nonwork into their job time by collectively controlling the work pace; they can monopolize to some degree the easier or more remunerative jobs; or they can increase their security of tenure.

The overall structure of the modern occupational world may be conceived as a range of variations in the possession of "political" resources for controlling the conditions of work and appropriating the fruits of production; hence it can be seen as a range of mixtures of productive work with political work. At one end are relatively unprotected laborers, subject directly to the market for productive labor; at the other are pure political laborers engaged in the activities of the ideological, financial, and governmental superstructure. The upper ranges of the working class and the middle ranges of the administrative class contain mixed activities, the former using the resources of organizational politics to reduce the strains and reap the benefits of productive work, the latter building an elaborate screen of administrative politics around a productive core of planning and distributive activities.

SINECURES AND POSITIONAL PROPERTY

Social classes may be distinguished by the amount of property they possess, but the most important form of such "property" is not limited to the traditional notion of material and financial possessions. Rather it is how "positions" are shaped that constitutes the most immediate form of property in the labor market, and it is by the shaping of such positions that income is distributed. The term *position* is only a metaphor (although it is widely accepted and taken for granted) for the seemingly object-like immutability of a collection of behavioral patterns that are reserved for particular individuals under particular conditions of tenure. Indeed, material and financial *property* is a similar metaphor, for the property relation is a behavioral one, a particular degree of tenure of action toward certain objects and persons, not a physical relationship of owner to thing. It is *property in positions* that is crucial in determining most of class organization and class struggle in everyday life. For material and financial property (if we except home ownership) is concentrated within a quite small group, but property in positions shapes class relations throughout the population and has a wide range of variations. The actual details of economic conflict are carried out on this level.

Technological change, within this context, has a peculiar result. It does not raise the skill requirements of most jobs very much; the great majority of all jobs can be learned through practice by almost any literate person. The number of esoteric specialties "requiring" unusually extensive training or skill is relatively small. The "system" does not "need" or "demand" a certain kind of performance; it "needs" what it gets, because "it" is nothing more than a slipshod way of talking about the way things happen to be at the time. How hard people work, and with what dexterity and cleverness, depends on how much other people can require them to do and on how much they can dominate other people. What the advance of technology *does* do, rather, is increase the total wealth produced and lead to intense struggles over the shaping of property in occupational positions, not because of the necessities of *production* but because of the struggles over the *distribution* of the increased wealth.

We live in an era in which our machinery and our organizational techniques are very powerful, capable of supporting everyone at a comfortable standard of living with relatively little physical effort.[3] This prospect has been contemplated for quite some time, sometimes with hope, sometimes with anger against the forces impeding it, sometimes with fear of ensuing boredom and purposelessness. But in fact, the shift toward a predominantly leisure society does not seem to be happening, or at least it is happening so slowly that it seems like little has changed. Most people still work a fairly long work week; at the highest job levels, very long work weeks (over 55 hours in a substantial portion of this group); a large proportion of married women work; many people hold several jobs (Wilensky, 1961).

Why? The paradox is resolved if we recall that the most prominent form of leisure in our society is the most undesirable: unemployment. People work because that is the main way that wealth is distributed. The welfare system for

---

[3]In 1850, 65% of the energy used in work in the United States was produced by people and animals, and 28% by wind, water, and wood. In 1950, all of these together produced only 1.6% of the energy, with all the rest coming from electricity, coal, and oil. At the same time, the energy output has multiplied tenfold (Lenski, 1966: 298–299).

the support of nonworkers, despite the outcries of its opponents, redistributes very little (Pilcher, 1976). The reason some people are wealthy is that they or their families have jobs that control the biggest organizations with the most money. Others have at least a middling foothold in the system of organizational property that supports us. People without jobs (or with a succession of marginal positions) are without power over the main property resources of our society (and usually without political influence as well), and that is the reason they are poor.

In relation to our hypothetical high-leisure technocracy, then, the crucial question becomes: *Who would control it?* The answer is clear: Those few who did work in a mass-leisure society would get most of the wealth. Michels's (1949) discovery that the persons who control the administrative machinery of a political party get most of the benefits from it is paralleled here on a larger scale. It is for this reason that we have not moved toward a high-leisure society, despite our technological capacity for doing so. We have elaborated a largely superfluous structure of more or less easy jobs, full of administrative make-work and featherbedding because modern technology allows it and because of political pressures from the populace wanting work. Thus we have the enormous structure of government employment (including education), the union sector protected by elaborate work regulations, and the huge work forces of our corporate oligopolies keeping themselves busy seeking new products to justify their jobs. In effect, leisure has been incorporated into the job itself. Advanced technology, far from demanding hard work and long training from everyone, has made occupational demands more and more superficial and arbitrary.

Bensman and Vidich (1971: 5−31) have given one set of reasons why it has been possible to move toward this "sinecure society": The very productivity of our technology has created the now widely recognized "Keynesian" problem of keeping up consumer demand and thus fending off economic depression. The massive expansion of government employment is one way in which this has come about. The support given by government to the tertiary sector by dispensing an increasing number of licenses for franchises and professional monopolies is another. Private sinecures also exist within the biggest manufacturing corporations, with their extensive educational requirements and staff divisions, their leisure perquisites in the forms of sales conventions and motivational and retraining programs. Much of the control apparatus of big organizations, even if it is established in the name of productive efficiency, increases the nonproductive sinecure component. Elaborate planning and cost-accounting divisions add their own expense to the organization and transfer wealth to their own members; so do agencies for compliance with insurance regulations and law enforcement. In all these areas, the struggle for control, both from above and from below, elaborates the political sector of organizations at every step. The more claims made upon insurance companies, the more union grievances or minority discrimination complaints, the larger becomes the institutionalized sector of positions that deal with such matters, adding yet more members of the organization who struggle to enhance their own positional property. The sinecure sector feeds upon struggles over control of itself.

One might ask why the rationality of the economic market does not drive out such wastefulness, forcing the organizations that engage in it out of business. In major sectors of the economy, this process does not hold. Government organizations are not subject to competition and are seldom subject to effective political pressures for economizing. And the large corporations are the very organizations that can best afford such internal redistribution, for they hold oligopolistic controls over their markets, often supported by favorable governmental policies; external competition does nothing to make them reduce their internal costs, while the scope of bureaucratic complexity and the separation of stock ownership from direct control make them accountable to no one but themselves. Ironically, it is these highly protected organizations that technocratic apologists like Galbraith (1967) think are prosperous because of their technological advance, whereas the smaller organizations that are not protected from the market are consigned to insecurity and relative poverty because of their technological backwardness. This is only repeating the gloating of the sinecure sector in the terms of its own ideology.

To speak of the prevalence of sinecures and of essentially "luxury" or "waste" production in a time of economic downturn may seem incongruous, but only from the point of view of a technocratic ideology. Economic crises due to inflation and deficiencies in aggregate demand may, in fact, be the very results of the inequality of a sinecure system. The coexistence of material wealth and leisure for some, with economic hardships for others, and perhaps anxiety for all, is hardly unprecedented in economic history. The high productivity of the technology does not disappear in an economic crisis, for crises are ultimately in the sphere of distribution, not of production.

The "political" realm, then, is found within all organizations and occupational networks, not merely in the formal government structure, and the major part of the redistribution of wealth, under the pressure of intermittent overproduction crises, has taken the form of reshaping property in occupational positions. This has come about both by expanding the numbers of people allowed into the political superstructure, especially the governmental and culture-producing sides of it, and by increasing the amount of nonwork within the occupational structure generally.

Weber would no doubt agree with this line of analysis. Although he had no opportunity to observe the power relations of advanced industrial society, his historical work makes abundant use of the concept of **prebends**—

y its own structure of
s instead of one: the
ket for culture. Eco-
and superstructure;
it is the means—the
e the lineups in strug-
conomic sphere at an
s that constitute "po-
where these barriers
haped by the cultural

e. In everyday life, it
d the expressions of
specially in conversa-
e, to set moods, to
es. Whatever subject
has a corresponding
emporarily dominant
social structure.
ge, the negotiation of
e empirical details of
he different sorts of
rely external relation-
tters, or more signifi-
discussion, ideologi-
Collins, 1975: 114—
then, are the forma-
izations. In different
ational communities,
called consciousness
ression of utterances
ersons involved.
munities rather than
e a variety of forms.
continually repeated
strong interpersonal
small local groups up
have direct contacts

zing their incomes. With
-style technocratic ideol-
often were openly bought
considerations and under
tury, the market for such
g a fundamental change;
educational credentials,
s of this cultural currency
various aspects of labor

in medieval society, for it
pope or king.[4] Today the
s of meritocracy by which
d. But the importance of
re important in a wealthy
the interior of virtually all
ious in the slow pace of
ive grind of some schools
ileges themselves. But this
nding conditions to avoid
ds to material results. The
nce, between the aristoc-
ce their position, and the
e aristocrats are struggling
nd commoners still exist,

determines how people in
t are the resources of or-
can we predict how such
me? The major weapon of
and to impress others with
of culture, and these effects

hout responsibility for the "cure of

ive and political labor is revealing.
ace, the standing jokes are usually
g professionals and managers, on
y, loaded down with outstanding
ve work are cynical and detached
nal politicians must play it straight,
d of course disguising these efforts

form their clearest pattern when culture is distributed b
exchange. We have, then, two important market realr
market for economic goods and services, and the ma
nomic and cultural markets are not separated as bas
they are distinguished only as ends and means, and
resources of group organization and struggle—that crea
gles for advancement. Cultural weapons penetrate the e
intimate level, shaping the behavior patterns and barrie
sitions." The appropriation of incomes is determined b
are formed. Stratification, on its most material level, is a
market, and it is to this that we now turn.

THE CULTURAL MARKET

Culture is both a good in itself and a social resour
takes the form of the style of physical appearances a
thoughts and emotions through communications and e
tion. Culture thus serves to dramatize one's self-ima
mentally re-create past realities and to create new or
holds the floor in a conversation, however fleetingly,
degree of shared mental reality. As such, it provides the
definition of the social situation and hence of operative

Conversation may be conceived as cultural exchan
partners to talk with and topics to be given sway. Th
social relationships of different sorts come down to
conversation that people carry out with one another: pu
ships confined to minimal exchanges upon practical ma
cant ties based upon talk containing larger proportions c
cal debate, entertainment, gossip, or personal topics
152). The consequences of everyday cultural exchange
tion and reproduction of social groups and formal orga
terminology, cultural resources are the basis of assoc
which Weber called status groups. They might also be
communities, since their distinguishing feature is the ex
in shared symbols with reality-defining effects for the p

One advantage of calling them consciousness cor
status groups is to remind us that such communities ta
They range in duration from brief, temporary relations to
ones, and they range in intensity from weak to very
commitments. The size of the community can vary from
through larger communities in which most individuals

with only a relatively few others, but who have the bond of being potential friends because of a common culture. The usual conception of a status group, or more loosely, of a social class, actually fits this latter case: This is not to say that everyone in the group knows everyone else, but their commonalities make their association easy when they do encounter one another. Ethnic groups are generally status groups of this kind. And finally, consciousness communities may vary in degree of self-consciousness, from associations carried on without explicit self-definition, through the self-consciousness that comes with the giving of group names, to the highly formalized group identity when a group institutionalizes itself with periodic meetings, regulations, and legal charters.

Cultural exchanges are the empirical means by which all organized forms of stratification are enacted and by which the class struggle over work and material goods is carried out. Culture produces both horizontal and vertical relations. Persons with common cultural resources tend to form egalitarian ties as friends or co-members of a group. Such groups, as we have seen, are major actors within the struggles to control organizations, whether over work pace, gatekeeping criteria, the definition of positional duties and perquisites, assessment of merit, or personal advancement. Such struggles need have little of a clandestine or conspiratorial tone to them; informal groups are manifested simply in casual conversation, usually without great self-consciousness or deliberation, but nevertheless can add up to very strong consensus about common courses of action. Formal and self-conscious versions of associational communities are also important in maneuverings for material advantage, as in the case of occupations that have organized themselves into professional or commercial associations or trade unions.

The ability of occupational categories to form consciousness communities of one degree or another is determined by how similar their cultural resources are, whereas the scope and power of the community thus formed depend in part upon the nature of their resources for defining reality, as well as upon the other resources that these mediate. Cultural resources enter into the process of stratification in another way as well. Hierarchical relations among nonequals are also immediately enacted in face-to-face conversational exchanges. Although background resources ultimately tend to determine domination and subordination in such encounters, they do so mainly by being brought to bear through the symbolic interchange of the moment. Cultural expressions are a way of defining reality and may define both a horizontal bond among equals and a vertical relation among unequals. Usually this is done by the dominant person controlling the conversational interaction, picking the topic and influencing what is said about it, affecting the underlying emotional tone, and thus controlling the cognitive and moral definitions of reality. Among the resources for doing this successfully are access to channels of information and other social networks and the vocabulary and rhetorical style to impress others with allegedly superior (and possibly esoteric) knowledge and power. Thus cultural resources not only form the groups that struggle over control of social organization, but also tend to determine the hierarchic relations among these groups.

Indigenous and Formal Production of Culture

Culture is produced in two different ways: in the experiences of everyday interaction themselves or by specialized culture-producing organizations. Indigenous cultural production goes on all the time in the worlds of work, home, and leisure alike. Every experience is potential conversational material, and every conversation generates further capacities to speak in certain styles and to peddle one's acquired information, entertainment value, and emotions in further exchanges. Much of these conversational resources, though, tend to be specific to particular individuals and situations. Information about one's own experiences or about the practical matters at hand, gossip about one's acquaintances, standing jokes and styles of joking—these are resources for local barter markets for culture. Such resources are not readily transferable to other situations; if cultural resources mediate group ties, indigenously produced resources produce local ties among limited numbers of specific individuals. If cultural resources construct shared social realities, the realities these create are inextensive and fragmentary.

Moreover, such resources may cumulate, but they tend to do so in a circular flow. Personal experiences and conversational contacts generate conversational resources, which can be used to keep up existing social relations and negotiate new ones of the same type. It is possible that individuals may move on the borderlines of their usual contacts and thus encounter new situations, thereby generating new conversational resources, which could be used to build different social ties. Such cultural and associational movement, though, is likely to be slow and sporadic when based only on purely indigenous cultural resources derived from the immediate situation. Thus indigenously produced culture tends conservatively to reproduce itself and a given pattern of social relations. Such cultures as a whole tend to change only when some exogenous processes, such as political or economic catastrophes, radically change the conditions of life. But even here, the circular flow of culture and group structure tends to stabilize any new developments. This kind of culture is not a force for change, or strictly speaking, an independent causal factor in its own right.

Culture may also be produced by specialized organizations. Churches and other religious associations were historically among the first such organizations in which full-time specialists devoted themselves to symbolic expressions. Professional entertainers constitute another type of specialized culture producer, as do, especially importantly for our purposes, schools. Such specialized agencies of cultural production have several effects. By comparison with indigenous cultural production, they can much more readily generate new forms of culture—partly because the internal exigencies and struggles over control within culture-producing organizations tend to shape their products in new directions, and partly because their members' full-time and self-conscious absorption with culture gives them much more refined skills. And cultural innovation, especially vis-à-vis any particular indigenous culture, is likely to be especially strong the more that specialized culture-producing organizations constitute a larger network or market among themselves. Such formal culture-producing agencies, then, become exogenous sources of change within the cultural sphere, and by extension, in the realm of group structures.

Thus developments of religious culture have been crucial in forming new political and economic organizations at various times in world history. In Weber's (1961) fully developed historical theory, the culture of the universalistic world religions transcended the family and tribal—ethnic base of organization, made possible the rise of the bureaucratic state, and eventually led to the "rationalized" capitalist economy. Similarly, it can be argued that the mass news media of the industrial era generated a new form of politics based on the ideologically oriented group (Gouldner, 1976) and that the popular music media were a crucial organizational basis for the youth revolt of the 1960s and 1970s. Schools have been especially important for forming new group structures, ranging from the creation of the gentry class of traditional China to the formation of specialized occupational enclaves in contemporary America.

Formally produced culture is not only more innovative than indigenous culture, but it also allows the creation of much larger and more self-conscious communities. This type of culture is propagated more widely across different local situations, tends to be made up of more abstract concepts and symbols, and it creates more generalized references. Formally produced culture deals less with specific individuals and situations and more with the commonalities across many situations. Its images, even if concrete, tend to symbolize every individual or to symbolize the aggregate of individuals as an organized unit. Formal culture is more widely useful than indigenous culture; it can relatively quickly negotiate ties among individuals who otherwise have little in common to exchange. Thus formal culture has been the basis for impersonal bureaucratic organizations, for generating political loyalties to an overarching state, for mobilizing mass occupational groups and large-scale social movements.

If indigenously produced culture supports local barter markets, formally produced culture operates more nearly as a monetary currency. It is more widely negotiable (i.e., it is a medium of exchange) and can be used on a much wider basis for assessing reputations (i.e., it acts as a store of value). A true currency-like system of cultural "money" only comes into existence with a further transformation, however: when formal culture-producing organizations not only broadcast their cultural products, but also give formal summary announcements of the quantity of cultural goods an individual has acquired from them (i.e., to develop the monetary analogy further, they act as measurable units of account). Thus religious attainments have sometimes been summarized by titles of sainthood and other distinctions, and the culture acquired in schools has been summarized by grades and certificates. Once these formal summaries are available, they may be substituted for the full display of the culture itself. In a further transformation, they may become subject to their own high-level economy, just as the value of organizational incomes can be transformed into stocks, which themselves are bought and sold on a specialized stock market subject to its own market forces. Once this occurs, the purely quantitative relations among these second- or third-order currencies become major determinants of their value and can affect their use in more primitive markets irrespective of their actual underlying content.

In other words, the more formalized the culture-producing organization, the more its culture tends to resemble a currency, and the more the cultural economy becomes subject to specifically monetary effects. The "price" of the social memberships that culture can "buy" may undergo inflation, due to an exogenous increase in monetary "supply"; conversely, price deflation is also conceivable. The conditions and effects of these, and their interdynamics with the material economy, will be considered next.

Determinants of Cultural Currency Production

How much cultural currency is produced is determined by several causes. First, it depends on how much material wealth is siphoned into specialized culture-producing organizations: that is, how much of the material economy is invested in the cultural economy. Thus richer societies in world history have generally been able to afford more churches and monasteries, more professional entertainment, and more schooling. Rich societies have not *necessarily* done this; the mobilizing and innovating effects of cultural organizations have sometimes been resisted by traditional rulers (as in various periods in the history of China and Russia, for example), and in some situations the populace has preferred to spend its wealth more heavily on direct material consumption. Wealth is a facilitating factor, not a determinative one.

Second, culture-producing organizations have been affected by inventions of special technologies for cultural production and transmission. The invention of writing itself, improved implements and paper, book printing, and the modern media of electronic communications and information storage have all affected the specialized production of culture. These effects, though, have not all been uniformly in the direction of increasing the amount of formal cultural production. Some of them (such as modern television broadcasting), because of their concentrated pattern of ownership, may have tended to keep cultural production within quite narrow limits and even to reduce the overall variety and amount of culture in society as a whole. Such technological changes have been relatively infrequent in world history and hence have operated primarily as background for more dynamic factors within any given historical time.

The major determinant of the amount of formal cultural production, and especially the determinant of relatively short-run variations in it, has been the degree of competition among cultural producers and also among cultural consumers. Both the history of religions and the history of education show the pattern: Religious movements and schools have proliferated where governments were relatively weak and decentralized; they have been kept under stricter limitations where centralized governments were strong (Collins, 1977). This is so even though centralized governments have often adopted a state religion, or, in modern times, a compulsory public school system, as a basis for bureaucratic administration and control of the population. But such governments have usually favored a single religion and repressed its rivals; their educational policies as well have tended to keep the educational system small. In contrast, it has been weak governments, unable to intervene to control the cultural market, that have allowed competitive cultural production to expand on its own.

In preindustrial times, the greatest proliferations of culture production have been in situations where an economically prosperous society was nevertheless politically fragmented or decentralized. Under these conditions, the potential consumers of a specialized culture were free to compete among themselves culturally and were indeed motivated to do so in the absence of an all-determining state that set the forms of stratification.[6] Although participation in schooling in such societies was generally confined to the aristocracy, the ideal of the cultivated gentry was most widely emulated in the decentralized rather than in the centralized dynasties of Chinese history, in the weaker rather than in the stronger Islamic states, and by the burgher-aristocrats of the fragmented competing city-states of Renaissance Italy rather than by rulers of the Roman Empire. The decentralization of demand for cultural resources thus tended to bring forth a corresponding supply of cul-

---

[6]A situation of relative internal peace as well as economic prosperity seems required too; otherwise competition is simply expressed militarily, not culturally.

tural producers, although in a variety of forms: private teachers in China, religious *madrasas* (mosque schools) in Islam, and private, sociable academies in Italy.

These decentralized conditions have had especially strong effects upon cultural production where a politically decentralized but economically mobilized society has been multiethnic. Ethnic groups are cultural groups *a fortiori,* constituted as identifiably distinct communities precisely because they have come into a situation of contact with other groups while continuing the indigenous cultures of their previous isolated situations. The struggle for economic and political domination in such a multiethnic situation focuses questions of social inclusion and group prestige on the most obvious cultural distinctions. Culture, even if only indigenous (rather than formally produced), thus becomes the object of self-conscious reflection, and ethnic groups become concerned over questions of cultural superiority or inferiority to each other. In this situation, groups are likely to welcome a generalized cultural currency by which to improve or consolidate their position, whether in the form of a new religion or a new educational system. Once such competition gets under way, it is likely to lead to mutual emulation by all parties and to a corresponding expansion of the set of culture-producing organizations.

Thus religious sects and their accompanying schools have proliferated throughout the prosperous periods of the history of India, especially in the decentralizing reaction to the crumbling centralized dynasties that had attempted to impose Buddhism as a single dominant religion (Weber, 1958: 123–133; Thapar, 1966: 136–166). Underlying this religious expansion was the enormous multiethnic diversity of India, channeled into a single system of economic domination and cultural prestige by the caste system. The system was rendered dynamic rather than static because political decentralization allowed castes to attempt to raise their status by emulating the higher culture. This fostered a large market for cultural entrepreneurs, in this case religious and secular teachers of all kinds. Similarly, the specialized culture of classical Greece was quite narrowly confined and informally taught during the earlier period, but it became transformed into a formal culture taught by a large network of schools established during the Hellenistic period when the Greeks had become the administrators of a number of conquest states around the eastern Mediterranean (Marrou, 1964). The multiethnic situation of the Hellenistic empires made the question of Greek identity versus the "barbarians" (who might just as well have been cultivated Syrians or Egyptians, for example) an especially salient one and made formal education an indispensable possession of the higher social classes.[7] Finally, it is worth recalling that

---

[7]The Roman conquest of these states, however, tended to reduce the salience of cultural stratification. The Greek culture, much more highly developed than the Roman (i.e., based on

Europe of the High Middle Ages was also a multiethnic society. Before the rise of the strong national states, the political unity of Europe was largely the business of the papacy, and the higher culture of Christianity, taught in church schools, provided a common cultural currency (and even a common language, Latin). The great proliferation of universities was a result of this situation, as different parts of Europe competed with one another in founding their own universities and drawing students from other ethnic locales.

In each of these multiethnic situations, cultural currencies became widely and increasingly produced and became significant bases for the formation of new group structures. In India, the successive transformation of the occupational castes was the result (Srinivas, 1955: 1–45); in Hellenistic Greece, the gradual development of governmental quasi-bureaucracies (Marrou, 1964: 400–418); in medieval Europe, the proliferation of specialized religious orders of papal and secular bureaucracies and of guilds and corporations organized under religious auspices (Rashdall, 1936; Southern, 1970). In several of these historical cases, an inflationary pattern resulted, and in at least one, an ensuing crisis of the currency system. These topics lead us more generally to consider the effects of cultural currency expansion.

Effects of Cultural Currency Production

A large-scale production of formal culture transforms the whole society. In effect, the populace invests large quantities of the goods derived from the material economy into the cultural economy with the hope of bettering their social position in all spheres. The struggle to control the occupational realm, whether by the direct shaping of positions, as in the modern world, or by building control over the economy through the development of a strong state (as is generally the case in the preindustrial world), can be carried on most effectively by groups that control superior organizational resources. A large and widely dispersed supply of cultural currency makes resources available to many groups in the population for organizing themselves in this struggle, which may then result in the proliferation of monopolized occupational enclaves. We see this tendency especially in late medieval Europe, as the expansion of formal religious currencies was followed by considerable organization building, both by local princes and by monopolizing guilds within an ever-increasing number of occupational specialties. Similarly, the continued ex-

more investment in culture-producing organizations), was generally adopted by the Romans as their specialized culture—but without a great deal of prestige being attached to possessing it, because it was the culture of a subordinated class. In many cases, Greek artists and entertainers were brought in as slaves. Roman social prestige was based much more blatantly on politics and wealth.

pansion of religious sects in India fostered a long-term tendency for castes to split into subcastes, as larger occupational groups split into religiously sanctioned subgroups. We shall see later in this book the way in which the increasing access to formal educational credentials has shaped numerous occupational enclaves in the modern American economy.

But the outcome of such a process of widening educational opportunities may bring little or no change in the order of stratification among groups. If previously dominant groups maintain a head start in the race for cultural resources, they may well end up with just as commanding a position in a culture-based stratification system as in a more primitive economically or politically based one. Moreover, the expansion of the entire system of cultural production, without a commensurate expansion in the number of desirable occupational positions, brings about an inflation in the cultural price of the older positions. For example, expanded numbers of students presented themselves for the civil service examinations in China from the sixteenth through the nineteenth centuries, but the number of government positions was kept virtually constant. Hence the cultural price rose—an examination system was elaborated, eventually becoming a series of examinations that might take a scholar 30 years to pass (Franke, 1960). Another period of credential inflation occurred around 1800 in Germany when a mass of applicants for government positions crowded the universities; the pressure resulted in a reform that extended educational requirements to more positions (Brunschwig, 1947; Schnabel, 1959, Vol. 1: 408–457). And Weber (1968: 998–999) noted the inflationary tendency in bureaucratic employment requirements in Europe in his day. In other words, the fact that cultural goods are resources for struggle over positions in the material realm means that there may be limits upon what various groups can buy, and hence overproduction crises are possible within purely cultural markets as well.

To study these sorts of possibilities, we must turn to the interaction between cultural markets and the economy of material production.

1. Increasing investment in cultural goods can bring about an expansion in material production. This can happen where cultural goods are used to build larger social networks of coordination and domination in such a way as to make possible greater economic exchange; thus the investment of cultural goods in building the superstructures of horticultural, agrarian, and the beginnings of industrial societies often tended to help expand the material economy and increase its productiveness. Or, within a modern industrial economy (and within agrarian economies too), a period of expansion of cultural markets may stimulate material production by creating an atmosphere of confidence and growth; it might especially help to overcome a chronic crisis of material overproduction—underconsumption by opening up a new area of material

investment (in the material basis of culture production) and by generally loosening stagnant organizational arrangements. This can happen even if the interaction between cultural supply and demand is the "inflationary" equilibrium noted above, in which the payoffs in domination that cultural investors seek do not come about because the relative standing of the investors does not change.

Such stimulating effects on the material economy depend upon there being unused material capacity for expansion. The potential resources and markets must be there; the situation should lack only the organizational interconnections or the wave of psychological confidence necessary to bring them together. Lacking this, an expansion of the cultural economy will have entirely different effects.

2. Increasing investment in cultural goods may bring about an increase in the degree of domination in a society. In one sense, this tended to be true in the long run for all the shifts from hunting and gathering, to primitive horticultural, to advanced horticultural, to agrarian types of societies; all of these, although they probably experienced an initial growth in material production through the organization of religious, or otherwise culturally cemented superstructures, ended up with a typical structure of material distribution that was markedly more unequal than the previous type (Lenski, 1966). Probably each went through an initial period of expanding overall production; then the investment of portions of this in a cultural and military superstructure resulted in greater inequality than before, and eventually the society settled into a pattern of economic stagnation. This was certainly the difficulty experienced by most agrarian societies in breaking through into industrialization; the structure of domination was such that markets were generally limited to luxury goods for the elite, and the mass consumer markets required to make mass production worthwhile had little chance of being established.

The shift to industrial society required that some pressures for redistribution take place in a prior agrarian society, and it is possible that cultural markets had a place in this. (Weber's thesis about Christianity might be interpreted in this sense.) In the long run, though, it is likely that industrial societies also undergo at least the structural possibility of repeating the earlier patterns: Cultural resources can become structured in such a way that they enforce economic domination and inequality rather than economic expansion, and hence they can contribute to economic stagnation. Industrial societies have not really existed long enough for us to have much evidence on these possibilities. One thing that seems clear is that the level of inequality enforced in industrial societies is lower than that in agrarian societies; but it is also clear that the new level does not recede constantly but reaches a plateau at which it remains fairly stable (Pilcher, 1976). For the United States, that plateau was reached by the time of World War II; the massive expansion of the cultural market since then has had little effect on the overall pattern of inequality. (This also seems to be the case in the histories of other twentieth-century industrial societies.)

Within the context of the material economy of material production, the growth of a cultural economy that settles into a constant level of domination will tend to exacerbate the underlying problem of overproduction — underconsumption. (In an agrarian economy, the similar use of culture for domination will block the growth of any mass market and hence any shift to industrialism; there are important elements of this in the stagnant quasi-agrarian — quasi-industrial economies of Latin America and elsewhere in the Third World today.) Thus we find that expanded cultural economies can result in economic growth or economic stagnation or even crisis. If the cause of the first alternative is the existence of unused material capacities and readily accessible markets, the cause of the second alternative may be the nonexistence of such conditions; or it may be a particular way in which the cultural economy is structured. About this second possibility, we know little as yet.

3. The cultural market might result in some redistribution of material goods. This seems to have been true in the early phase of industrialization and perhaps in some periods in earlier societies as well. This comes about first by the redistribution of goods to the segment of the middle class that is involved in cultural production; a growth in the number of teachers (or priests, monks, etc.) is itself a widening of the number of people employed in the superstructure. The general expansion of the culture-producing industries throughout most of the twentieth century in the United States is thus one element in redistribution of material resources that otherwise would have gone to the previously smaller group of dominants in the political sector. Furthermore, educational credentials have been invested in expanding autonomous professional enclaves, as well as the productively superfluous component of the administrative sector, and have helped shape occupations in such a way as to help leisure migrate into the interior of jobs. The growth of the nonproductive, white-collar sector has been achieved above all through the mechanism of investing cultural resources (educational credentials) in occupational property. Thus an expansion of the cultural market, even though it has not changed the overall proportions of the distribution of wealth, has led to an expansion in the number of people who are dependent upon the "political" sector (the "sinecure sector"), who receive their material goods by way of the structure of domination rather than the structure of production.

Once that revolution was carried out, it has seemingly had no further effects. Yet the number of people employed in the sinecure sector has constantly risen, even during the period when the degree of inequality in distribution has changed little. There are probably two offsetting processes going on simultaneously here: (*a*) the shift into the sinecure sector has brought about a continuous redistribution; and (*b*) at the same time, the tendency of the sector of domination as a whole versus the sector of production has been to create greater inequality. The continuous process of technological overproduction and financial centralization has kept the economy in a chronic state of operation below capacity, since it has kept down overall consumer demand. The growth of the sinecure sector has been just enough to offset this, to maintain a rough equilibrium around a constant degree of inequality. Short-run shifts in employment in either sector, wars, and other such phenomena have moved the economy briefly and marginally on either side of this equilibrium, but the long-range pattern is remarkably constant.

4. Finally, we may imagine the possibility of an extreme redistribution of material goods brought about by an expansion of cultural markets. This might happen, for example, if cultural movements became so widespread that they mobilized virtually the entire active population. The organizations that would be built upon these cultural resources could no longer be so hierarchic; cultural resources would be so common that no one would be unduly impressed by those held by others. This tendency might be considered to be a revolutionary one. But any revolution that maintained a centralized organization would itself be antithetical to the centripetal tendencies of universal cultural equality and would either act to set up a new cultural elite (for example, by establishing new standards of culture, such as revolutionary party membership, whose eliteness is upheld by the resources of domination) or would fail to maintain its own centralization. For the interests of individual investors in cultural resources are always in the direction of inflating their own subjective prestige; this is done, if possible, by trying to dominate others in the objective world, but lacking that, it is done by creating one's own autonomous enclave in which one's personal cultural standards alone have to be noticed. In a situation of mass mobilization (one that is more than an ephemeral episode), individuals might come to see that their increase in relative status vis-à-vis the previous dominants is no longer of any value except to make the former elites equal to the majority; the tendency would then be to withdraw into private spheres in which their own personal idiosyncracies make the best subjective impression. Under these conditions, we may expect that the social organization would tend to fragment. There would no longer be any dominant cultural currency; ethnically or religiously heterogeneous empires would fall apart into monoethnic states;[8] modern status groups would go their private ways and

---

[8]For example, the unity of multiethnic medieval Europe under the papacy disintegrated into national states. The devaluation of the spiritual credit of the centralized church played a central part in this disintegration—a disintegration that we have come to take for granted so much that we forget that Europe in the thirteenth century could very well have laid the basis for modernization as a single unified state. But the universities, the key to the emerging papal bureaucracy,

ignore the prestige claims of others. A true cultural revolution is inherently anarchistic; the attainment of any very high degree of equality of cultural resources tends to result in social decentralization.

The various material results of cultural markets, then, are often likely to be disappointing for the investors. Sometimes, if excess material productive capacity is there to be brought into action, an expanding cultural market will help the overall productiveness of the economy. But cultural goods are above all resources of domination; especially in an inflationary cycle of relative status competition, the result is likely to be the crystallization of a pattern of domination at a level of relative material inequality that cannot be broken. It is possible that at some periods the cultural market does bring redistribution, at least for those who can use it to enter fully into the "political" sinecure sector, but this redistribution is likely to be episodic, limited to shifts in goods from the higher to the middle sectors of the elite, and offset in modern economies by a countervailing tendency for economic processes to increase inequality. Finally, in the areas and cases where a truly equal distribution of cultural goods is approached, the result is likely to be the destruction of the standardized currency and a dissolution of the system into many smaller parts.

Sensing these various outcomes, various groups may attack, withdraw from, or try to limit or destroy the cultural market. Dominant elites, fearing redistributive consequences, may attempt to hold down cultural production; ironically, however, it is often their own policies of external military expansion that force them to rely on cultural mobilization of their own population as a motivational and economic fund-raising device (as in nineteenth-century Russia), and thus bring about their own downfall. It sometimes happens that a new internal middle class, heavily investing in the means of cultural mobilization, has displaced an older upper class by instituting a regime of their own

---

underwent enormous inflation in the price of their credentials, as the number of years to achieve the higher degrees giving employment in the higher ranks of the church increased from 6 to 16 years. From the fourteenth century onward (and lasting until the nineteenth century in many places), student enrollments dropped sharply, a number of the higher faculties disappeared in many places, and intellectual and cultural life migrated to other institutions. With the destruction of its former monopoly over culture production, the centralizing papacy was severely weakened and eventually lost its monopoly even over religion to a series of schisms in the fourteenth and fifteenth centuries and to the Protestant churches of the sixteenth century. The final split, interestingly enough, was set off by a reaction to the devaluation of an even more explicit form of spiritual currency, the sale of indulgences—certificates of spiritual pardon for sins, redeemable in purgatory. These were sold in larger and larger quantities as time went on in order to meet deficits in the papal budget. Martin Luther led the attack on one particularly blatant selling campaign in Germany as their monetary prices and moral acceptability declined with increasing volume; the result was the end of the unified cultural currency entirely and the end of the papal efforts at a pan-European state. See Schachner (1962: 135), Southern (1970), Chadwick (1972: 40–63), McEvedy (1972: 24, 36).

domination. Sometimes there has been a popular revulsion against an inflationary credential market, leading to a refusal to buy any more cultural goods and even leading to a violent destruction of the culture-producing agency. In its most extreme form, this is exemplified by the Protestant reformation; in milder forms, it is exemplified by a somewhat earlier reaction in medieval Europe against the selling of credentials by the universities, and a similar development in America in the early 1970s.

The underlying cause for this revulsion against an inflationary credential market is probably to be found in the interaction between the cultural market and the material market. Perhaps the short-term cycles in the material economy and the more long-term cycles of the cultural economy coincide at particular points that makes it no longer materially promising, or even bearable, for people to invest very heavily in cultural goods. A downturn in the material economy coinciding with a point of particularly obvious overinflation of the costs of cultural prestige may be the formula for an anticultural revolution. And since cultural resources are the crucial building blocks of what is distinctive about societies, these crises may be very important indeed. Given a reaction of sufficient proportions, these may turn out to be the major turning points in history.

CONCLUSION

The cultural market, then, is a key to the class struggles over control of material production. To the extent that competitive cultural and economic markets exist at all, the success of any particular contenders in these struggles is determined not so much by their own resources as by the relationships between production and consumption of all groups in both the cultural and economic spheres. The differences between an expanding cultural market that leads to material expansion and one that leads to crisis or fragmentation are largely quantitative variations depending on the interplay among a number of conditions. In general, one might suppose that simultaneous crises of cultural and economic markets would be the equivalent of the epoch-making revolutionary crisis in Marxian theory. This may be true, although a theory of revolutions of this scope has hardly begun to be worked out.

But in more limited ways, the expansion of the cultural economy seems to move counter to the Marxian model of increasing class mobilization. The Marxian model proposes the development of a homogeneous culture among workers, brought to self-consciousness of a common interest through participation in a common economic struggle against a single enemy. The culture that is thus elevated into a general proletarian consciousness is not an abstract and externally imposed one, but is based upon the commonalities of the everyday experience of the worker. In this sense, as Lukacs (1971) stated, the proletarian class consciousness is the destruction of abstract and reified consciousness. But the expansion of formal cultural currency has precisely the opposite effects. A formal currency is doubly abstract—both as a specialized set of symbols transcending ordinary local experience and in the cryptic marks of cultural attainment summarized in educational degrees. Consciousness in a cultural currency system of this degree of formalization is directed away from the material realities of work experience and into the purely relative values of the cultural currency at that point in its market's history.

The effects of widespread cultural currency upon the occupational realm are not to unify it, but to divide it. Specialized occupational groups come increasingly into possession of resources for monopolizing positions for their own local advantage. At most, cultural currency leads to the development of self-conscious and organized groups of workers within particular specialties. This, too, is a form of class conflict, for the workers can be seen as struggling in the throes of a capitalist economy for economic survival, as well as for economic advantage. The difference is that a cultural currency makes the conflict irreparably multisided, each occupational group against the other, and tends toward increasing fragmentation rather than toward consolidation into two opposing blocs. A common cultural currency, while it may reduce ethnic differences, thus reproduces the equivalent of an ethnically segregated division of labor. Education, as I have argued elsewhere, might very well be called pseudoethnicity.

A theory of cultural markets, then, may prove relevant to salvaging Marx's insights on class conflict and revolution, although in a far more cynical form. Class conflict may be even more pervasive, and less historically revolutionary, than had been supposed.

4

The United States
in Historical Time

The social structure of the United States has a shape of its own. It is not a typical industrial society. Nor is it distinguished from others simply by virtue of being more advanced on an evolutionary scale, showing the face of the future to the rest of the world. Its most striking features are its great industrial productivity and its world-leading level of consumption; its rate of educational attainment and its number of institutions of higher education, by far the highest in the world; and its enormous expansion of the credentialed professions and concomitantly of the horizontal, decentralized form of bureaucratic organization. These features have usually been taken as a package, exemplifying the knowledge-based postindustrial society toward which the world is tending. Other features of America—its relatively nonideological politics, its degree of governmental democracy—have been claimed to be further cosequences of this evolutionary stage as well. But we have seen that the detailed evidence does not support this model of a technocratic meritocracy; the chain of causality does not run from education-based skills to economic productivity, and the other links among the parts are equally dubious.

Generally speaking, an evolutionary stage theory means a monocausal theory. One factor is assumed to have such overriding importance that changes in it define entire stages of social development. The technocratic—

functional theory, in effect, is one such model, placing central importance upon the skills demanded by a particular level of productive organization. More general evolutionary models (e.g., Parsons, 1966), emphasizing a trend toward the natural selection of more efficient organization, also rest upon a single underlying dynamic, which makes the different institutional sectors—economic, political, educational, and cultural, etc.—all correspond to each other. Marxist evolutionism as well posits a single factor of such overriding intensity—the trend in the economic organization of production—that all other institutions follow in its wake, and the only major differences among societies are historical ones among levels of development.

This kind of monofactor emphasis is very misleading. To be sure, most models recognize a variety of conditions and variations, but these are left untheorized, regarded as minor elaborations upon the main pattern. In fact, there are major differences among societies even within the great historical and archaeological categories of economic subsistence levels, and it has usually been these *differences* that have been crucial for the patterns of world history. Max Weber (1951, 1952, 1958), doubtless the foremost exponent of a multicausal view of society, placed great emphasis upon the differing forms of cultural and political organization found in the agrarian societies of China, India, the Middle East, and Europe as the key to the subsequent industrial revolution. At a lower level of economic production, there are major differences among various types of horticultural (and even among hunting-and-gathering) societies.

Hence it should hardly be surprising that industrial societies should differ among themselves, or that their political and cultural institutions are not simply hinged to a common economic pattern. Clearly, the politics of industrial societies vary structurally from centralized-bureaucratic or personal-patrimonial dictatorships to decentralized republics, and political economies vary among communism, capitalism, mixed welfare-state socialisms, and ethic—racial fascism. Wishful thinking aside, there is no clear trend from any of these to any other. In addition, industrial economies themselves can be diversified or based on a single major product, they can be wealthy or relatively poor, stable or unstable. Similarly, educational systems vary among elitist and mass, sponsored and contest mobility forms.

It is not so useful, though, to go to the opposite extreme and abandon any search for patterns whatsoever, for this means giving up the possibility of explanatory generalization. A long list of causal factors can soon become a burden upon one's capacity to see any pattern at all. What we need is a multifactor perspective composed of a manageable number of variables. Combining these, we may be able to see a wide range of alternative outcomes as the products of a few distinct conditions.

Some main dimensions of variation, in fact, are implicit in the theory of cultural markets presented in Chapter 3. That model proposed that stratification is determined by the intersection of the material production process and the cultural economy, especially to the extent that culture is produced by specialized organizations, independently of the everyday transactions that make up social life. Hence we have two main sets of causes: the conditions of the material economy and those of the cultural economy. Since the two spheres interact, let us attend to the distinctive features of each by itself. A high production of cultural currency, it was proposed, is determined by the level of material resources invested in it (which is one of the ways in which it is dependent upon the level of material production) and by the development of technologies of communication, which is an independent causal factor. But technologies, especially of this sort, tend to diffuse throughout the world fairly rapidly and hence tend not to differentiate among societies. Where societies *do* differ sharply in their cultural markets is in the degree of centralization or decentralization of cultural production and hence in the degree of competition among culture producers. It is here that the main dimensions of variation cut across the level of economic production.

The centralization or decentralization of cultural production is ultimately a matter of the intersection of history with geography. That is to say, particular parts of the world, because of local geographical peculiarities and their degree of connectedness or isolation from other places, develop particular cultural patterns. When people carrying these patterns come into contact through migration or conquest, a multicultural society is generated. These separate cultures may eventually assimilate to a common pattern, depending upon various conditions. But this does not happen inevitably, for there are countervailing forces to the forces of cultural assimilation—notably the processes by which history is encapsulated in cultural institutions. Ethnic communities that find themselves in or are forced into particular economic sectors, and especially distinctive positions of domination or subordination, tend to be continuously reproduced by the process of stratification; this is even more so if they have the resources to generate specialized culture-producing organizations, such as in the fields of religion, education, and entertainment. The solidarity of ethnic cultures is a weapon of social domination, which continues long after the initial forces that first stratified those groups have disappeared. Past traditions continue to complicate present societies because groups struggle to carry on institutions shaped in the past. History calls no time out; people living at any point in time continue to use whatever advantages they have inherited, whether in the form of cultural, organizational, or material property.

Thus a decentralized and hence highly competitive cultural market depends, through a chain of causal conditions, upon initial geographical differences and their historical encapsulation by stratified economic factors—that is, on traditionalized cultural bases of economic appropriation—and on specialized tradition-reproducing organizations. The degree to which competitive cultural markets can be active, moreover, depends upon how much the coercive power of the state allows them to do. This leads us again to a chain of causality involving geography and history. For states can strongly affect the pattern of economic stratification among cultural groups (by sheer conquest, as was so prominent in agrarian societies; or by legal enforcement of patterns of ethnic—racial job monopoly, by controlling terms of immigration, etc.). States can also directly act to foster or prohibit churches and schools. But again, the power of the state to do these things is affected by its own geographical setting and by its own encapsulation of prior historical patterns. Strong states have been those whose geography has given them a favorable military situation externally and favorable conditions of transportation and communication for internal unification.[1] And the type of state itself—its degree of centralization—decentralization and of democratic sharing of power—often involves the encapsulation of the patterns of a prior period of history. Hence geographical conditions and self-perpetuating institutionalizations of historical patterns are crucial in the realm of the state, making it both a factor in its own right, varying independently of (though interacting with) the economy and also making a causal link by which geographical and historical variants affect the operation of the cultural economy.

In this perspective, every modern industrial society has its own unique combination of factors. None should be regarded as representing an evolutionary stage through which all the others will pass. For although technologies may be exported fairly easily, the other factors cannot. The type of economic production, the degree of activity of a cultural currency, and the structure and actions of the state are independent conditions, and the latter two may be quite locally particularistic. The United States is distinctive because of its geography and historical background. Other technologically advanced societies are different because of the structural forms carried over from their histories: Russia with its post-Czarist despotism, Japan with its clanlike business corporations, France with its Napoleonic centralization, Britain with its lingering gentry, and so on.

Indeed, even the level of economic production is partly determined by local conditions—and in more than the sense that it is affected by its interaction with the local conditions expressed through the cultural market and the state. For a material economy is based not only on a technological type, but also on the natural resources and geographical conditions to which it is applied. Thus the United States has been the wealthiest of all industrial societies, not because it is technologically and organizationally the most ad-

---

[1] The argument is too complex to be developed here. For an exposition and historical evidence, see Collins (1978). Weber (1951: 20–30, 1958: 328–343) points to geographical differences between the easily centralized greater river valleys of China and the multiple heartlands of the ancient Middle East as underlying causes of the political, and hence the cultural (religious), histories of those regions.

vanced, but most importantly because it controls the wealthiest territory upon the earth (Bartholomew, 1954: 20–21). In terms of rich and varied agricultural land, mineral and fuel resources, abundant sources of water power and inland and coastal waterways for transportation, the territory is an extremely favored one for economic development. Hence the United States' world leadership in GNP (both absolute and per capita) must be attributed to geographical peculiarities that cannot simply be imitated by other countries.[2] This fact has often been lost in discussions of economic development that attribute the observed world patterns to social organization or culture, and which hold out the United States as a stage through which all societies will pass. In explanations of current American social structure, it is important to see that the high level of economic productivity is determined by factors other than the output of the educational system or by the shape of the modern professions; indeed, these appear primarily to be luxuries that a resource-rich society has been unusually able to afford. Thus introducing geographical peculiarities into our view of an economy enables us to see the direction of causality more clearly.

The pattern of development in the United States is attributable to several key conditions: Like many other societies today, American society is based upon industrial technology, and hence it shares with them the familiar features of a high level of urbanization, a politically mobilized populace, primarily nonagricultural employment, pervasive literacy, generally bureaucratic organizational style, and so forth. Its geographical resources, however, are especially rich, allowing an unusually high level of production and consumption, great military might, and the possibility of considerable spending on a sinecure sector. The United States is also very sharply distinguished from most other industrial societies because it has been among the most pervasively multiethnic societies in the modern world, especially at a crucial formative period in its institutions.[3] This has meant that the United States has had an extremely volatile and competitive cultural market, initially with effects upon religious movements, and then more significantly, producing the largest and most inflationary educational system in the history of the world. The cultural market has been especially volatile because the geographical pattern has also favored government decentralization, and thus state effects have amplified

---

[2]The fact that the United States has been overtaken in recent years in GNP per capita by oil-producing but institutionally preindustrial Kuwait illustrates the point *a fortiori*.

[3]A recent calculation based on ethno–linguistic fractionalization (Taylor and Hudson, 1972) places the United States at .50 on an index of 0 to 1.00, below Canada (.75), the USSR (.67), and Belgium (.55), but far above the United Kingdom (.32), France (.26), the Netherlands (.10), Sweden (.08), Italy (.04), West and East Germany (.03 and .02), and Japan (.01). Moreover, these are contemporary estimates; for the importance of ethnic conflict in the later nineteenth-century United States, before the cutting off of immigration began to reduce the level of ethnic multiplicity, see Chapter 5.

rather than inhibited cultural competition. Finally, the United States is politically distinctive. It has inherited the basic institutions of republican government, and in an unusually decentralized form at that, as the product of the
geographical conditions and historically crystallized institutions of the struggles
of late medieval England (see Rosenberg, 1958: 1–25; Huntington, 1966).
Moreover, the sheer size of the United States and the historical pattern set
under the limited conditions of transportation in the institution-forming period
of its history have helped extend this decentralized pattern. And in content,
American politics has been especially capitalist in its emphasis, whereas its
economic conflicts have been centered less on class-wide confrontations and
more on smaller ethnic, regional, and limited occupational interest groupings.

Some explanations as to why the United States is the most capitalist
country in the world, and why it has had its peculiarly fragmented class
struggles, will emerge as we pursue the analysis of the development of the
American economy and cultural market and their mutual interpenetration.
The expansion of the cultural market will be the subject of the next chapter,
especially in relation to the ethnic immigration and conflict that overshadowed
its formative period in the late nineteenth and early twentieth centuries. The
outcomes of this for the occupational structure and for the political side of the
class struggle generally will be reviewed in Chapters 6 and 7. But it is important to keep in mind that the United States has not always been a multiethnic
society and that a crucial formative period for the organization of the material
economy took place earlier, under different influences. Thus the United
States is a mixture of several institutional structures: the structure of the
oligopolistic corporations in the productive economy, already formed before
the rise of the credential system, and the overlay of credentialism and
credential-based occupational enclaves that arose in the succeeding period of
multiethnic conflict and an inflationary cultural market. In order to avoid
mistaking the latter for the cause of the former—of seeing the educational and
professional expansion as the cause of the corporate oligopolies—it is worth
examining briefly the rise of the national economy itself. This prelude to the
analysis of the rise of the credential system will make up the remainder of this
chapter.

THE TWO AMERICAS: NINETEENTH AND
TWENTIETH CENTURIES

The main structures of the American economy are the product of
nineteenth-century developments, especially the favorable geographical conditions and the transportation revolution that produced the first waves of
industrial growth. These economic forms were laid down shortly after the Civil

War and have changed relatively little since then. Only the long decline of small farms has changed the organizational face of the private economy, and their lengthy survival into the twentieth century may be explained by the political effects of geographical decentralization (and partly by the politics of cultural conflict with the immigrants). The national corporate economy and the survival of small-scale local businesses and professions are features of a naturally wealthy, geographically far-flung, politically decentralized nineteenth-century society. The science-based technologies of the twentieth century have not fundamentally changed this structure; they have only contributed to the economic overproduction strains within it and to the expansion of the sinecure sector. The basic economic organization of American society was laid down with a relatively simple industrial technology; the bureaucratic national corporation did not have to wait for the advanced electronic and chemical industries following the 1920s and 1930s to link scientific research and development to the industrial process. And the basic shaping of industrial society in America was carried out with a relatively uneducated work force; the meshing of the extended educational-credential system and bureaucratic employment is something that came later and largely outside of the nexus of technological demand.

The second, twentieth-century, America is the result of massive and ethnically diverse immigration, especially in the late nineteenth and early twentieth centuries. Its earlier outlines may be seen in the response to Irish immigration before the Civil War; the results of the importation of African slaves during the colonial period were largely delayed until their mobilization into urban society in the mid-twentieth century. These cultural conflicts contributed above all to the expansion of the culture-producing sector—and in particular the expansion of the educational system, which was used both as a means of control and of monopolization by the Anglo-Protestant bourgeoisie, and eventually as a path to creating positions and to occupational mobility by many immigrant groups themselves. The credential system became the basis for struggles over the control of occupations by professionalization and the model for other forms of licensing and position monopolizing. Educational bureaucracies themselves led the trend of increasing government employment that has characterized the twentieth-century labor force in response to continuous overproduction pressures and the mobilization of ethnic politics.

Thus we have two sets of factors underlying present-day American social structure. The conditions that we may somewhat glibly refer to as "nineteenth-century America" are those of geographic isolation and political decentralization upon a resource-rich territory. The conditions that may be called "twentieth-century America," because their main impact was subsequent to and building upon the earlier economic and political structure, are the massive immigration that transformed America into a multiethnic society and the improvements of twentieth-century technology that brought about our economy of overproduction and occupational sinecures.

The Nineteenth-Century Basis

The U.S. economy was already centered on industrial enterprise by the time of the Civil War (Gates, 1960; Cochran and Miller, 1961; North, 1961; Struik, 1962: 175–199, 303–333). Agriculture was being mechanized; the factory system of manufacturing was already extensive; the mining and heavy metals industries had been established; the national railway network was near completion. The 35 years after the Civil War were less a period of industrial foundation than of consolidating a national economy under the control of large corporations. Although the settlement of the trans-Mississippi West continued through the 1880s (with attendant wars on the indigenous Indian population), modern industrial America was clearly established by the last quarter of the nineteenth century. The railway network was complete, providing national marketing for all commodities. Agriculture was not only commercial, but also organized by large enterprises using mechanical equipment; the smaller farmers began to be squeezed out and the rural populace began to diminish as a proportion of the whole.

As Table 4.1 shows, the proportion of the labor force in agriculture has declined steadily since the early nineteenth century. It dropped below 50% of the labor force in the 1880s. Conversely, manufacturing and construction increased, making their biggest leap between 1850 and 1900. The shift is not quite as severe as one might expect, however. Even in 1820, about one-sixth of the labor force was in manufacturing and construction, although mostly in preindustrial craft or small-scale enterprises. This sector increased to about one-third of the labor force by about 1920 and the proportion has stayed approximately steady ever since. Contrary to the expectations of mid-nineteenth-century observers, modern society has not become dominated by industrial workers, but neither have they tended to disappear. The late nineteenth-century pattern, for the core of the industrial system, has turned out to be an enduring one.

This was true with respect to organizations as well. After the 1860s, concentration set in very rapidly. By the end of the century, oil, steel, tobacco, and other industries had become divided among a few large corporations. The national scope of business was crucial in this development (Chandler, 1959: 1–31; 1962). Those firms that organized a national distribution system had a competitive advantage over local business, thus forcing the trend to bigness. The meat-packing industry led the way, with a refrigerated railway distribution system centered in Chicago. Manufacturers of such products as reapers, typewriters, sewing machines, bicycles, and later automobiles, hit on

Table 4.1
Industrial Distribution as a Percentage of the American Labor Force, 1820–1970

Type of industry	1820	1840	1860	1880	1900	1920	1940	1950	1970
Agriculture, forestry, and fisheries	72	69	59	50	37	27	17	15	5
Mining	NA	.3	1	2	3	3	2	2	1
Manufacturing and construction	12	15	18	23	25	31	29	33	31
Transportation, trade, finance, and real estate	NA	NA	7	12	17	20	24	29	32
Services and government	NA	NA	12	12	11	16	21	21	33
Not allocated	16	16	.7	.1	.1	.9	6	—	—

Sources: *Historical Statistics of the United States*, Series D, 57–71; *Statistical Abstract of the United States, 1971*, Tables 341 and 342. Figures should be treated as approximations, since not all sources and time periods use the same definitions of enterprises nor do they all have data of equal reliability. Totals may not add up to 100% due to rounding.
    NA indicates not available.

the advantages of vertical integration. Instead of relying on independent wholesalers for their distribution, major companies set up their own distribution and repair networks, driving out their less efficient small competitors as a result. Expansion backward to incorporate sources of supplies added further stability to the enterprises' production, thus rounding out the bureaucratic structure of American industry. Another reason for concentration was financial; the large national enterprises needed huge amounts of capital, and by the end of the century the elaborate corporate devices of the trust and holding companies were dominated by the major Eastern banks.

By 1900, the modern pattern was set. The period of competition among numerous small businesses was largely over, and every major sector of the economy was a controlled market, dominated by a few oligopolistic organizations. The "trustbusting" period of reform politics that followed the turn of the century did not reverse the trend, but it stopped concentration just short of monopoly—in some cases breaking up monopolies such as Carnegie's in steel and Duke's in tobacco. The resulting level of concentration has remained constant ever since. The new industries (automobiles, electrical equipment, chemicals, aircraft) have quickly taken on the same pattern. Thus in 1920 (the earliest year for which figures are available), the largest 5% of business companies took in 80% of business income, both in manufacturing and finance; this proportion has held steady since then.[4]

The basic shape of the national economy was thus established early in the industrialization process. The pressures of technology are not crucial in this development; the monopolistic national corporation emerges in tobacco and other agricultural products as readily as in steel and machinery. Rockefeller's monopoly in oil was established first in the technically crude market supplying oil lamps and became transferred to the automobile market that emerged fortuitously several decades later. Rockefeller's strategy was typical in that it drew on financial manipulations in the national arena against locally oriented business, and this was done in explicit alliance with the national railroads. Somewhat similarly, the Dupont Corporation's dominant position was established first by capturing a commanding position in the manufacture of traditional gunpowders as a result of long-standing government contracts, and then enhanced by financial manipulations such as that which enabled it to acquire temporary control of General Motors during World War I; its position was merely extended by the opportunities created by the chemical discoveries in the 1920s and 1930s.

In effect, the geography of the United States, interacting with its demographic and political structures, was crucial for the shape of industrial society. The fertility of the land and its suitability for large-scale agriculture provided an initial basis of wealth and incentive to commercialization; the favorable conditions for long-distance transportation and the abundance of mineral resources made possible a very rapid and productive industrialization. The main limiting factor was the small population, especially early in the nineteenth century. But in an indirect way, the population problem proved to be an added spur to industrialization. It provided an incentive to mechanize agriculture and craft production, and it also tended to keep wages high (relative to labor-rich Europe), ensuring a large consumer demand and hence a spur to mass consumption industries. And these, of course, are the industries in which American innovations are best known: changing the automobile from a luxury of the European upper class into a mass production item; turning photography into mass-entertainment motion pictures; organizing electric power, telephones, radio, and television for mass consumption; pioneering food packaging for large-scale, long-distance storage and delivery; developing synthetic (plastic, nylon, rayon) substitutes for previous luxury goods (porcelain, silk) and thus opening them up to mass consumer markets.[5]

---

[4]*Historical Statistics of the United States* (Series V45−56); *Statistical Abstract of the United States* (1971: Table 713). In 1968, the richest 2.8% of the businesses took in 78.7% of the income.

[5]The internal combustion engine, photography, the electric dynamo, the telegraph, radio, refrigerator, and first plastics (celluloid) are European (mainly British and German) inventions, as

The twentieth century has seen a continuous series of such expansions, but the pattern was already established in the more traditional products of the nineteenth century.

The relatively thin population and the geographically far-flung economic resources that developed simultaneously in the nineteenth-century boom gave a special prominence to the national transport system. Itself financed on a national scale (and originally an international one, especially through British investments), the railroads provided the basis for a national financial center, which in turn provided the resources that put national corporations in quasi-monopolistic control over most major industries. The large-scale bureaucratic form followed from this geographic scope and was already in evidence in the late nineteenth century (Chandler, 1968: 220–237).

National finance and business were not only better organized for direct economic competition than other economic interests, but they were better organized to gain political influence as well. American government continued the decentralized traditions of the colonists, and westward expansion in the democratic atmosphere of the early nineteenth century resulted in a large number of state governments. These attracted the attention of local speculative interests, especially in local banking. National business, however, concentrated relatively early on the federal government; in the absence of any well-organized opposition, it won major concessions not only in the form of enormous grants to the railroads, but also in the form of favorable policies on finances, immigration, and labor control.[6] State governments were generally left to local interests while the plural structure was turned to advantage in the legal maneuverings to find favorable sites for the financial devices by which monopolistic corporations and holding companies were organized. Centralized business prospered vis-à-vis decentralized government.

Against this organizational advantage, labor was especially weak. The peak period of industrialization, the 1880s, was also a period of labor militancy, but the breaking of the strongest union in the Pullman strike in 1894 through the intervention of federal troops symbolized the decisive advantage

---

is the basic science on which some of them rest. The telephone is an American invention, while the long-lasting and inexpensive evacuated light bulb was simultaneously invented in England and America, based upon the previous British electric-arc lamp. It is the commercial development of inventions that is notably American. See Mason (1962: 474–485, 503–526).

[6]The major opposition to national business influence was from Southern agriculture interests in the first half of the century over the issue of the tariff, but the power of this group waned at about the time the railroads began to develop. It was the national business group that apparently provided the strongest support for the Union cause in the Civil War, no doubt in recognition of the threat of Southern succession to the national scope of the economy. We do find the domination of major cabinet posts, above all in the Treasury and the War departments, by members of the national financial group (Wall Street financiers and lawyers) firmly established since the Lincoln administration; see Mills (1963: 110–139); Domhoff (1967: 58–62, 84–114).

of national business. The hostility and active intervention of the national government against the unions left the American labor movement relatively weak until the 1930s, a very late period in its industrial history by contrast to European societies.[7]

Yet the size and natural wealth of the territory, and above all the large consumer markets, left numerous opportunities for smaller business in America; as we shall see, smaller entrepreneurs have held their own in more modest sectors of the economy right up through the present. The "Reform" movement of the turn of the twentieth century was above all a mobilization of the Anglo-Protestant middle class, reacting against the pressures of the new economy and culture, but its greatest successes were against the immigrants in culture and politics, and relatively little was achieved in direct confrontation with the power of the trusts. Middle-class political power was successful primarily on the state level in protecting small entrepreneurs in retailing and services, establishing regulations that favored local price fixing, and giving monopolistic powers to professional associations (Cutler, 1939: 851–856; Gilb, 1966; Wiebe, 1967).

For the shape of economic stratification as a whole, the geographic conditions of America thus had their effects by around the end of the nineteenth century: the power of national finance over major productive processes, its special influence over the national government, the corresponding weakness of organized labor, and the sheltering of small entrepreneurs and professionals within localized enclaves.

Twentieth-Century Outcomes

Early industrialism shows the main patterns of later industrialism. Subsequent increases in the productivity of technology and its linking, for the first time, in a regular fashion to the results of scientific research, produce comparatively minor changes. The developments of the twentieth century do not take place in the basic structure, nor do they greatly change the patterns of class and ethnic stratification, nor the fundamental modes of social selection.

Let us examine what has changed and what has remained the same (see Tables 4.1 and 4.2). The percentage of the labor force in agriculture dropped from 37% in 1900 to 5% in 1970. The proportion in the industrial sector (mining, manufacturing, and construction) has hardly shifted: 28% in 1900,

---

[7]The ability of business interests to profit from escalating ethnic conflicts was a related factor. "Americanization" and antiradicalism were usually a single issue, with such consequences as the FBI crackdown on labor in the "Red Scare" after World War I, coinciding with the mass hysteria that brought a legislative end to immigration (see Johnson, 1976).

Table 4.2
Occupational Distribution (%), 1900–1970

Type of occupation	1900	1920	1940	1970
Professional and technical	4.2	5.4	7.5	14.2
Managers, officials, and				
proprietors	5.8	6.6	7.3	10.5
Clerical	3.0	8.0	9.6	17.4
Sales	4.5	4.9	6.7	6.2
Craftsmen and foremen	10.5	13.0	12.0	13.0
Operatives	12.8	15.6	18.4	17.7
Nonfarm laborers	12.5	11.6	9.4	4.7
Service workers, except				
private household	3.6	4.5	7.0	10.3
Private household workers	5.4	3.3	4.6	2.0
Farmers and farm managers	19.9	15.3	10.4	2.2
Farm laborers and foremen	17.7	11.7	7.0	1.8

Sources: *Statistical Abstract of the United States,* 1971, Tables 347 and 348; *Historical Statistics of the United States,* Series D, 72–122.

32% in 1970. The decline in the agricultural sector has been absorbed entirely within the tertiary sector, with transportation and trade and finance growing from 17 to 32%, and services and government from 11 to 33% of the labor force during this period. Since 1950, the only important growth sector for jobs has been in government employment (Table 4.1: a jump from 21% to 33% between 1950 and 1970 in the services and government sector), especially with the expansion of the military, welfare, and eductional bureaucracies. The same points may be illustrated with occupational (Table 4.2) rather than industrial breakdowns: The industrial working class (craftsmen and foremen, operatives, and nonfarm laborers) has stayed virtually the same (totaling 35.8% in 1900, 35.4% in 1970), while the largest increases have been in the clerical (3.0% to 17.4%), professional and technical (4.2% to 14.2%) and service (3.6% to 10.3%) categories. In the wealthy industrial society of mid-twentieth-century America, less than one-half of the active adult population engages in the extraction or the production of goods, while the rest are involved either in distribution, administration, luxury services, or the welfare services and sinecures of government employment.

New industries have continued to appear. Electricity began to be used for light and power in the late nineteenth century, and later for phonographs, movies, and radio. In the early twentieth century, there was the automobile with its effect on the production of oil, rubber, glass, paint, and highway construction. In the 1930s came the chemical industries with the invention of plastics, nylons, cellophane, vitamins, and drugs. After World War II came the invention of jet planes and military rockets and a second wave of electronic developments, such as transistors, computers, and television, and the continued expansion of national chains into retail distribution of groceries, clothing, and meals.

But the level of business concentration has stayed much the same.[8] In some areas, such as automobile production, the industry began with competition among a large number of small manufacturers and eventually concentrated around the few well-financed corporations that achieved vertical integration most swiftly. In others, such as electrical utilities, major financial interests dominated the industry from the outset. In virtually every area, the industry came to be dominated by a few big corporations within two or three decades of the first commercial offering of a product. In the major areas of production, above all heavy industry, the quasi-monopolistic national corporation has been the organizational pattern since the late nineteenth century.

This is not to say that the small independent business has disappeared. In the 1960s there were 11 million businesses in the United States, 90% of which had 20 employees or less (*Statistical Abstract,* 1971: Tables 710, 720). Most of these were unincorporated and concentrated in retail or services (restaurants, bars, laundries, home repairs, or business services) and in construction and real estate. There also remain a few small commercial farms, although the twentieth century has seen a steady trend toward large-scale concentration in agriculture, virtually completed in the 1960s. Outside of agriculture, however, the proportion of small businesses has held fairly steady since the establishment of oligopolies around the turn of the century.

There are several reasons why the small business sector has been able to maintain itself in an economy overwhelmingly dominated by large corporations. Certain enterprises based on local markets—for example, bars and restaurants—are accessible to very small capital investments, and in the case of bars and liquor stores, are protected by local licensing policies. Other areas—for example, the entertainment world—are highly volatile, marketing a series of continually innovative, short-term projects. Although large-scale corporations dominate distribution in records and movies, the production aspect is often highly decentralized. Such areas of high risk can most economically be externalized by large corporations; thus recording studios and franchise dealers of autos, appliances, or gasoline can survive as independent (or semi-independent) small business (McCauly, 1966: Hirsh, 1972: 639–659). Very modern areas of highly technical innovation such as electronics

---

[8]On trends in industrial concentration, see *Statistical Abstract* (1966: Table 1147); see also Cochran and Miller (1961) and Chandler (1962).

are often pioneered by small businesses, usually by engineers or applied scientists striking out on their own. These new areas have usually been consolidated under the control of a few large corporations in a few decades, but the continual innovativeness of the American economy has constantly produced a certain number of small businesses, however unstable, at any given time.

How do we look at the structural changes that *have* taken place in twentieth-century America—the decline of agricultural employment, the growth of government, of education, of clerical, professional—technical, managerial, and service sectors generally? The increased productivity of twentieth-century technology operates within the same basic structures laid down by nineteenth-century American capitalism under the new conditions of vehement ethnic struggles. The nationally organized bureaucratic corporation in the major productive sectors, and small business and independent professionals in the local ones, usually state-protected enclaves of finance, distribution, and services—these have been enduring features of American stratification for about a century now. The massive increases in productivity of twentieth-century technology have taken place within this structure. Its effect on the skill and educational levels technically required for maintaining material production has turned out to be rather small. What it has produced is a continuous problem of aggregate demand, a reversal of the chronic labor shortage of the nineteenth century into the chronic unemployment pressures of the twentieth. The growth of the tertiary sector and of white-collar employment has been the response—to the pressures for employment opportunities from the labor force and to industrial demand for a prosperous economy capable of buying its products.[9]

The mechanism by which the tertiary sector has absorbed technically surplus labor has generally been indirect; WPA-style hiring of the unemployed poor has been the exception. Rather, it has been by going along the path of least resistance—expanding military and welfare expenditures, following the politically popular slogans of equality of educational opportunity and higher technical quality in education (e.g., the Sputnik crisis), increasing the proportions of specialized professional branches, and allowing the proliferation of clerical bureaucracy within governmental and corporate organization—that tertiary employment has been built up. The expansion has been as great at state and local government levels as at the federal level, thus maintaining traditional decentralization, even in a new form; the proliferation

---

[9]See Bensman and Vidich (1971: 5–31). O'Connor (1973) argues that the industrial upper class supports this policy because the increased tax cost is passed on to the consumer through quasi-monopoly prices and through other devices that kept it from being a burden on their personal incomes.

of "professional" specializations and of record-keeping complexity itself has
contributed to internal organizational decentralization. In this ethos, federal
and state government have continued to expand the self-protective privileges
of business and professional associations and have continued to support
private industry by loosely monitored contracts for equipment, construction,
and services. All this has been carried out, against a background of general
political approval, through the more immediate activity of the status groups
that actually inhabit government organizations, private businesses, and professional communities. Hence it has been the best-mobilized status groups of
the upper middle and middle classes that have secured the largest and most
immediate benefits from this policy of unconscious Keynesianism. But the
effects must have been to reduce the employment problem indirectly at lower
levels—by keeping open the market for personal services, spurring industrial
employment (now turned increasingly toward essentially luxury goods), and
keeping members of higher classes from invading lower labor markets.

The ethos of technocracy is the ideology by which the sinecure society is
legitimated. Rising educational requirements for employment, the proliferation of professional and technical degrees and their control over specialized
work enclaves, the massive clerical enterprise of personnel management in a
credentialized system—all of these are devices whereby the tertiary sector
expands upon itself. Being remote from the sectors in which actual material
production takes place, outputs in this sector have only arbitrary criteria by
which they can be measured;[10] the only guidelines for its efficiency come from
the contending forces of the political budget, itself balanced between pressures to keep up aggregate demand and the defenses of particular social
classes concerning their own taxation. The technocratic ideology favors the
forces of sinecure expansion at the same time that it hides their actual nature.
The result is an elitist Keynesianism, maintaining a system of stratification that
has been quite stable for a number of decades.

But what of the decline in the number of agricultural enterprises? Here
we may note that the twentieth century has only brought about the pattern
that has existed in other major areas of material production for the national
market since the late nineteenth century. The small business sector that has
survived throughout this period is at the other end of the economic process, in
local enclaves and concentrating in distribution, services, and luxuries. The
enduring small business sector has been protected against large-scale eco-

---

[10]This holds for all large and internally complex bureaucratic organizations. The counterpres-
sures of market competition have been alleged to prevent sinecures in private employment, but
this pressure can hardly be strong in the oligopolistic national corporations, especially where
government contract work is done. When these corporations do respond to market fluctuations, it
is by laying off manual workers, whose output is indeed measurable, while the invisible-output
white-collar workers are retained.

nomic competition by state protection and other favorable niches; much of it, albeit indirectly, is in the sinecure sector of economic organization, where essentially luxury consumption and inefficient modes of production are favored as a sort of tax the highly productive core of the economy can afford (and is politically required to support).[11]

What is remarkable about the concentration of agriculture is not that it has come about, but that it has been delayed so long. What has allowed it to survive, on the national markets for processed and refrigerated foods and against the resources of the national financial establishment, has been essentially its favored status group connections within American stratification and politics. It was the Anglo-Protestant farmers, as we shall see, who were the bulwark of cultural opposition to the immigrant working class from the mid-nineteenth century through the mid-twentieth century; the use of the political ideology of Anglo-Protestant Americanism to hold together the coalition with the big business upper class has required continual political concessions to the farmers. The long-term trend since the *early* 1800s, though, has been a *continuous* decline in the agricultural labor force (see Table 4.1) as the market forces of a system of national capitalism have steadily eroded the position of the small farmer. One might guess that without the political alliances engendered by late nineteenth-century immigration, the process would have been pushed to its conclusion half a century ago—or else would have provoked a successful populist revolt to curtail the power of big business.

The hypothetical case is of general significance. The cutting off of non-Anglo immigration in 1860 instead of 60 years later would have made an immense difference in the American social structure of today. Given its geography and its natural resources, America would still be unique among industrial societies (although one difference might be that the United States would be less industrialized). The thought-experiment sharpens a more particular point: the emphasis which a multiethnic society puts on cultural stratification and the uses to which these weapons can be put in the organization of its economy and policy.

Nineteenth-century America is thus the basis of our society of oligopolistic national corporations and a decentralized local bourgeoisie. Twentieth-century America is the overlay of credentialism, government employment, and widespread sinecures that has arisen due to the active cultural market of massive ethnic conflict and the overproduction pressures of an advanced productive technology. The ramifications of the credential process will be taken up in Chapters 5 and 6.

----

[11]If we regard independent professions as service businesses, lawyers provide a particularly clear example of a government-created monopoly (in this case over access to judicial pleadings, delegated to the lawyers) that reaps the surplus wealth for essentially sinecure positions within the economy (see chapter 6).

5

The Rise of the Credential System

The big change in the social structure of the twentieth-century United States has not been in the organization and control of the productive sector of the economy, but in the superstructure built upon it. We have seen an enormous expansion of what I have called "political labor," the rise of a huge "sinecure sector" of government employment, massive educational institutions, and the growth of the tertiary sector generally. An underlying factor allowing the growth of this nonproductive sector has been the economic pressures for keeping up aggregate demand as productive technology has grown steadily more powerful while proportionately fewer workers are required. But the most direct agent of this expansion has been the growth of the educational credential system. The schools themselves have been a major component of government employment (42% in 1975, and 10% of all employment, see *Statistical Abstract of the United States,* 1976: Tables 452 and 569). The extension of school attendance has kept increasing proportions of the potential labor force occupied elsewhere (often, as in the case of college students supported by financial aids, in a condition of disguised welfare support). Educational credentials have been the means by which much of the sinecure sector has been built up. It has provided the means of building specialized professional and technical enclaves, elaborated bureaucratic staff divisions, and in general has served to monopolize jobs for specialized groups of workers and thus insulate them from pressures for directly productive work.

The United States is the most credentialized society in the world, and its educational system is correspondingly unique. Where most industrial countries have had relatively small secondary school systems, the United States has not only long pushed toward universal high school attendance, but in the 1960s also came close to universal completion of high school by the teenage population. College attendance built up to close to one-half of the young adult population, college graduation came near to one-fifth, and postgraduate studies have expanded at an unprecedented rate. Moreover, as we have seen (Table 1.1), these trends have been building up steadily since the late nineteenth century.

The U.S. educational system has been different not only quantitatively, but also structurally in comparison with most industrial societies. Most others divide their secondary education among two or three institutions—an elite organization (the English public school, the German *gymnasium,* the French *lycée*), teaching traditional high culture and leading to university attendance; a commercial high school preparing students directly for business or clerical work; and sometimes a third technical school for engineers and technicians, or at a lower level, a vocational arts school for the potential working class (when these are not simply released from school if they fail the differentiating examination at the beginning of their teens). These forms have been described as a **sponsored mobility** system, in that once the branching point has been reached, the rest of the student's career is set, and the student who passes this point is sponsored through successive levels without much attrition (Turner, 1960).

The U.S. system, by comparison, is described as a **contest mobility** system. There are no crucial branching points. There are no sharp divisions among different types of secondary schools, or even among different sorts of undergraduate colleges. It is fairly easy to transfer among different sorts of programs or to re-enter the system after dropping out (Eckland, 1964). The main pattern is one of continuous attrition from year to year, from high school on through advanced professional training, as the "contest" continues indefinitely. Moreover, there are no fixed end points. The occupational consequences of education in this system are purely relative. Where the European type of branching into specialized training produces distinctive types of careers at early choice points (e.g., medical or legal training are entered directly at the end of secondary school), the U.S. system continually puts off final professional identification to the very end of the sequence. This end point has changed continuously as once-elite high school degrees have become near-universal, common undergraduate training has been supplanted by graduate-level education, and for the lucrative specialties, increasingly by postdoctoral specialized training.

In brief, the contrast is between a system in which elite occupational access is marked off early by horizontal branchings and one in which there is a continuous set of vertical ranks, formally accessible to everyone with sufficient perseverance, with elite occupational status attached to sheer longevity within the system.[1] There are also differences of quality among different schools at each level of the American system,[2] but these form a continuous progression rather than sharp divisions, and individual students can and do transfer horizontally among them as the contest goes on. Moreover, as we shall see, the lower-prestige forms have continuously changed to emulate the high-prestige forms.

The American system exemplifies the workings of a volatile cultural market. For this, it has had the determining conditions in abundance. A cultural market appears when material resources are invested in specialized culture-producing organizations. The more decentralized and competitive these organizations, the more competition there is in the realm of cultural consumption, especially if at the same time culture is attached to stratification, by which economic and political domination are organized on the basis of cultural group membership. In the United States around the turn of the twentieth century, these conditions approached an extreme. America's geographical and political decentralization not only prevented any particular group from

---

[1]Note the following figures from the early 1960s for the percentages of the population in the industrialized countries that complete various levels of education.

Country	Percentage completing secondary school[a]	Percentage attending university	Percentage graduating from university
United States	75	39	18
USSR	47	19	9
Japan	57	11	12
France	30	11	—
England	12	6	5
West Germany	11	6	—

Sources: Bereday (1969, 80, 281); Havighurst (1968, 55–56); Blewett (1965, 113, 118, 122, 158–159).
[a]Percentages refer to relevant age groups.

[2]It has been suggested that internal tracking within American high schools (Rosenbaum, 1976) and distinctions among junior colleges and 4-year colleges (Karabel, 1972) are the equivalents of the "sponsored mobility" form. The difference between the U.S. and most European educational systems is one of degree, as there are elements of "contest-like" attrition in the latter as well. The figures given in Footnote 1 show that the USSR also has a "contest mobility" pattern; Japan has a significant contest point for university entrance, but "sponsored" mobility thereafter. One should bear in mind that the character of the different systems cannot be captured entirely by such figures, for different types of secondary schools, where they exist, are lumped together in one column.

monopolizing control of the educational system (as was very nearly the case in most European societies), but also actively fostered the founding of schools at all levels, by state and local governments, church denominations, and private entrepreneurs. Not only was there no state church, but also competing denominations emulated one another in founding schools. Middle-class organization of new communities behind the receding frontier could also be accomplished by establishing schools on local initiative. And most importantly of all, the United States underwent a period of the most massive and diverse ethnic immigration in the history of the world. In the situation of political and geographical decentralization, this multiethnic society generated a tremendous struggle for cultural hegemony, which was fought out especially by building a massive school system.

The decentralization of control over this system meant that any specific purpose for which schools might be intended would be swallowed up by the competition among groups and institutions. Business owners might favor schools to socialize the work force (Bowles and Gintis, 1976); the average Anglo-Protestant citizen might favor them to Americanize offensively alien cultures (Katz, 1968). The plutocratic elite might build exclusive private schools to keep their children separate (Baltzell, 1958: 337–348); Catholic communities or other religious and ethnic minorities might build separate schools in the interest of their own cultural pride (Curti, 1935). But the surrounding context would not let any school alone; its students found themselves in a larger world where more and more education was becoming visible in the populace, and higher and higher levels of education were needed for occupational entry. Schools came to imitate one another's programs: secondary schools in order to enter their graduates into high-prestige colleges, the varieties of colleges and professional schools to make themselves part of the sequence that would allow their students to claim at least a chance of attaining the highest social positions. American schools thus came to form a unified hierarchy, and one that expanded continuously in a vertical direction.

Although the competing cultures of America were most sharply distinguished originally in ethnic and religious terms, the specific content of education has become increasingly less important. As the system elaborated, the value of any particular kind and level of education came to depend less and less on any specific content that might have been learned in it, and more and more upon the sheer fact of having attained a given level and acquired the formal credential that allowed one to enter the next level (or ultimately to pass the requirements for entering a monopolized occupation). Cultures of specific groups were gradually transformed into abstract credentials. In theoretical terms, the particular cultures of everyday social transactions were transmuted into a general currency. This cultural currency became increasingly autonomous, increasingly subject to organizational forces within its own sphere of

production. The process of bureaucratization within schools themselves
would further shape the nature of the cultural currency into directions far
removed from the original ethnic and religious contents, and indeed removed
as well from whatever scientific and technical content various reformers attempted to add to it.

The rise of a competitive system for producing an abstract cultural currency in the form of educational credentials has been the major new force
shaping stratification in twentieth-century America. Beginning with the internal organization of schools themselves, credentials have permeated the occupational structure, from elite professional monopolies on down, and have
been the decisive impetus to the elaboration of super-complex bureaucracies
in all spheres. Just as the ethnic struggles shaped the other social struggles of
the late nineteenth and early twentieth centuries, the permeation of educational credentials into the occupational world has shaped the major issues of
stratification in recent decades.

Does this mean that ethnic and cultural issues have submerged economic
class conflict? To put the question in this way would be to misunderstand the
nature of social organization. Economic classes do not exist in one compart-
ment, cultural groups in another. Empirically, the world consists of the interaction of individuals maneuvering *individually* for whatever goods and favorable social positions they can attain. Not only are cultural goods weapons that
individuals can use in obtaining and monopolizing economic positions, but
cultural goods also make all the difference in determining how individuals will
ally with others in order to fight for advantages. To put the matter another
way: There is no pre-set number of economic classes struggling as blocs for
economic survival or supremacy. The "working class" and "bourgeoisie" are
only statistical categories formed in the mind of a theorist, except insofar as
real people actually form alliances to act as such groups. The forming of such
groups is a cultural matter (as sophisticated Marxist theorists have recognized
well enough when they see class formation as a question of mobilizing groups
by "raising consciousness"). In fact, economic struggles have almost always
been fought out among a much larger number of smaller groups, as cultures
that have united them have usually extended only locally, within particular
organizations or occupational sectors, or within particular ethnic groups.
Ethnic groups, or segments of them, *are* economic interest groups when they
occupy common occupational positions. The "ethnic division of labor"
(Hechter, 1974) or "eth-classes" (Gordon, 1964) have been far more common economic actors than Marxian class-wide fronts. And the same holds for
the groups that have emerged in the twentieth century based upon the
abstract cultural currency of educational credentials. In describing the conflict
of cultural groups, then, I will be describing the actual shaping of class struggles in America.

The aim of this chapter, then, is to outline the rise of the educational credential system in the United States and the conditions that have shaped it. This involves looking first at the immigration that made the United States into a multiethnic society and the way it has shaped American political and economic conflicts ever since. Then we examine the growth of educational organizations, from the minimal schooling of monoethnic colonial America, to the growth of elementary and secondary schools as ethnic conflict escalated, and concluding with the development of colleges and universities. The vicissitudes of professional education and its eventual linking to a unified credential system will be left for Chapter 6.

MULTIETHNIC CONFLICT IN AMERICA

The thin population of the United States, relative to its geographic size and economic resources, created a huge demand for labor in the nineteenth century. Eventually, the cultural conflicts of the immigration, the most diverse in the history of the world, would force a closing of the state barriers around the territory. The open immigration policy of the intervening period was virtually unique. The colonies of France, Spain, and Holland were reserved for their own citizens, and their territories already contained sizable native populations, thus eliminating any sizable demand for external labor and limiting immigration to a single elite. But in North America, in the absence of an indigenous labor force working at a subsistence level, an expensive labor force had to be imported, with resulting impetus for mass consumption industry and rapid economic development.[3] Against the background of initial settlement by radical Protestants and the conditions favoring their middle-class cultural style in the colonial period, the alien cultures of the period of mass immigration provoked a crusade for cultural domination. The institutional consequences of that crusade make up a major part of the uniqueness of American social structure.

The American population in 1790, at the beginning of the republic, was about 4 million (*Historical Statistics of the United States*, Series Z20). About 66% were of English-Scottish background; another 8% were Irish (mostly northern Irish Protestants); another 10% were Dutch or German. In total, about 85% of the country was Protestant and probably English speaking, with the remaining 15% black Africans, most of them slaves.

---

[3]For a comparative economic analysis showing the advantages of an expensive labor force, see Emmanuel (1972). Hartz (1964) describes the political consequences of the settling of relatively unpopulated territories, although ignoring the specific effects of ethnic traditions and conflicts on American social structure.

The United States had one of the most rapidly growing populations of the modern era. The population was under 4 million in 1790; it had risen to 23 million in 1850, 76 million in 1900, 151 million by 1950, and about 205 million by 1970 (*Statistical Abstract,* 1971: Table 1). Part of the increase was due to internal growth, but most of it was due to immigration. The 4 million people who carried the culture of the early United States, an overwhelmingly white, Protestant, English-speaking group with their black slaves, faced a long series of immigrations from alien cultures that threatened to swamp them.

The cultural threats of immigration built up progressively throughout the nineteenth century. As Table 5.1 shows, by 1850, 10% of the people in the United States were foreign born (extrapolating from the only available figures, those for males). It is not known how many others had foreign-born parents. The black population was about 15%; thus, by the mid-nineteenth century, the old native majority was down to about 75% or possibly below. The great shift, however, occurred after the Civil War. In 1900, about 14% of the American populace was foreign born, about 20% had foreign-born parents, and the black population was down to about 11%. Together this adds up to 45%—close to a majority of the population not of the original stock. Only in the twentieth century was the tide turned back so that by 1950 only about one-third of the population was foreign born, of foreign parentage, or black.

This conveys some notion of the pressure that Anglo-Protestant America has felt over the last century and a half, but the following figures make it even stronger (*Historical Statistics,* C 218–283; H 538–543). In 1850, 70% of the foreign born came from northwestern Europe or Canada. Hence they were usually Protestants, although some of them spoke German or Scandinavian languages. By 1900, half of the foreign born in the United States came from northern Europe. The general trend during this period is for immigration to come from "alien" cultures. By 1890, 40% of the United States was Catholic

Table 5.1
Percentage of Native, Foreign, and Black Population (Adult Males), 1850–1950

	1850	1900	1950
Native-born white males of native parents	75	55	68
Foreign-born white males	10	14	7
Native-born white males of foreign parents	—	20	15
Black males	15	11	10
Total adult male population (millions)	12	38.5	74.4

Source: *Historical Statistics,* Series C, 218–283.

and about 5% was Jewish. Since blacks were mostly Protestant, this means that by 1890 the Catholics and Jews probably outnumbered the white Protestants in the United States.

The conflict arising from the situation was especially severe because many of the groups were organized on widely differing cultural styles. Their backgrounds ranged from those of Anglo-Protestant independent commercial farmers, Catholic peasants from the autocratic agrarian societies of Europe, traditional Jewish merchants and artisans from the cordoned-off *shtetls* of Poland and Russia, to African slaves from horticultural tribes, and indigenous Indian tribes, many living in hunting-and-gathering cultures. In effect, the United States was not only a transplanted polyglot Europe, but also a sampling of cultures from most of the major types of societies that have existed in world history, all pushed together simultaneously.

Such major differences in political, economic, and community organization do not merely produce superficial differences in language, cuisine, and style of dress, but much more profound differences in styles of work, attitudes toward power, religion, and personal interaction. The bulk of the Anglo-Protestant population, for example, held ascetic attitudes toward work, savings, play, and sexual behavior (Main, 1965; Morgan, 1966). These attitudes fitted small independent communities where moderate economic respectability could be attained by most people, and the market enforced continuous discipline. Many of the Catholic immigrants, in contrast, came from the bottom levels of societies dominated by aristocratic landlords; in these circumstances, hard work and frugality were externally enforced rigors, not internalized ideals, and an attitude of fatalism went along with the ideal of period celebration and largesse (Thomas and Znaniecki, 1918; Arensberg and Kimball, 1948; Banfield, 1958; Gans, 1962). Similar differences held in political style: Whereas the Anglo-Protestants were used to co-management of community affairs and stressed public enforcement of religious moralities, the Catholic peasants had a heritage of political subordination that gave them mainly familistic and patrimonial standards of political loyalty (Weber, 1968: 458–472, 1006–1067). From these sorts of differences flowed sharply opposing conceptions of morality: The Anglo-Protestants regarded the immigrants as lazy, dissolute, and politically corrupt; the Catholics' view of their hosts is not recorded, but it is likely that they viewed them as fanatical, priggish, and disloyal to the claims of family and friends.[4] In personal style as well, there was likely a further antagonism: The Protestants no doubt found

---

[4]Woodrow Wilson thus considered it morally respectable to prosecute the ethnic political machine with whose support he won the governorship of New Jersey in 1911; for the ethnic politician, this constituted an example of Protestant untrustworthiness (Hofstadter, 1948: 251–253).

the patrimonial style of the immigrants too emotional and boisterous, perhaps even sinfully loud; the Catholics, Jews, and blacks must have regarded the market-conscious Protestants as inhumanly cold and self-righteous.

In short, the boundaries among these diverse groups were upheld by deep cultural differences. To be sure, some groups were not so far from each other, and there was comparatively rapid assimilation among some groups with similar cultural styles. German and Scandinavian Protestants, deriving from commercial farming and small-town backgrounds rather like those of most Anglo-Americans, assimilated fairly quickly to them;[5] the Catholic groups tended to assimilate to each other (Kennedy, 1952; Greeley, 1970; Laumann, 1969, 1973). But the stronger the cultural differences, the less likelihood of assimilation and, indeed, the greater the overt cultural antagonism. Thus the different emotional, sexual, and sociable styles of Africans,[6] and the equally remote cultures of the Indian tribes, were regarded with near total condemnation by all of the European groups and used as justification for treating them as inferior or even subhuman. In general, then, the cultural diversity of late nineteenth-century America produced not merely culture shock, but also profound feelings of emotional antagonism and moral outrage. Communities built upon opposing conceptions of morality now fought over control of a common economy and a democratic polity in which they were all formal participants. It is no surprise that the Protestants took increasingly stronger measures as their domination was threatened.

In the late nineteenth century, the conditions that had made middle-class Protestantism a sealed cocoon of cultural authority were breaking down. The rise of big cities, the growth of the national economy, the big bureaucracies, the mass media, the challenge of the immigrants—these removed the mechanisms whereby the Protestant middle class had established its culture of

---

[5]This fact illustrates the superficiality of language differences. Compare the much longer resistance to assimilation of Irish Catholics, who did speak English.

[6]The survival of African culture under the effects of slavery and subsequent conditions has been vigorously debated (Metzger, 1971; Lyman, 1972). The high degree of sociability, verbal facility, physical vigor, sexual freedom, and emotionally expressive styles of entertainment and religion of working-class black communities have been interpreted as responses to poverty and discrimination, a kind of compensating hedonism (Liebow, 1967). Nevertheless, that there is a distinctive ethnic component is apparent by the marked differences between black and white lower- and working-class cultures. Blacks are far more likely to belong to social groups than whites of the same class (Orum, 1966; Olsen, 1970) and have lower rates of psychosis, alcoholism, and suicide, and higher measures of happiness and self-esteem (McCarthey and Yancey, 1971; Farley and Hermalin, 1971). These seem to follow from a more sociable and emotionally expressive culture, and this is what is found in the background of highly participant and relatively democratic African tribal communities (Murdock, 1959: 17–19, 64–100, 222–264; Oliver and Fage, 1962: 102–124).

businesslike respectability as the linchpin of everyday belief. This decline in cultural resources meant a loss of control over labor; economic interests became threatened as the cultural resources by which they had been upheld declined. The close-knit communities of the early colonies had been able to enforce their public standards with an iron discipline. This power was eroded more and more as settlement moved west and the economy developed. By the turn of the twentieth century, Protestant culture had not only softened, but also its adherents had lost the power to enforce what was left of it through traditional means.

Yet the conditions still existed to support some version of Protestant culture and to provide a basis for organizing a counterattack. There were still respectable middle-class communities and opportunities for social mobility through hard work. The restrained tone of Anglo-Protestant culture was still a force to be reckoned with in one's everyday associations. It was still a mark of respectability that would get one a good job from Anglo employers, a loan from Anglo bankers, and professional repute among Anglo clientele.[7] The ongoing struggle to advance one's career in a world in which Anglo-Protestants controlled the major economic resources kept the culture relevant.

A many-sided struggle went on over just which standards would prevail. The more traditional Anglo-Protestants struggled against the slackening standards of urban Protestants; business interests invoked the old virtues to legitimate their class control; liberals invoked traditional moralism to justify reform. All of these made a larger bloc struggling to keep its cultural advantages over the immigrants.

The Protestant counterattack took two forms. There were the hostile, conservative efforts to repress or exclude non-Anglo groups entirely, and there were the self-consciously "liberal" efforts to assimilate the immigrants and the Protestant backsliders into conformity to traditional Protestant culture. Conservative reactions pervaded both political and economic spheres. Most extreme were the nativist political movements, often with a violent tinge, extending from the anti-Catholic and anti-Masonic Know-Nothing Movement of the 1840s to the Ku Klux Klan revival of the 1920s and subsequent right-wing ideologies (Billington, 1938; Solomon, 1956; Jones, 1960). None of these exclusively nativist movements was ever very successful politically, but the nativist tone found its way into the programs of more important parties. Its most important practical proposal, the prohibition of immigration (except from white Protestant homelands) was finally enacted in the 1920s. It was not

---

[7]Max Weber (1946: 302–322) noted this phenomenon on his visit to the United States in 1904.

carried out earlier in large part because of the opposition of American business leaders, who actively fostered immigration by sending agents to arrange
passage for workers.

This meant that ethnic divisions shaped the lines of class stratification.
Administrative jobs were reserved whenever possible for Anglos. Immigrant
ethnic groups were confined to manual labor or, at best, foremen of labor
gangs. Within the ranks of labor, various ethnic groups fought for position—
generally with the Irish coming to control the skilled positions, Italians and
Slavs the unskilled, and blacks confined to service positions. Ethnic solidarity
became the basis for workers' resistance to their employers. Studies as late as
the 1940s show the continuing pattern: The groups of workers acting to
control work pace usually were made up of ethnic Catholics; rate busters—
individuals who ignored group sanctions and produced near their personal
maximum—were likely to be Anglo-Protestant (Collins *et al.*, 1946: 1–14;
Hughes, 1949: 211–220). Union membership, similarly, was usually drawn
especially from the ranks of immigrants, and union organizers and ideologies
often came directly or by example from European socialist movements. Anglo
businessmen, in turn, used private guards such as the Pinkertons, judicial
powers, and federal troops to crush strikes and destroy union organization
(Johnson, 1968: 104–143; 1976). The failure of industrial labor organizations before the 1930s, when national government power finally shifted in
response to ethnic voters, was due largely to this vigorous suppression.

The other form of response was self-consciously gentler, although its
cultural ends were much the same. Its keynote was "reform." In the political
sphere "reform" meant an effort, under the name of "good government," to
destroy the power of Catholic political machines and return urban political
power to more genteel Anglo elites (Gunsfield, 1958: 521–541; Banfield and
Wilson, 1963: 138–167). Since cities in the United States are legal creatures
of the state government, Anglo control of state legislatures could be used to
take local autonomy away from urban governments and return it to the state
legislature. Other reforms, such as the creation of a post for city manager and
the replacement of precinct representation on city councils (which represented local interests) by at-large elections, were designed to reassert Anglo
control; the introduction of civil service regulations for government employment was similarly designed to break the power of bosses' patronage. Reform
governments in office used police power to attempt cultural control: Raids on
burlesque houses and attempts to crack down on prostitution and gambling
were carried out under the Protestant ideology of "suppression of vice."

The more grass-roots effort at the reform of urban culture was organized
largely under religious auspices. A wave of Protestant revivals reestablished
middle-class respectability among the former frontier areas before the Civil
War. After the war, the revival movements turned to the cities. It is unlikely

that the unending series of crusades from Billy Sunday to Billy Graham had a notable impact on ethnic cultures, but these crusades may well have served to shore up the declining faith of the Protestant migrants to the cities. The fact that urban crusades were partially financed by urban business elites, including men such as Morgan and Vanderbilt, who were not otherwise noted for their personal piety, suggest the coalition of anti-ethnic and anti-working-class forces in action (Hofstadter, 1963: 110). Closely associated with the urban revivals were the Salvation Army and the YMCA movements. The latter was staffed by upper-middle-class Anglo-Protestants from the religious colleges, as was the growing social-work movement. The efforts of settlement houses were to Americanize the immigrants by teaching English, respectable forms of culture, manners and morals, and generally to extirpate "vice and delinquency." The program of teaching English seems to have had an impact since it provided a skill the immigrants could use to acquire citizenship and political rights. The other aims of the welfare workers were by no means so welcome and had little effect (see Whyte, 1943: 98–104; Platt, 1969).

The more militant wing of Christian reform was expressed in the movement to prohibit alcohol (Gusfield, 1963). Puritan culture always regarded drunkenness as evil, but its traditional emphasis had been on moderation. The Puritan colonists regarded a mild use of alcohol as possibly medicinal and only a minor vice. Alcohol grew into a major issue only in the late nineteenth century, when it came to symbolize the wholesale challenge to the traditional Protestant values. The movement to use the force of the state to cut off alcohol by a constitutional amendment gained ground in the years just preceding World War I: Prohibition was finally enacted in 1919. The timing was not accidental. Decades earlier, Protestant culture was still locally dominant and needed no such action to assert itself. A few decades later, the action would have been impossible; rural America was losing its majority, and indeed by the 1930s the urban and ethnic forces were strong enough to repeal Prohibition. The struggle over alcohol symbolizes the crisis period of the ethnic struggle, the decades on either side of World War I. H. L. Mencken, the Scopes trial, and F. Scott Fitzgerald symbolized the cultural conflicts of the era.[8]

---

[8]Mencken was, of course, an urban German, Fitzgerald an Irish Catholic, and the works of both men were focused on the ethnic conflicts surrounding them. The history of American literature shows the ethnic transitions very sharply. The classic writers of the nineteenth century were all Anglo-Protestant—Hawthorne, Cooper, Melville, Whitman, James, Howells—and generally from the old Eastern oligarchy; their themes for the most part were reflections on Puritan moralism and a concern for cultural decline. The major writers of the early twentieth century were ethnic aliens: Germans (Dreiser, Steinbeck, Mencken, Gertrude Stein, Henry Miller); then Irish and other Catholics (Fitzgerald, Eugene O'Neill, Dos Passos, Hemingway). The only major Anglo-Protestant novelists, for some reason, are Southerners—Thomas Wolfe, Faulkner. The

The most significant effort to assert Anglo-Protestant culture was in the realm of education. Public schools, with their compulsory attendance laws, spread precisely in those states facing the greatest immigration influx; the claims of educators to Americanize the immigrants was a major force in getting public support. And in other ways as well the struggle for social precedence in late nineteenth-century America began to shift toward an increasing reliance upon educational credentials. The results have ramified, not only in the schools, but also in the professions and the entire occupational structure.

Eventually, the ethnic conflicts were to recede, although as of the late 1970s they had not yet disappeared. The high point of multiethnic diversity came just before World War I; just afterwards, most culturally alien immigration was cut off. In succeeding decades, assimilation has diminished some of the cultural differences and broken down some of the group barriers (Lenski, 1963, 1971; Schuman, 1971). Not all cultural differences have disappeared, to be sure; ethnic communities have much more resilience than sociological theory traditionally gave them credit for, and major ethnic differences can still be found in occupational levels and occupational enclaves (Glenn and Hyland, 1967; Wilensky and Ladinsky, 1967; Duncan and Duncan, 1968; Jackson *et al.*, 1970), as well as in marriage and friendship patterns (Greeley, 1970; Laumann, 1973), political participation (Greeley, 1974), social attitudes (Featherman, 1971), and emotional expressiveness (Zola, 1966; Zbrowski, 1969). Moreover, cultural diversity has been replenished, although on a smaller scale, by continuous migration from Mexico, Puerto Rico, and Latin America, and by the mobilization of blacks in their movement from the rural South into the large industrial cities. The conflicts to which these movements have given rise in recent decades are well known.

In order to explain the American cultural market, it is not merely sufficient to describe how much cultural diversity still exists, and hence how strong group boundaries are. The most crucial effect of multiethnicity in American history has already happened: the creation of an institutional pattern, a "contest-mobility" credential system, which has gathered the diverse particulars of American cultures into an impersonal cultural market with its own

---

Anglo-Protestants hold onto the realm of poetry longer: Eliot, Frost, Pound, Jeffers, Cummings, Williams, Stevens, most of them from the old Puritan cultural center, Harvard, and most propounding the most extreme disillusionment with the cultural "decline" of the surrounding society. (In Eliot, this often reveals the ethnic bias very blatantly—"apeneck Sweeney" and so forth; Hemingway counterattacked with a deadly characterization of a snobbish and repressed poet in "Mr. and Mrs. Elliott," in *In Our Time,* 1926.) After World War II, Jews and Catholics took over both in the world of novels (Mailer, Roth, Bellow, Salinger) and of poetry (the Beats—Kerouac, Ginsberg, Ferlinghetti, Corso). It appears that cultural creativity is focused in the ethnic group most highly mobilized, either to defend a slipping domination or to break into national prominence for the first time.

abstract currency. Even if ethnic differences were completely to disappear today, this institutional structure would still be with us and still occupy a central place in our stratification. The fact that ethnic diversity *does* still exist and that Chicanos, Puerto Ricans, blacks, Asians, and various white ethnic groups (even self-conscious, backlashing Anglo-Protestants) make demands for precedence within the credential system today merely *accelerates* the pattern of development of that system in channels laid down several generations ago.

AMERICAN EDUCATIONAL INSTITUTIONS: EARLY BACKGROUND

The height of multiethnic conflict in the United States was reached in the early twentieth century. But the process of cultural conflict, and hence the building of the cultural market, grew up gradually and over a number of generations. In broad outlines, we can say that ethnic cultural issues came to permeate the stratification struggle not long after the Civil War with the tremendous increase in non-English-speaking immigration at that time. But Irish Catholic immigration, which picked up in the 1830s and became considerable in the 1840s, had already provided opposition, and there were cultural issues involving class relations within the early Anglo-Protestant community even earlier. For a strong relative contrast, it is worthwhile to go back to the educational institutions of America at the turn of the nineteenth century in a situation of near ethnic homogeneity.

In contrast to the lengthy sequences and complex branchings of modern American education, the school sequence at the turn of the nineteenth century was short and simple, and the system was small.[9] The basic skills of literacy and arithmetic were taught in several locations: at home (by parents or, in the wealthier families, by tutors), in church, in the apprentice's work place, or at local public and private schools. More advanced education based on the classical curriculum (the medieval *trivium* and *quadrivium*) were offered by colleges. There were also a very small number of academies that offered a classical curriculum beyond the elementary level.

These three types of educational institutions did not form a sequence. Colleges and academies taught substantially the same curriculum, and graduation from an academy was not necessary for college admission; as in medieval Europe, bare literacy was the only requirement at many colleges.

---

[9]For more information on the material that follows see Bailyn (1960); Curti (1935); Hofstadter and Metzger (1955); Rudolph (1962); Folger and Nam (1967); Greer (1972).

Elementary schools did not provide social certification, and attendance at such a school was not a prerequisite to college enrollment. Schools other than colleges carried with their training little or no additional social status; they existed for the limited and functional purpose of inculcating literacy, the possession of which was deemed sufficiently obvious to require no official announcement. The early American colonies were literate societies, but the literacy was accomplished by the largely informal acquisition of obviously useful skills. The main difference among types of schools was their social class composition: Elementary schools and apprenticeship were for the artisan class; the Latin grammar schools and the colleges (as well as home tutoring) for the upper class; and academies emerged in the eighteenth century, with a somewhat less classical curriculum, for the urban commercial middle class.

College education was essentially a secondary education at this time. Unlike elementary education, it served no clear technical purpose, but it did have the power of certification: Colleges were legal entities, chartered by the state and deriving from their charters the right to grant the traditional degree of the European university, the B.A. The earliest colleges of the seventeenth century had the traditional powers to grant higher degrees (Master and Doctorate), including the subjects of medicine and law, but this vocationally important certification power was rarely exercised. In the fluid frontier society with its volatile labor market, the teaching of medicine and law came to be carried out primarily through apprenticeship, and college control over entry into professions disappeared. The earliest colleges had been founded primarily to provide educated men for the ministry; this vocational function was preserved, although seminaries were also founded to give expressly theological training. (In a sense, American colleges had become secondary schools for preparation for the "higher education" of seminaries.)

American formal education in the early nineteenth century was rudimentary. There were growing numbers of locally supported elementary schools, teaching the classical curriculum but providing no certification; an unusually large number of colleges, which taught a curriculum essentially the same as that of the academies and offered a bachelor's degree; and finally, there were a few seminaries, which recruited from college graduates but also from those without college degrees. Requirements for entry into any of these institutions were minimal and did not depend upon certification by any other educational institutions: The only restrictions placed upon entry to academies, colleges, and seminaries were sex (only men were admitted), literacy (sometimes in Latin and Greek as well as in English), ability to pay the modest fees, and adherence to the orthodoxy of the religious denomination in charge of the school. Age was not a requirement, and hence the age of college students varied from early adolescence to the mid-twenties. The number of years of college study was not rigidly adhered to, although the traditional medieval term of study was 4 years. Only seminaries provided a certification relevant to any occupation, and even they did not monopolize paths into the ministry, as ordination by evangelists was another common route, especially on the frontier. The colleges provided a certification in the form of a degree, but it was acquired by few of those who entered college (most dropped out when they felt they had enough education) and seemed to carry with it little vocational advantage.

Formal education was important for only two occupations: the ministry and school teaching. In the coastal areas, especially in New England, where the status and pay of ministers remained high, the link between the colleges and the clergy was fairly close. The elite Congregational and Anglican clergy were virtually hereditary castes, their sons practically monopolizing the specified cultural training at home and in schools (Main, 1965: 139–141, 275). If ministers in the older areas were well off, however, the teachers were not. School teaching was an ill-paying and hazardously unstable occupation, and teachers barely clung to the bottom rungs of the lower-middle-class life style, often at the cost of foregoing marriage. School teaching was not a very desirable occupation. Although it seems to have attracted many college graduates as a temporary job on the way to the ministry, the educational qualifications of teachers were acceptable at far below the college level (Bailyn, 1960: 96). Thus even for teachers, formal school certification was not highly stressed.

In general, the educational system in the colonies before the American Revolution comes close to an ideal type of an educational system in which organizational restraints and symbolic certification counted for nothing. Upon this base line we may trace the growth of a system in which, as the technical importance of training grew in some areas, the social edifice surrounding it grew even faster.

THE RISE OF PUBLIC EDUCATION

The first step toward a system of educational certification in the United States was the creation of free public elementary schools. Even though the elementary schools were not themselves certifying agencies, they provided the basis for a sequence of years of public instruction that was eventually to culminate in the certificate of a high school degree and to be unified by school attendance laws.

Colonial education at the elementary level took place in many contexts: home, apprenticeship, church, private schools, tutoring, and some public schools. Public schools were a small part of this group. They were supported by local townships, but they often required a small fee from the parents of their students, and truly free education was provided primarily for the children of families willing to declare themselves indigent. As a result, public school attendance was fairly low and confined largely to the most prosperous New England and Middle Atlantic states. Basic education could be acquired outside the schools; the overall efficiency of the system was indicated by the fact that between one-half and two-thirds of the adult male populace was literate.[10]

Beginning around the turn of the nineteenth century, states began to require local townships to establish free public elementary schools, and somewhat later began to support them with financial aid. By 1860, most New England states had created free elementary school systems; southern states did not begin to do so until the northern pattern was imposed by the Reconstruction after the Civil War. Western states and territories began to do so soon after they were formally organized.

The impetus for the foundation of public elementary schools came primarily from upper-class and upper-middle-class professionals, especially ministers, educators, and lawyers. This was the class of religious leaders of earlier days; in the more secular climate of the nineteenth century, they turned to humanitarian crusades, as if to restore their old cultural dominance through moral reforms. The influx of ethnic aliens, beginning with the Irish Catholics in New England of the 1830s and 1840s, gave a special opportunity for cultural entrepreneurship. Public education was but one cause among many. This same group of professionals was also active in crusades against slavery, war, intemperance, imprisonment for debt, harsh penal conditions, inhumane treatment of the insane, and harmful labor conditions. They agitated for child labor restrictions, public hospitals, and social welfare, as well as for free schools.

The reformers used a wide variety of arguments to gain political support for public education, claiming that education had good effects on labor productivity, political stability, and moral character. Some of these arguments were echoed by a few supporting industrialists, but most manufacturers and merchants were hesitant to support free education, primarily because of the tax expense. The lower classes in general were rather opposed to it. On the frontier, the lower class and the farmers tended to oppose public education on the ground that there was no need for it (Curti, 1935: 66–68, 87–90). Urban workers were also generally apathetic, especially since the public schools were attended most heavily by the children of the upper classes and imposed upper-class notions of deference to authority upon wayward working-class youths. In Beverly, Massachusetts in 1860, for example, work-

---

[10]Folger and Nam (1967: 112). Female illiteracy appears to have been much higher.

ers mobilized by a shoemakers' strike voted overwhelmingly to abolish the new public high school, whereas the upper class voted to retain it (Katz, 1968: 19–93).

There were some contrary currents. Labor union programs sometimes called for free unified schools serving all social classes, usually linked with the demand for restrictions on the competition from child labor (Ensign, 1921: 41, 52; Curoe, 1926: 13–15, 29–31). But labor was not the main mover or even a consistent supporter of public schools. Its influence was more likely indirect, through the support of child labor laws. These in turn raised the question of great interest to upper-middle-class moralists: What was to be done with the unoccupied children?

It is apparent that mass elementary education was created not primarily in response to industrial demand nor in response to a publicly felt desire for its practical benefits, but rather in response to the political influence and persistence of the descendants of the colonial clerical elite who made the political alliances and ideological appeals necessary to further their cause. In the New England states where the movement began, its leaders gave the impression of being on the defensive, acting to preserve a traditional moral culture that was being challenged from several directions: by the speculative ethos of commercial and industrial expansion just under way; by the rise of a working-class culture mobilized by urbanization and by trade unions; and by the beginnings of alien immigration, especially of Irish Catholics. This was not simply a matter of fighting against status decline in a purely cultural battle. The clerical and professional elite of New England was an actual subclass, with economic and political interests to defend and with which its cultural prestige was intimately bound up. It found itself in a situation in which other social groups were increasingly mobilized to challenge its social domination in economic, political, and cultural respects alike. But these other groups were by no means united among themselves; and by making appropriate alliances, the old clerical class was able to sell other groups the apparent advantages of a formal and compulsory education in the traditional culture.

Perhaps the most significant of these other groups can be found most clearly, not in the old coastal settlements, but inland, where waves of religious revival had been spreading westward intermittently since the late eighteenth century. The early period of the frontiers was dominated by land speculation, violence, and uninhibited masculine carousing. Once the frontier moved farther west and land became settled for routine commercial agriculture, the middle-class ethic of disciplined, ascetic work and familial morality began to be reasserted. Religious revivals were the vehicle for this movement to reorganize once-frontier communities on a respectable *petit bourgeois* basis. Thus, although the population shift beyond the Appalachians at the end of the eighteenth century had reduced religious adherence to perhaps only 10%

of the population, revivalism swept the inland areas, especially from the 1830s onward (Hofstadter, 1963: 55–141). The agents of these revivals were itinerant Methodist and Baptist preachers, who by 1850 had made their denominations the largest Protestant groups. Along with religion, and frequently in the persons of the same entrepreneurs and congregations, came education.

Education, then, was adopted by a newly expanding middle class, which was creating a commercial society upon territories that had recently settled down from the violent and much less tightly organized days of frontier conquest. Traditional Anglo-Protestant culture, in the form of religion and education, was used to create solid middle-class control—indeed, for the new commercial settlers to constitute themselves initially as a locally dominant class. Cultural organizations were their weapon against what they saw as the "barbarism" of their more adventurous and individualistic predecessors. It was this source of demand for traditional culture that gave the clerical class new opportunities, although they would act no longer in the role of undisputed community leaders, but as entrepreneurs selling culture, and thus laying the basis for a public cultural market.

In the first half of the nineteenth century, the basic pattern of elementary education was established. It would be extended without important modification to the South and to the new states of the West. The main purpose of elementary education was to inculcate moral values and the basic social skills of literacy. To that end, its curriculum remained religious and classical, its methods rote learning and discipline. Public feelings about the value and necessity of education continued to be ambivalent. On the one hand, attendance rates rose, even in the absence of compulsory attendance laws, to perhaps 40% of the youthful populace in 1840 and 60% in 1880.[11] On the other hand, attendance did not seem to be an urgent matter, as the ages of elementary school students varied from 5 to 18 (Folger and Nam, 1967: 6–8). Since retardation rates were highest in rural areas, where high schools developed latest, it seems likely that before the introduction of free public high schools, parents sent their children to elementary school only sporadically. Rigid age-grading did not become important until elementary school came to be treated as a step toward secondary education.

We may conclude that elementary education by itself met a mild public demand. If the public did not care enough about education to pay tuition for each child's education, it would take advantage of free elementary schools, if and when the services of the children were not needed on the farm or in the

---

[11]Folger and Nam (1967: 3–4). These figures refer to the entire 5–18 age group; because of the high level of retardation in grade, they apply primarily to elementary rather than to secondary schooling.

shop. No doubt the enactment of child labor laws in the late nineteenth century made the school attractive as a caretaking institution. The sporadic attendance pattern suggests that children attended until they achieved what seemed a sufficient degree of literacy, then dropped out unless they planned to go on to high school. For the majority of the populace, free public elementary schools operated primarily as a training ground in basic literacy, and particularly in the frontier areas, as a device for establishing a basic level of middle-class respectability. Only with the rise of the public high school did the formal certification become more prominent and the elementary school itself become transformed.

UNIFIED SECONDARY EDUCATION

Publicly controlled, tax-supported high schools began to appear in eastern states such as Massachusetts, New York, and Pennsylvania by 1860, and spread throughout the rest of the country during the remainder of the nineteenth century. The political battle for public secondary education was fought by the same group of upper-class and upper-middle-class humanitarian reformers who had won public elementary schooling. As in the earlier instance, all manner of public benefits were alleged in favor of this innovation. In 1877 an educator declared that the schools alone had saved America from the terrors of the French commune, and another leader in the struggle for public support declared: "The remedy for agricultural depression, bad roads, the discontent and thriftlessness of youth, for many of the ills of which we complain, is a well-sustained school system [Curti, 1935: 274; see also 209–210, 216–218]." Every political crisis and issue was seized upon as indicating the need for more public education.

Diverse coalitions were involved in establishing state-supported secondary schools, with one central element remaining constant: the educators themselves. The public schools created in the first half of the century themselves provided the major element in the growth of free secondary education in the second half of the century: an articulate and highly dedicated group of men who strongly believed in the value of education and were skilled at gaining political support for it, the administrators and state educational officials. Once established, the educational system, like other organizations, struggled to extend its size, resources, and influence. To this end, educators succeeded in having state after state adopt laws not only establishing secondary schools, but also requiring school attendance between certain specified ages. The first such law was passed by Massachusetts in 1852, the second by Vermont in 1867. Such laws were enacted by 25 states prior to 1890; most of the other states (concentrated in the South and West) did so by 1920 (Folger and Nam, 1967: 24–26). At first the laws specified ages 6 to 14, but the upper age was gradually raised to 16 and in places to 18. Efforts to enact and extend child labor laws at about the same time undoubtedly helped bring labor support to the humanitarians and educators in their battles for public support and attendance laws.

The arguments for public high schools and for compulsory attendance were much the same as those advanced for public elementary schools. Industrial benefits were alleged on occasion, but the principal reationalizations referred to good citizenship, political stability, and moral qualities. Generally speaking, compulsory attendance laws must be seen in the context of group conflict. The schools were established by upper-middle-class reformers, and their content and methods were designed to inculcate the virtues of an idealized rural society. Voluntary attendance in high school around 1860 was highest among Anglo-Protestant middle-class rather than working-class children. Greater proportions of children attended in the more traditional (and predominantly Anglo-Protestant) New England small towns (28%) than in medium-sized towns (15%) or cities (8%).[12] But although the schools appealed most to carriers of middle-class and rural culture, the effort to establish public high schools was strongest in the cities (Katz, 1968: 48). This was partly a matter of securing a greater tax base for urban schools, but mainly it reflects the challenge of urban immigrant working-class culture for which the public school was a response.

The pattern by which compulsory attendance laws developed makes this clear. Compulsory attendance laws grew out of two related issues: truancy and control over recalcitrant youths. Elementary school administrators complained constantly of irregular attendance, and legal means for apprehending absent students were urged. The first state law against truancy was passed in Massachusetts in 1850, 2 years *before* the first compulsory attendance law. But even earlier than this, the Massachusetts State Reform School was established in 1848, the main purpose of which was to provide a place where rebellious students could be committed. That the issue was cultural conflict was indicated by the most prevalent offenses for which boys were committed; in order of frequency, among 440 boys committed, 1850–1851 (Katz, 1968: 175): 394 "had used profane language"; 350 "had been idle previous to admission or had no steady employment"; 303 "had attended the theater and similar places of amusement"; 259 "had used obscene language." The typical scenario of what was regarded as delinquency, as recounted by Katz (1968), went as follows:

---

[12]Katz (1968: 39). It should be borne in mind that Massachusetts at this time had more high schools than the rest of the states combined.

> The first crime was often truancy from school. The truant became familiar with
> "horse racing, the bowling saloon, the theatrical exhibitions and other similar places
> of amusement, debauchery and crime." In the bowling alley, "initiated by being
> employed in setting pins," he soon acquired "the desire to act the man" and became
> a "juvenile gambler." Profanity, drunkenness and licentiousness soon followed, hur-
> rying him forward in the path of crime and ruin [172–173; see also 164–185].

The "criminals" were for the most part boys of the urban working class, many of them Irish Catholics. The solution for the reformers was the reform school, set in the morally pristine countryside and having compulsory religious instruction under the direction of a Protestant evangelist minister. It was in this mode that compulsory school attendance laws developed. Massachusetts seems to have led the way, both because it had the upper-middle-class leaders and the traditions of community moral control over individuals and the earliest cultural challenge of alien immigration. The spread of compulsory school attendance laws after the Civil War seems to have followed the lines of immigrant and urban challenge. As the conflicts between native Protestants and immigrant ethnic groups built up, the importance of school as a weapon of control increased. From compulsory elementary schooling in the nineteenth century followed compulsory secondary schooling in the twentieth.

Secondary education was conceived primarily as socialization, and the curriculum as initially established emphasized the classical studies, quite remote from commercial life. But here arose a tension within the plans of the secondary educators. On the one hand, they were committed to providing an education consisting of cultural socialization, but this socialization was to take place at a level beyond that of elementary school and hence must have some distinctive content. This content could be found in the traditional subjects of higher education: classics, languages, literature, history, science. On the other hand, this content was already given by the existing colleges, and as we shall see in the section dealing with colleges and universities in this chapter, the colleges were widely available in America even before the push for high schools. Thus high schools and colleges competed with each other because age-grading had not yet developed and they both drew upon the same age range of students.

Compulsory schooling laws, which began from truancy laws around 1850 as part of the moral socialization crusades of that time, specified *ages* at which children were to attend school but not the level of study or the type of school (Folger and Nam, 1967: 24–26). Grade levels, the 4-year high school, the 8-year elementary school, and above all, regular yearly promotion, did not develop until the 1870s. There was considerable retardation in grade: As late as 1910, a majority of the students aged 14–17 were still in elementary school; approximately 25% of the elementary school population was over 13 years of age, and 80% of secondary school students were over 18: high school students might be as old as their twenties (Folger and Nam, 1967: 6, 8–10). And colleges, following the medieval model that prevailed in America until the late nineteenth century, also had a range of students from their early teens to their mid-twenties. They did not require prior high school or even elementary school attendance as long as students were literate (sometimes in Latin and Greek), and many colleges established their own preparatory departments for students who needed to work up these prerequisites.

Moreover, both types of schools competed with professional training in this same age range. Professional training in medicine, law, divinity, and engineering in the middle of the nineteenth century was largely carried out by apprenticeship, again beginning anywhere from the early teen years to the twenties. Where professional schools did exist, they would admit students (as had the medieval European universities, the British Inns of Court in which lawyers trained, and so on) without prior educational requirements except literacy, and at any age from the early teens on.[13]

Under these conditions, it is not surprising that all of the traditional contents of education were frequently attacked by the public as useless drill in irrelevant subjects. The alternatives proposed most often were some form of new, vocationally relevant education for the modern age. Some educators opposed this, but others began to organize vocational high schools in the 1880s. The ideal of a utilitarian education had been raised even earlier. Before the Civil War, an idealized view of manual training flourished among upper-middle-class philanthropic reformers as part of the effort to recapture the virtues of rural life. Thus manual labor was first introduced in seminaries training missionaries for their evangelical ventures in the West (Fisher, 1967: 16). Manual labor was the main course of training in reform schools, where it was regarded as the best remedy to crime and delinquency, and the moral value of manual training could still be extolled late in the century by social workers such as Jane Addams, who argued that it would give a sense of meaning to the lives of prospective industrial workers (Fisher, 1967: 47).

---

[13]In other words, distinctions among secondary, higher, and professional education did not exist prior to the development of a bureaucratic sequential school system in modern times. In Europe before the nineteenth century (and even later), the term "college" was used indifferently for a nonchartered local school and a component of a university. When the differentiation of levels was made, it was done by a fairly arbitrary division of contents. Thus in Germany and France, the emerging secondary school took a larger portion of the university curriculum than in England and the United States: The former taught university subjects such as philosophy, whereas the latter merely extended the elementary school studies of grammar (Aries, 1962: 141–161). These differences indicate that there is no intrinsic necessity for teaching particular subjects at particular ages.

In the period of heavy industrialization after the Civil War, however, this sentimentalized philanthropic view receded, and advocates of vocationalism began to argue that vocational training could provide a new elite of engineers. The foremost advocate of this position was Calvin Woodward, a Harvard graduate and Dean of the Polytechnical Institute at Washington University in St. Louis, who set up a Manual Training High School designed to replace the traditional vocationally irrelevant education. Woodward's school attracted much attention, especially in the atmosphere of Horatio Alger ideology then popular among businessmen.

Nevertheless, engineers themselves were not friendly to the manual training programs. The engineering profession was just separating itself from the apprenticeship-trained occupation of skilled mechanic, and the Morrill Act in 1862 opened up land-grant colleges to them. Accordingly, they were not eager to have engineering training established at the secondary level. "No standard of gentility, no patent of nobility can be too high for a profession which leads the civilization of the world . . . " declared the President of the American Society of Engineers in 1891, in an address entitled, "The Engineer as a Scholar and a Gentleman" (Fisher, 1967: 66). The American Society of Mechanical Engineers was cool on manual training schools and in the late 1890s began vigorously to support the manual trade school as an alternative, nonelite conception of vocational training.[14]

In the early twentieth century, vocational educators swung back to the ideal of education for the lower occupations, advocating separate trade schools or programs for the working class. The program came to be supported after 1900 by the American Society of Mechanical Engineers, the National Association of Manufacturers, and the National Education Association. The manufacturers and engineers regarded the extension of trade schools as a crusade to break the power of foreign-controlled trade unions, which kept American boys from learning a trade. Frederick Taylor, the advocate of scientific management as a solution to labor strife, tended to equate the notions of "education" and "production." According to Fisher (1967):

> This is evident in Taylor's testimony before a special Congressional committee, where he described how shovelling could be made scientific. When one of the shovellers in a gang was having trouble or producing below par, said Taylor, a "teacher" was sent to show him how to do the job most easily and quickly. "Now

---

[14]Career patterns of graduates from Woodward's Manual Training School tended to bear out the skepticism of those who did not expect high school education to lead to truly elite status: Approximately half were bookkeepers, general assistants, accountants, or draftsmen; fewer than one-eighth were engineers. Others did achieve white-collar positions in manufacturing, sales, and the professions (Fisher, 1967: 77).

gentlemen," Taylor continued, addressing the committee, "I want you to see clearly that because this is one of the characteristic features of scientific management, this is not nigger driving; this is kindness; this is teaching; this is doing mighty well what I would like to have done to me if I were a boy trying to learn how to do something" [89; see also 115–131].

Given this view of trade education, it is not surprising that Samuel Gompers and the trade unions generally regarded it with suspicion and hostility, even though they had some status interests in dignifying manual labor by giving it a place in the school curriculum. It is apparent from the evidence cited in Chapter 1 that vocational education was never of great practical importance. Its advocates were always most strongly motivated by ideological issues, and programs were actually put into effect in periods of political crisis. Thus the Smith–Hughes Act, giving federal support to vocational education, was passed during the antiforeign fervor of the American entrance to World War I. Further extensions occurred in 1933 and 1934 as part of New Deal efforts to handle the "youth problem" and again in the NDEA Act of 1958 during the nationalist upsurge of the Cold War Sputnik issue and an economic recession.[15]

The leaders of American secondary education have generally been hostile to the vocational school movement (Curti, 1935: 317, 348; Cremin, 1961: 27ff.). They saw vocational education as undermining the ideals of a culturally socializing education and of education for citizenship, and they doubtless felt the accompanying threat to their status. In principle, vocational high schools or their curricula might have replaced entirely the high schools more oriented toward liberal arts, or the school system might have become bifurcated along class lines. Educators generally opposed the second threat as well as the first. The political difficulties of funding the liberal arts schools in competition with a superficially more appealing technical education must have seemed a threat, and their commitment to the moral and social value of education made them oppose any structural split that would dilute their moral influence and undermine the political inclusiveness of schooling.

---

[15]Fisher (1967: 213) describes the arguments of the Federal Board of Vocational Education in 1934 as follows:

> There were more "socially maladjusted people" in this country than ever before, the Board (quoting liberally from the *Reader's Digest*) suggested; "crime and disobedience to the law" were on the upswing; thousands of Americans were killed and maimed every year in automobile accidents. The nation could take a vital step in the direction of solving these problems by providing more vocational education; the crime rate could be lowered and the many Americans handicapped by accidents could be rehabilitated.

As it turned out, vocational education never posed a serious threat, since it had major weaknesses of its own. Vocational education might seem attractive on comparison to the rote learning of the classical curriculum, but vocational schools themselves lost out in competition with occupational realities. Training for manual labor could just as well be acquired on the job or through apprenticeship, and training in purely manual skills apparently reduced the value of education to the student below that of liberal arts education. The prestige of education was lost, but little advantage was given over to the manual laborer who gained his skills on the job. The slogan was put forward that technical skills would dignify labor, and much was made of the distinction between "arts" and "trades." Nevertheless, such efforts to give status to manual labor did not convince. Students such as those at Booker T. Washington's Tuskegee Institute objected to manual training in place of learning the middle-class culture that would raise their social status (Curti, 1935: 293). In general, manual training was associated in the public mind with the rehabilitation of criminals (Fisher, 1967: 78–79).

The combination of these two faults—the lack of competitive advantage of manual education over on-the-job or other informal training and the fact that manual education provided no social mobility for students into middle-class culture—meant that manual arts education was bound to lose out to the liberal arts course. Students preferred to take liberal arts or drop out altogether. High school education did take on an increasing vocational value as the number of clerical jobs increased, especially with the introduction of the typewriter and the subsequent hiring of female clerical help around the turn of the century. The commercial arts course was more successful than the manual arts course, although its main appeal was confined to girls. In content and in status, however, it remained close to the liberal arts curriculum and thus prepared students for the middle-class culture as well as for the technical skills required of clerical jobs. Vocational schools themselves did not flourish. There were fewer than 100 in 1950, and only the NDEA Act of 1958, operating in a period in which schools had become a major means of keeping unemployed youths off the streets, brought a serious expansion of vocational training (Fisher, 1967: 218).

In retrospect, we may view the vocational education movement as an attempt of some sectors of the educator community to adapt to the influx of lower-class students into the high schools resulting from the introduction of compulsory attendance laws. Having fought for such laws to extend their influence, educators found that their teachings were irrelevant to the lives of many of their students, but instead of relinquishing them by giving up on compulsory attendance, they sought for a rationale to justify keeping them in school. The same interpretation may be roughly applied to the Progressive movement in education, which attempted to substitute a rather vague "life adjustment" training for the classical curriculum. Some of its innovations, such as athletics and other extracurricular activities, no doubt served an internal function for the school itself—providing some diversion for their unwilling captives and hence some control over them, especially through school athletics.[16]

Progressivism's reforms have had a greater long-term effect than those of vocationalism, partly because they have not threatened the status socialization and mobility functions of schools. While providing some needed outlets for restless children, the shift away from emphasis on academic subjects eased the pressure of teaching a large and hostile body of working-class students. These pressures were especially strong in the largest cities. In 1909, 58% of the pupils in the 37 largest cities had foreign-born parents, and it was in these cities that Progressive education first took hold (Swift, 1971: 44).

Progressivism provided, for a time, a useful ideology to counter criticism of the uselessness of the curriculum, and its emphasis on scientific pedagogy and on scientific tests gave some basis to claims of professional status for teachers. Once college attendance became a widespread goal in the United States, high school education no longer needed to be defended as an end in itself, and Progressivism declined as a popular ideology (Cremin, 1961: 175ff; Trow, 1966). Nevertheless, its practices remained prominent, both in the emphasis on athletics and the extracurriculum and in the values prevailing among students. Thus Coleman's 1957–1958 study of 10 midwestern high schools found that athletics and leadership in social activities were most looked up to, scholarly competence relatively little, and that these attitudes were strong even among the middle-class students who planned to attend college (Coleman, 1961). Indeed, the antiacademic values were highest in an upper-middle-class suburban high school where going to college was the norm. Studies of high schools in the 1920s found that the Progressive innovations in the extracurriculum had been heartily accepted by students and teachers alike, making the schools into a kind of social club for the middle-class students and their parents (Lynd and Lynd, 1929: 188–205, 211–222; Waller, 1932: 103–131).

The attack on the practical uselessness of secondary education was thus blunted by a few relatively minor reforms. The demands for a vocationally relevant education were only a convenient form of rhetoric for expressing dissatisfaction in a period in which the organizational relevance of any of the competing forms of schooling was dubious. This was especially true of the newest form, the high school. The underlying issue was one of career sequences and the status value of particular kinds of education for moving along such a sequence. But the public (or for that matter, the educators) had no

---

[16]See the summary of studies by Bidwell (1965); see also Swift (1971).

such abstract insight into the nature of the educational market. Their dissatisfaction was real enough, but for solutions they fell back on the most common style of "practical" argument. Their actual response to vocational training, when it was offered, shows the roots of their behavior more truly.

With the growth of high schools in the 1870s, organizational problems became a dominant influence on the nature of education. Following the lead of Superintendent William T. Harris of St. Louis, the high school was organized into a 4-year sequence with promotion by regular examinations. The large numbers of pupils necessitated standardization of instruction sequences and means of evaluation; schools emphasized rote learning, attendance records, and general principles of efficiency in moving students through in large batches (Cremin, 1961: 19–21; Swift, 1971: 67–77).

At the same time, schools became larger administrative units. Unification of school districts began in the 1870s. This meant the decline of the one-teacher school with children of all levels in the same room, still the most typical pattern in 1870. School principals and superintendents began to emerge, and by the early twentieth century, schools had become huge in both the number of students and administrators. Once the bureaucratic organizational form was established, its own logic of development became dominant: Between 1920 and 1950, the number of students in public schools grew 16%, the number of teachers 34%, and the number of administrators 188% (Swift, 1971: 81). As a result of age-based attendance laws and the effects of bureaucratization, schools began to standardize by age, and the age range of students dropped sharply, both in high schools and elementary schools. In 1910, an estimated 25% of the elementary school students were over 13 years, and 80% of the secondary school students over 18 years, whereas in 1950, the figures were 2.4% and 4.2%, respectively (Folger and Nam, 1967: 6, 8–10). This has meant that the flexibility of time for school attendance has sharply decreased for the student; it also implies that students move through schools largely by aging rather than by scholastic achievement.[17] Interests of administrative efficiency were prominent in this transformation: Retardation in grade was explicitly attacked as an unnecessary expense, and administrators in the Progressive urban schools took the lead in establishing criteria of efficiency based on high promotion rates (Callahan, 1962: 168–169).

The American secondary education system thus took shape: a unitary sequence, open and compulsory for all, preparing primarily for college educa-

---

[17]The declining rate of retardation in grade cannot be accounted for by the increased number of dropouts, since the rate of high school attendance has *increased* from 12% of the 14–17 age group in 1910 to 75% is 1950. The other possible explanation—that students have been learning more efficiently—is highly implausible.

tion, rigidly age-graded, with a heavy emphasis on moving students through in orderly phalanxes. The entire trend of twentieth-century public schooling, though, is not simply a matter of bureaucratization in response to internal problems of control and large numbers. Both primary and secondary education finally found a modest but firmly established place in careers as part of a steadily lengthening channel leading through higher education. Thus it became less and less important whether students learned any particular academic content at the lower levels or even if they were moved through without real examination at all. The occupationally relevant distinctions were pushed further and further ahead to the higher levels—entering college, then completing college, eventually entering graduate or professional school, and so on. Rising school completion rates at the lower levels were simply part of a larger pattern of expansion at the higher levels.

It is to this pattern that we now turn.

COLLEGES AND UNIVERSITIES

The United States has always had a large number of institutuions of higher education. At the time of the Revolution, there were 9 colleges in the colonies; in all of Europe, with a population 50 times that of America, there were perhaps only 60 colleges. With the turn of the nineteenth century, the United States experienced a wave of new foundations, bringing the number of colleges in existence in 1860 to approximately 250. By 1880, there were 811 colleges and universities; by 1970, there were 2556 (see Table 5.2). The United States not only began with the highest ratio of institutions of higher education to population in the world, but it also increased this ratio steadily, for the number of European universities was not much greater by the twentieth century than in the eighteenth (see Ben-David and Zloczower, 1962: 44–85).

The difference in numbers of colleges does not appear to lie in the public demand for higher education, for the supply of colleges in the United States has for most of its history been far ahead of demand, a fact which has had important consequences for the place of higher education in American society. Rather, we must look at the impulses and conditions that fostered and allowed the large number of college foundations in the United States. The conditions allowing such widespread foundations were political decentralization, the disestablishment of state churches after the Revolution, and the emerging legal tradition that liberally granted corporate charters. (The Dartmouth College case, after all, is a landmark in corporate law.) American democracy and local government made it easy to obtain state permission to found a college; in Europe, the centralized and autocratic governments limited the sources of charters, and the connection of European universities to

Table 5.2

*Institutions of Higher Learning and Ratio
to Population of the United States*

Year	Colleges and universities	No. per million population
1790	19	4.9
1800[a]	25	4.7
1810	30	4.2
1820	40	4.2
1830	50	3.9
1840	85	5.0
1850	120	5.2
1860	250	7.9
1870	563	14.1
1880	811	16.1
1890	998	15.8
1900	977	12.8
1910	951	10.3
1920	1,041	9.8
1930	1,409	11.4
1940	1,708	12.9
1950	1,851	12.2
1960	2,008	11.1
1970	2,556	12.5

Sources: *Historical Statistics of the United States,* Series A-1 and H-316; *Statistical Abstract of the United States* (1971: Table 198); Tewksbury (1932: 16); Rudolph (1962: 486). There are slight discrepancies among alternative sources.

[a]Numbers of institutions for the years 1800 through 1860 are estimates rather than exact counts.

the established church made the founding of new universities a matter of church politics.

The American political situation made it easy to start new colleges; competing political, regional, and religious groups took advantage of the opportunities. The original modest proliferation of colleges in the colonies was due primarily to rivalries between denominations—an orthodox reaction against liberal Harvard led to the founding of Yale; a Presbyterian split led to Princeton, the Baptists founded Brown, the Dutch Reformed founded Rutgers, and so on. To some degree, the rash of college foundings was also due to regional sentiments for a college conveniently located nearby. After the Revolution, and especially during the period of expansion to the West, local and state pride led to a large number of new colleges. Moreover, the frontier produced not only a widening of the franchise, but also a weakening of the influence of the respectable Eastern churches and of the cultural monopoly of the colonial upper class. In this fluid situation, the status-bearing institution of the Puritan aristocracy, the college, became available to the poorer sector of the populace. The evangelical lower-class churches, the Baptists, Methodists, and others established colleges of their own in every locality in which there was a sizable group of church members or a threat from the college of a rival denomination. In this situation, a figure arose who was to dominate higher education in America until well into the twentieth century: the college president, an educational entrepreneur.

The colleges that proliferated across the American landscape in the early nineteenth century were imitations of the original colonial colleges; innovations on the narrow classical curriculum were rare until the second half of the century. This curriculum had originally been taken from the liberal arts section of the European universities and led to the traditional degree of B.A. In the medieval university, the arts instruction was essentially a preparatory school for the true university studies in theology, medicine, and law; the medieval university, as the institutuion of higher education in a society that otherwise possessed only local church-run elementary schools, combined the functions of a secondary school and a set of professional schools. (The upgrading of the B.A. curriculum to a level above that of secondary schools occurred in Europe only in the early nineteenth century, at a time when true secondary schools began to develop.) The American college, however, had lost the professional training and certification functions at the outset. British legal tradition, on which Americans drew, trained lawyers outside of the universities; Protestant denominational opposition to the established church forms of university theology schools resulted in the elimination of a theology faculty; and the tiny and widely dispersed American medical profession precluded the establishment of university medical faculties. The colonial college was essentially the equivalent of a secondary school, and the nineteenth-century colleges were faithful imitations of the original models.[18] In the absence of secondary schools in America, the college acted as a substitute; moreover, the range of ages of the college students—from the early teens to the mid-twenties—was in fact equivalent to that of the few secondary schools that began to emerge in mid-century.

The nineteenth-century American college was primarily an instrument for inculcating religious piety, according to the tenets of particular denomina-

---

[18]The high proportion of colleges in early America, then, should not really be compared with the proportion of universities in Europe, at least those (such as the German universities) that had already undergone reform. But these American colleges were to become upgraded into true tertiary education, in the *structural* sense, extending the years of educational certification for a proportion of the population unprecedented in the world.

tions, and for conferring whatever status still remained in the concept of a college and its degree. Only the status certification function of the college was important at this time, for the training inculcated via the classical curriculum and stern discipline was of little intellectual or practical value. The college was distinguished from the secondary school only by its name and its degree, not by its substance. The origins of the large number of American colleges cannot be attributed to the demands of the economy nor to the demands of the industrial revolution; not only did the colleges precede the economic expansion, but also their training was in no way designed for practical skills.

By the 1850s, the American colleges faced a crisis. The colleges were small and continually in financial difficulties. The failure rate was high: Feverish entrepreneurship in the educational sphere had founded perhaps 1000 colleges before the Civil War, of which over 700 failed (Rudolph, 1962: 47). Clearly, there were far too many colleges for the demand. But in mid-century, the crisis appeared to be worsening: Colleges not only failed to grow, but they also shrank in size; the number of college students in 1870 in New England had been declining for some time, both absolutely and in proportion to the population (Rudolph, 1962: 218). Moreover, attacks began to be heard upon the colleges and the curriculum as irrelevant to the lives and interests of the vast majority of the populace. Yet this was a period of rising literacy in the populace, a time of the consolidation of public elementary schools, and the beginnings of public secondary schools. A larger potential clientele was becoming available, yet the colleges' situation was becoming worse rather than better.[19]

The crisis was clearly a result of overextension; the United States, with perhaps five times as many colleges as the rest of the world together, had far too many colleges for the demand. Still, this overextension had surely existed throughout the nineteenth century; the crisis also seems to reflect a change in the nature of the value of the college education and the rise of an external source of competition for the colleges. It appears that the *status value* of a college education had become diluted by the large numbers of colleges. Offering little besides an imitation of the high-status New England colleges, the newer colleges succeeded only in reducing the value of a college degree by making it more widely available, much as an exclusive club loses its desirability by being thrown open to the public: Its charm existed largely in its

---

[19]It has been argued by Potts (1977) that there was no crisis, at least before 1860; he bases his argument on the grounds that data on enrollment trends are fragmentary and some tabulations show increases during the 1800–1860 period. But the total figure of 25,000–30,000 students in 1860 was not large, and it is clear even from Pott's discussion of the local support expressed for colleges that threatened to move away for economic reasons that, in fact, removal was a problem in this period.

closed doors; once inside, the public was likely to find that its armchairs were musty and uncomfortable. The educational entrepreneurs who traveled the country from college to college, often founding and abandoning several, had finally debased the currency they had hoped to build into status fortunes.

The expansion of secondary schools may have contributed to the crisis. To be sure, secondary schools shared the liabilities of the colleges in providing little educational substance for which there was a real demand; but they had the advantages of child labor laws, the elementary school movement and its related compulsory attendance laws, as well as freedom from tuition and location near the homes of their clientele. Moreover, the age range of secondary school and college students was substantially the same; only a small proportion of the population attended *either* type of institution (see Table 1.1), so they competed for the same limited pool of students.

The colleges' only weapon was its certification power, but that was waning because it was based on the status appeal of an exclusive medieval institution that was rapidly losing its exclusiveness. The curriculum of the college met little public demand, and professional training in the ministry, law, and medicine could be obtained outside the colleges. The first answer of the educational entrepreneurs was to initiate a few cautious experiments with a vocational course, but this in itself met little success. The old curriculum was repeatedly attacked as providing no useful training, yet when nonclassical programs were introduced (such as at Miami, Virginia, and New York in the 1820s and 1830s) as alternatives to the classical B.A. course, they failed for lack of students (Rudolph, 1962: 126–129, 238–240). The old method of certification was becoming less respected, but new methods that based their appeal *solely* on the technical training provided (the programs mentioned did not culminate in the B.A. but only in a certificate of proficiency) evoked even less demand than the classical course. Utilitarianism seemed an easy solution to a few reformers, but the conservatives saw more clearly when they clung to the old forms of status conferral. As one college president put it: "While others are veering to the popular pressure . . . let it be our aim to make Scholars and not sappers or miners—apothecaries—doctors or farmers."[20] The function of the college was primarily certification and not training; to advertise college education purely on utilitarian grounds was to lose even its certification power.

In the 1870s, the leading entrepreneurs hit on a reform, a shift from the "classical" college to the modern university. In the 1880s, the new form spread rapidly, and the fortunes of American higher education began to

---

[20]Rudolph (1962: 240). Notice the denigration of doctors at this time before their successful status revolution at the turn of the twentieth century (see also Chapter 6).

improve. The rate of failures fell off sharply, the numbers of institutions increased rapidly into the twentieth century, the size of student bodies and of faculties increased, and the ratio of students rose steadily from 1.7% of the 18–21-year-old population in 1876 to 53% in 1970. The innovation was initiated by a few new universities such as Johns Hopkins and Cornell in the 1870s and 1880s and by some older colleges such as Harvard, which reformed themselves into universities. The success of these leaders resulted in rapid emulation. In the background, of course, was the increasing conflict of ethnic–class cultures, which gave the old cultural institutions a new urgency in a period of stepped-up immigration.

Curricula were changed and postgraduate (M.A. and Ph.D.) studies were added to the B.A. program. The curriculum change was brought about primarily by the introduction of the elective system in which the student was given a choice of a variety of course offerings (Rudolph, 1978). This necessitated going beyond the classical curriculum and resulted in a great expansion of courses in the sciences, modern languages and literature, social studies, and eventually in vocational fields. The creation of graduate schools had a similar effect on the curriculum: the superseding of the classical curriculum by a variety of specialized scholarly and scientific fields of study.

As Vesey has shown, these reforms were carried out in the name of a variety of ideals: practical utility, pure science, and scholarship, or high culture (1965). Although the proponents of these ideals were often quite antagonistic to each other, none of them was able to prevail over the others, nor indeed to have much effect in shaping the lives of the students. Nevertheless, these ideals appear to have played a crucial part in overcoming the crisis in higher education; they provided the necessary public relations to revive the prestige of the college degree and attract large numbers of students.

The utilitarian ideal had been tried before but although usefulness may provide a good standard by which to declare classical curriculum a dismal failure, it does not attract students when schools offer training they can get just as well outside (see Chapter 1). By emphasizing training alone, universities stand in danger of losing their main value, status certification. Although utilitarian rhetoric was used to pass the Morrill Act (setting up land-grant colleges) in Congress in 1862, little attention was paid to organizing practical courses in agriculture, and when such courses were started, they attracted few students (Curti, 1935: 212). The only utilitarian claim for a university education that seemed successful was the claim to educate a political elite in the arts of public statesmanship, an ideal that was successfully used at Cornell and later at Princeton and elsewhere.

Science, scholarship, and high culture appealed primarily to those who wished to perpetuate the old cultural elite. Interestingly enough, these tended to become a specialized occupational group: those who expected to become university teachers. Since this was a period of the expansion of universities, the demand for teachers was great enough to make possible the expansion of graduate schools, which would be justified as training teachers. The undergraduate emphasis on scientific and scholarly subjects probably had little more effect in training the minds of most students than the classical curriculum had, but it at least carried with it the prestige of a small but prominent and growing profession, that of the scientific researcher. Thus, by offering an education described glowingly, if vaguely, in terms of some larger utility, and carrying the prestige of science for students who would not themselves become scientists (nor, generally speaking, study science very hard), the educational entrepreneurs managed to revive the status of the college degree.

The main appeal of the revitalized university for large groups of students was not the training it offered but the social experience of attending it. The older elite was being perpetuated in a new, more easygoing form. Intercollegiate sports grew up at the same time as the university revolution was being carried out, and the same elite institutions led both innovations (Rudolph, 1962: 373–393). Through football games, colleges for the first time became prominent in the public eye, and alumni and state legislators found renewed loyalty to their schools. At the same time, fraternities and sororities became widespread, and with them came college traditions of drinking, parties, parades, dances, and "school spirit."[21] It is little exaggeration to say that the replacement of the pious, unreformed college by the sociable culture of the university was crucial in the growth of enrollments, or that football rather than science was the salvation of American higher education.

The two developments—the rise of the hedonistic and ritualistic undergraduate culture and the transformations of curriculum—need not be opposed in this way, however, because they occurred together as part of the same effort to revive the status of the colleges. The rise of the undergraduate culture indicates first of all that college education had come to be treated as consumption by the new industrial upper classes, although it also attracted growing numbers of the intellectually oriented and those seeking careers in teaching. College attendance had become an interlude of fun in the lives of upper-class and upper-middle-class young Americans, and the rise of enrollments must be partly attributed to the rising standard of living. But the rituals of undergraduate life had another important aspect: They were direct expressions of the informal side of stratification, sociability. Through participation in the parties and pranks of college life, young Americans formed and consolidated friendships. Sororities arose, as Scott has shown, through the

---

[21]This is not to say that carousing was entirely absent earlier. Fraternities also date back to the 1820s in some places. But on the whole, the shift in tone was considerable.

efforts of parents to promote class endogamy (1965: 514–527). Fraternities, which had already existed in the 1830s, became all-important. The collegiate culture took the function of bringing together the children of the upper middle class, forming them into groups of friends bound together by sentiments of college activities and eventually intermarrying (see Baltzell, 1958: 327–372). The new style football-and-fraternity college thus became important in forming elite status groups in America, recapturing in secularized form the status of the early colonial colleges.

That the initial success of the new university model was more a result of its status appeal than its efficiency in training is shown by the defeat of the "acceleration" movement in the 1880s. Some utility-minded administrators attacked the 4-year curriculum as a useless tradition inherited from the medieval universities, and they introduced reforms to allow students to move through college at their own pace, acquiring their training on an individual basis (Rudolph, 1962: 446–448). This effort to put training back as the central function of the college was a failure. Students did not want to disturb the rituals of freshman and sophomore class rivalries, junior dances, and senior privileges. The leaders of the acceleration movement, taking too seriously their own rhetoric of reform, misconceived the appeal of college education to many of their clients: Most students found the essence of college education to be the enjoyable and status-conferring rituals and social life of college rather than the content of classroom learning.

The internal form of the university was shaped by its history of seeking students and catering to their desires for enjoyment and certification. The 4-year curriculum remained because of the value placed on traditional forms of certification. As a result of the long period of seeking students, the colleges had become largely secular and nondenominational; they could not afford to exclude students because of their religion. Similarly, until well into the twentieth century, admission standards were low or nonexistent. The need for a clientele also broke down sex requirements. With the period of university reforms, coeducation was introduced and spread widely in most of the larger and more successful schools, a process that fed upon itself since as the marriageable males concentrated in the colleges, the women had a strong incentive for following. The expansion of credentialed employment in the public schools at this time also drew many women by offering the prospect of careers in teaching.

A prestige hierarchy began to emerge among American colleges and universities for the first time during the period of reform. The schools that led the reform—the original colonial colleges, the heavily endowed new private universities, and the well-supported midwestern state universities—soon set themselves apart from those who were slow to follow. As the period of expansion set in, the leading schools began to attract thousands of students while those that lagged behind in reforms remained tiny. Financial differences followed suit, as did intellectual differences, due to the quality of the faculties that could be attracted by schools of varying resources. With the rise of football and its accompanying undergraduate culture, Yale, Harvard, and Michigan became household words. Once this prestige hierarchy was established and buttressed by financial success, what Riesman called the "academic procession" was formed, and the conservative colleges at the rear were forced, however unwillingly, to emulate their wealthy and famous rivals (Riesman, 1958: 25−65; Jencks and Riesman, 1968).

The leading universities were now in a position to set standards throughout the educational world and began to rise to a position from which they dominated all other forms of education: secondary, professional, and teacher training. In the 1890s, the leading universities, organized in the American Association of Universities, began to exercise accrediting power over secondary schools by setting up standards of admission. Secondary schools became more clearly separated from elementary schools, and a specifically defined age group for each was enforced by the universities' newly instituted requirement that 12 years of school precede college admission (Rudolph, 1962: 281−286; Wechsler, 1977). It was Harris's response to this pressure from the universities (see page 117) that caused him to oppose vocational instruction in the public high schools. Thus college education linked itself specifically to the 12-year secondary school system. Aptitude and achievement tests came later, in the twentieth century. A high school diploma was the first formal requirement for college admission and remains so even today, when standardized tests geared to individual attainment could take its place.

Through the prestige of its social and curricular innovations, the new American university became the major influence in the world of education. This influence was expressed in several ways. Those schools that could do so attempted to become universities themselves. Other schools, such as those for professional and vocational training, attached themselves to universities or were annexed by them. Competing forms of education had to establish niches for themselves that did not draw on the same group of students. This was done by tailoring their curricula as either preceding or following the university's B.A. program.

As Jencks and Riesman (1968) showed, specialized forms of higher education, from teacher-training schools to fundamentalist colleges, Catholic universities, women's colleges, and community-oriented junior colleges, all have come to emphasize the same scholar-dominated disciplinary sequences as the leading universities have. Beginning in the 1890s, normal schools (teacher-training institutes) developed the standard 4-year B.A. curriculum requiring a high school diploma for admission. In this way, many state normal schools transformed themselves into state colleges, and decades later some of these colleges succeeded in establishing graduate departments and renaming themselves universities. Similarly, the state Agricultural and Mechanical universities set up under the Morrill Act tended to downgrade their vocational functions and to expand their arts and sciences offerings in imitation of the proliferating specialties of the growing major universities with their large numbers of research-oriented scholars. Even the junior college movement, designed expressly as a community service and vocational venture in direct opposition to the scholarly curricula of the universities, could not uphold its distinct curricular ideals. The irresistible force was the students, who greatly preferred the liberal arts, transfer-preparatory programs to the job-oriented terminal programs. Designed as an alternative to the university, the junior college became a last chance for educational mobility for students with poor secondary school records and an agency for "cooling out" those who would not make it into the university (Clark, 1960: 569—576; Jencks and Riesman, 1968: 480—509).

The most dangerous potential rival to the early American university was the professional school, particularly since it drew from the same pool of students. In the late nineteenth century, it was nowhere required to have a B.A. in order to attend a school of law or medicine, and the criticism of the uselessness of the classical college education might have led to a shift of students away from the colleges and toward immediate training in the professions. But instead of substituting for college education, the professional schools became subordinate to the B.A. program. Universities moved to found their own professional schools and make them into graduate schools, requiring a B.A. for admission. This eliminated the competition for students and increased the attractiveness of the B.A. by giving it a palpable value for a visible, if somewhat artificial, career sequence. Professional schools did not resist, for they had troubles of their own, as we shall see in Chapter 6. Professions, after all, maintain sometimes precarious monopolies over practice, especially by controlling entry into their ranks, and the professions in America were wracked by internal status conflicts in the late nineteenth century. The old traditional Anglo-Protestant status of the universities was a handy weapon for the professional elites, defending their holds against ethnic and lower-class intruders. Thus an alliance was forged and the power of the universities established.

THE ESTABLISHMENT OF THE
EDUCATIONAL SEQUENCE

The universities thus consolidated their newly reestablished prestige and firmly established the 4-year B.A. curriculum, or analogues of it in some vocational fields (engineering, business administration, education, nursing), as a universal stage in a sequence toward post-high-school certification. Whatever the amount of training necessary, 4 years of it was to be required; moreover, any field aspiring to high professional status must establish itself in the sequence after the B.A. First with law and medicine (and trickling down within these professions from the most prestigious professional schools to the others by emulation), and later in engineering, business administration, and education, the post-B.A. program became the route to prestige, formalized in employment requirements.

Forms of education that competed with the universities never acquired any status: Correspondence courses and commercial technical schools (such as those offering limited training in engineering specialities or commerce) led a marginal existence, attracting enough students to make a steady profit only in fields of very short labor supply (such as computer programming in the 1960s), or jobs of low status (auto mechanics, secretaries), or by resorting to unscrupulous advertising and financing plans (see Hollingshead, 1949: 380–381; Clark and Sloan, 1966). Such schools emphasized only training; they required no high school degrees (which, after all, may be quite irrelevant to learning a specific technical skill); they did not prolong instruction for 4 years, nor include extraneous, nontechnical courses, nor take up time with extracurricular activities; they certified only the specific skill trained, not a diffuse social status. Yet it is the name of the college degree, the medieval terminology of the B.A. and its modern elaborations, that carries the prestige and attracts the students. Here, as elsewhere, certification prevails over training.

By the mid-twentieth century, the universities had realized a self-fulfilling prophecy. By continually harping on the unspecified but great usefulness of the college degree for "success," universities had succeeded in surviving, and growing, until the point at which college education could be seen to have specific payoffs. With the rise of extensive graduate education, both in the professions and for scholarly careers (the latter having become increasingly attractive because of the continual expansion of positions for undergraduate teachers), the B.A. program was transformed into a link in a sequence, to be justified by pointing to the next link. Thus colleges traded on their old status skillfully enough through a period when a college degree had no links to further education until that further education arose to justify the undergraduate course.

History helped the universities to cover their tracks in another respect. By continually telling the public that its education led to elite positions and by offering the opportunity for social mobility, the university attracted most of the members of the populace who had any chance to reach elite positions. The colleges now were able to declare the truth of their prophecy, since having attracted most of the upper-middle and upper classes, and then the middle class and the most ambitious and intelligent members of the lower class, they could point out that the elite positions in American society were increasingly filled by college graduates; they neglected to mention that there were now large numbers of college graduates who did not reach high-status positions. By their very numbers, college graduates could no longer count on elite status, since they came to exceed the number of elite positions available (even including those positions they could create).[22] But the colleges had carried out a *fait accompli,* and there was no turning back. Now college graduation had become the requirement for many positions for which no such education had been required before. College education, once an incidental accompaniment of high status, now became the prerequisite of mere respectability.

Educational credentials, as we have seen, first became established within the school system itself. The crucial point was when the elite universities began to accredit high school programs for college admission, thus resolving part of their struggle for an amorphous common age group of potential students. The other half of this struggle was resolved when the universities' other rival, the professional schools, began to link themselves to colleges by making a bachelor's degree prerequisite to entering their programs. Thus educational credentials first became formal requirements for advancement of students within a sequence of schools.[23] At first, then, degrees, like grades and test scores today, had no directly negotiable value in the occupational realm but did determine one's movement to a higher level of schooling. The advanced school levels then began to take on occupational significance in particular professions as these obtained state-licensed monopolies incorporating credential requirements. The process by which this developed and the further spread of educational credentials outward into the rest of the economy is the subject of the next chapter.

The major impetus for this whole development, I have argued, was the severe multiethnic conflicts of American society after the mid-nineteenth century. Insofar as the school system was created to resolve the strife by reducing cultural diversity, one can say it has met with a degree of success. It did manage to make training in Anglo-Protestant culture and political values compulsory for all children up to a certain age, and it did make it *virtually*

---

[22]In 1967, 7.9% of the skilled manual workers and 5.7% of the operatives had 1–3 years of college, and 1.6% of the former had college degrees (U.S. Department of Labor, 1967). See also Folger and Nam (1964: 19–33) on the declining association between years of school (through college level) and occupational success.

[23]Schools have subsequently become the leading user of credentials for employment as well (Collins, 1969), not only for entering teaching and administrative positions, but also often basing pay scales upon completion of additional units of academic credit.

compulsory for a continually increasing period beyond this if the student wanted to be economically successful. Yet one could not call this a total success in its own terms. The creation of a massively inclusive educational system has caused schools to become internally bureaucratic parts of an indefinitely lengthy sequence of obtaining a negotiable cultural currency. Hence the content of education has become increasingly irrelevant, except in the very short run of passing a particular course or even cramming for an exam. The results have been stored almost entirely in the cryptic records of credits, grade-point averages, and degrees. The system that was to preserve Anglo-Protestant culture has thus also tended to destroy it.

At the same time, the diversity of ethnic cultures in the populace has given way only gradually. Ethnic cultures are still at least mildly in evidence today, three full generations after the cutting of mass immigration in 1922. And newly mobilized and rather sharply divergent ethnic cultures—black and Latin—have put renewed pressure upon the legitimacy of the culture imposed by the schools. But for all their vehemence, these conflicts are now safely channeled *within* an institutionalized system. For all their rhetoric of ethnic cultural preservation and even separatism, the main result of these conflicts has been to make the abstract bureaucratic credentials easier for members of their ethnic minorities to obtain. Even this has had ironic consequences. Easier passage through lower or intermediate levels of the educational system has had the aggregate effect of devaluing those levels of the credential currency and mounting pressures for yet higher levels of attainment. However these ethnic struggles are resolved, the expansion of the credential system quite possibly has reached nowhere near its outer limits.

6

The Politics of Professions

Professions and related occupations have been the fastest growing sector in the American labor force: from 4.3% in 1900 to 14.2% in 1970 (*Statistical Abstract*, 1971). Not only have the traditional professions expanded—teaching, engineering, science, medicine, law—but also other skills have up-graded themselves and new ones have emerged. We now have social work-ers and licensed realtors; undertakers become morticians and business school spokesmen talk of the development of business administration as a profes-sion. This proliferation is all the more remarkable because the earlier trend in the American labor force—from the Revolutionary War until late in the nineteenth century—moved in the opposite direction. This earlier develop-ment of the American economy saw the breaking down of the closed corpo-rate controls of the traditional professions and a general democratization of occupational access. The shift back to professionalism began in the atmo-sphere of a nativist counterattack in the late nineteenth century against the influx of culturally alien immigration and political reform in defense of the local powers of the Anglo-Protestant middle class; the revival of closed profes-sional enclaves went hand in hand with the consolidation of the culturally elite universities in control of an expanding educational hierarchy. For as we shall see, far from indicating the triumph of technocratic meritocracy, the development of the modern American professions is only a new variant on the familiar processes of stratification through monopolization of opportunities.

The rise of professional associations was carried out under the popular slogans of modernization and reform, and this idealized image has continued to dominate not only the public but the academic views as well. The most widely accepted sociological description has been an idealized one. A profession is a self-regulating community (Goode, 1957: 194–200). It has exclusive power, usually backed up by the state, to train new members and admit them to practice. It practices its specialty according to its own standards without outside interference. It reserves the right to judge its own members' performance, and resists incursions of lay opinion; it alone can decide whether to punish or disbar an incompetent member because presumably only it can decide what technical competence is. It has a code of ethics, claiming to dedicate its work to the service of humanity, pledging disinterested and competent performance, and condemning commercialism and careerism.

With this description, it is not surprising that professions have been regarded as the saviors of the modern world.[1] Of course, not all "professions" quite live up to the model. The ideal definition is taken especially from medicine and extends fairly well to science, law, and architecture. It becomes strained when applied to engineers employed in large corporations or to teachers in bureaucratic school systems. With the increasing employment of traditional professionals like lawyers and scientists in bureaucracies, the sociology of professions has given much study to the problems of role conflict (e.g., Kornhauser, 1962; Miller, 1967: 755–767). Related issues involve pseudoprofessions like social work and psychiatry, whose professional status is left problematic by their lack of demonstrable efficacious skills.

It is clear that not all occupations can become professions in the strong sense of the term. What we have instead is a continuum, or rather several continua of characteristics conducive to a self-regulating occupational community. Special conditions are necessary (Wilensky, 1964: 137–158). A strong profession requires a real technical skill that produces demonstrable results and can be taught. Only thus can the skill be monopolized, by controlling who will be trained. The skill must be difficult enough to require training and reliable enough to produce results. But it cannot be too reliable, for then outsiders can judge work by its results and control its practitioners by their

---

[1]During the ideological battles of the 1930s, Talcott Parsons (1939) argued that professions provided a third way between the selfishness of individualistic capitalism and the repressive collectivization of socialism. More recently, we have been told that the growth of professions has reversed the trend toward dehumanization in industrial bureaucracies, and professionalization has been held out as the answer to police brutality at home and military dictatorships abroad, as if to professionalize the agents of violence would turn them into paragons of altruism.

judgments. The ideal profession has a skill that occupies the mid-point of a continuum between complete predictability and complete unpredictability of results. At one end are skills like those of plumbers and mechanics, which do not give rise to strong professions because outsiders can judge whether the job is well done; supervisors know whether the machinery runs or not, although they may not know why. At the other end are vague skills like administrative politicking or palm reading; these cannot be monopolized because they are too unreliable or idiosyncratic for some to successfully train others in them. Other so-called skills may be entirely nonexistent, such as the case of the social worker, whose professional rhetoric covers up activities as welfare functionaries, or of psychiatrists, whose cures do not exceed the proportion expectable by chance. And, of course, the activity must be strongly desired by clients so that they are willing to allow its practitioners a high degree of autonomy and respect in carrying it out.

This narrows down the ideal-type professional to a smaller group. But it still gives too idealized a view of the "real" professions of medicine, law, and science, and it fails to explain the rising tide of pseudoprofessions in modern society. For the appropriate level of skill predictability is not the only variable involved in achieving a monopoly over practice. There are also sheer political power and techniques for manipulating symbolic status.

Political power is involved in almost all successful professions; they achieve their monopoly and self-governing rights by getting the force of the state to license them and back up their collective authority over members. Medical examining boards and bar associations control their respective professions through the ultimate sanction of the police (Gilb, 1966).[2] Hence, variations in political resources are responsible for the prevalence of professions and pseudoprofessions alike. The proliferation of both in modern America is due to the widespread availability of organizational resources by which occupational groups can gain political influence. It is fostered by American democracy and its structure of federalist pluralism, in which unorganized publics are little represented, but organized interest groups bargain with each other over favored niches. It has been intensified by American ethnic diversity and resulting group conflicts in which professional organizations have been used as a publicly legitimate control device. The extension of licensing powers to various occupational groups has gone on under the banner of liberal reform, fostered by a large lobby of mutually supporting professional groups.

---

[2]Science is the major exception: a profession in which the skill is intrinsically so esoteric that those who would learn it must put themselves under the tutelage of a practitioner, and in which careers depend continually on the community's judgments of the significance of each individual member's work for the advancement of the entire field.

There is also the sheer mystification that goes along with groups acquiring resources to keep outsiders out. The earliest profession was that of the shaman or sorcerer with his secret training in occult powers. The powers themselves were essentially the powers to mystify; without the secrecy and the show, the sorcerer could not play on people's emotions and influence their subjective construction of reality and thus bring about the psychological suggestibility that produced results. Priesthoods combined these techniques with conscious moral and political leadership of the community. It is out of their collegial organization and their training institutions (the medieval universities) that most other professions (teaching, medicine, law, science) branched off.

The other traditional profession was that of the military officer. It grew out of the institution of knighthood, which arose in stratified societies containing a small dominant class owning heavy weapons and armor with which to equip themselves or land and serfs. The position became enshrouded in a mystifying and self-glorifying ideology: the legends of the Round Table and the troubadours, the heroic code of chivalry (Bloch, 1964: 283–331). These altruistic and gentlemanly ideals went along with the standard of a noble (noncommercial and nonmanual) style of life, which eventually became combined with an emphasis on family heredity to produce the closed aristocracies of late medieval Europe. Weber cites the rise of the European aristocracy out of the profession of arms as his major example of a closed status group developing upon the basis of a class; his other example is the Indian upper caste arising from the Brahmin priests (1968: 932–937). The model of professional monopoly is thus a subcase of the more general process of forming self-consciously exclusive groups—what Weber called "status groups."

Status groups are formed on the basis of common and distinctive experiences, interests, and resources. Status communities may derive both from occupational and territorial (ethnic) situations: Class-based status groups derive from occupational experiences, common interests in struggles for power and wealth, and differential resources for life style, for group mobilization, and for cultural idealization. Ethnic-based status groups derive from the common experiences of once-isolated community settings, the common interests of such groups in struggling against other ethnic groups with which they come into contact, and the resources of their own cultures and ritual procedures that mobilize them as operating groups. Professions are occupational communities; they are thus a type of class-based status group except that the community is organized explicitly within the realm of work itself rather than in the sphere of consumption. Its basis is the practice of certain esoteric and easily monopolized skills and the use of procedures that by their very nature work most effectively through secrecy and idealization. The experiences of selling such services and striving to protect their esoteric quality and ideal image give a common basis for an associational group to form; the interests of the members in wealth, power, and prestige motivate them to institute strong collective controls over insiders and to seek monopolistic sanctions against outsiders; and their resources—esoteric skills, techniques and opportunities for playing on laymen's emotions, wealth, and personal connections that can be translated into political influence—enable them to organize an occupational community with strong controls and defenses.

These processes have operated in the development of professions in modern America. Many of the techniques by which the professions of today became organized originally and achieved their high status were based on mystification and secrecy regarding their real skills and use of their status background rather than their technique per se. The elite professions in America grew out of older gentry elites: their communal organization from upper-class clubs and their legitimating ideology from the traditions of upper-class altruism and religious leadership. The ups and downs of professions have reflected changes in the balance of political power as well as the threats of rival ethnic and class cultures in Anglo-Protestant America.

Modern technology has contributed to the proliferation of professions in America, although not necessarily because of the intrinsic importance of technical specialization. As Weber pointed out, bureaucratization gives great power to middle- and even lower-level officials because of the mass of paperwork and administrative complexity that shield them from their superiors (1968: 987–988). In the centralized and autocratic European bureaucracies, this has made for a great deal of rank consciousness throughout organizational hierarchies and has led to characteristic inertia and conservatism. The geographically far-flung and economically competitive American organizations, on the other hand, have been a good deal more decentralized, and employees at middle levels have increased their autonomy by claiming professional status. The proliferation of staff departments separate from line authority and the emphasis on the rhetoric of technical expertise in modern America are results of an ongoing struggle in which control becomes ever more dispersed among middle-level functionaries (Barnard, 1938; Chandler, 1962; Crozier, 1964: 231–236).

The rise of the professions in America, then, is an extension of the age-old struggles of self-interested groups using refinements of traditional tactics. They do not represent the technical needs of a new technocratic society. The various industrial societies have diverse forms of professional organization, reflecting their political histories and the sequence of organizational resources available to different factions in the struggle for wealth, status, and power.

What of altruism? Is the image that is projected of the dedicated medical researcher inoculating himself with diphtheria merely a fraud? We should

recall, of course, that most professionals do not behave like this. Their sac-
rifices are confined to spending a few years in medical school—which in fact is
as hard in reality as it is in popular myth; medical schools may now be difficult
to get into, but they are extremely hard to flunk out of.[3] Professionals do work
longer hours than the average person, and they may work considerably
beyond the 9-to-5 routine. But this is characteristic of all powerful and ambitious people—it is true of business promoters and politicians as well—since
their work is well remunerated with high incomes, and pay is usually on a fee,
not on a salary basis (Wilensky, 1961: 32–56).[4] The altruistic professions, in
fact, are among the highest paid, and their "altruism" gives a further payoff in
the form of status and deference.

A better explanation of professionals' altruistic codes of ethics is that they
are defenses against the potential distrust of their clients (Wilensky, 1964).[5]
An occupation that monopolizes an important skill and reserves the right to
judge its success or failure can provoke considerable antipathy among those
who depend on it. When the doctor or the lawyer is called in, the client is
usually helpless and distraught. Moreover, the outcome is often in doubt,
even with the best of skilled performance; the disease may be incurable, the
case may be unwinnable. In order to protect themselves against the anger of
unsatisfied clients (or their surviving relatives), the occupational groups pro-
fess strict standards and enforce them against practitioners who bring the
entire group into disrepute. As Zilboorg (1941) puts it, it was the public who
created the Hippocratic Oath rather than the doctors themselves.

There is great variation in how much the self-interest of professionals
requires them to enforce their code of ethics and with what emphases. Codes
of ethics among lawyers and doctors serve quite well to reinforce a restrictive
club based on genteel manners, to prevent competition, and thereby to keep

---

[3]Information supplied by the Pre-Medical Career Counseling Office of the University of
California, San Diego, in June 1974, indicated that the noncompletion rate for entering medical
students in America is approximately 5–7% (compared to the approximately 50% attrition for
college students indicated in Chapter 1, Table 1.1).

[4]The "fee" system means a very short-term contract for services and hence represents a
much more volatile market than a labor contract on a wage or salary basis. It is striking that
occupational groups should have to exercise great monopolistic powers to be able to sell their
services on a market of this degree of openness; but then it appears that the monopolization of
such a market by a small group of practitioners means it can be most profitably exploited in this
way.

[5]Berlant (1973: 83–159) points out that it has been doctors, not aggrieved patients, who
have called for monopolization as a protection against incompetent practice. Monopolistic sanctions have not been used for this purpose, however; professional discipline or revocation of
license on the basis of malpractice has been extremely rare, on the order of less than 1% of the
cases (1973: 101–102), while most cases in which sanctions have been applied involve status
offenses such as drug use, writing illegal prescriptions, or violations of economic norms, including
participation in group health care plans.

fees high. The introduction of stringent ethical standards among professionals has always resulted in an improvement of their economic and social position and a restriction of access to their ranks.

Perhaps some individuals have gone through their careers guided subjectively by noble ideals. Some professionals, such as medical missionaries, have not been much interested in wealth. But it is a mistake to explain people's behavior simply in terms of their own interpretations of it, or to exempt their subjective ideals from sociological explanation. Esteem is a goal like any other. Usually it goes along with a desire for power, especially over the reality-constructing activities of other people's minds. Medical missionaries have been the imposers of self-satisfied Western culture upon weaker societies, and of Western political dominance as well. We would do well to recall that altruism as an ideal emerged with the rise of organized priesthoods, claiming to speak in the name of the community; at the same time, these priesthoods have been major factors in the history of political struggles. Altruism per se is just as much a part of the conflicts that make up most of history as violence and property.

Professions are no exception to the conflict theory of stratification used in this book. The distinctive forms of mobility channels in modern America are due, to a considerable degree, to the way professions have developed, and this is a matter of understanding the sequence of conflicts that has shaped and continues to shape them. In this chapter we take up three of the biggest and most important professions in modern society: medicine, law, and engineering. A fourth, teaching, has already been considered in Chapter 5.

The evidence that follows ranges more widely in historical time and space than elsewhere in this book. There is an important reason for this. The rise of the professions to very near the top of the stratification ladder has been the primary evidence used by proponents of technocratic interpretations of modern society. Hence, if an alternative interpretation of their rise can be established in terms of credentialism and monopolization via political resources, it will constitute an *a fortiori* proof of the superiority of one theory over the other. Comparisons are of the essence of any such proof. Hence, I examine several dimensions of comparison.

There are comparisons in time, showing the ups and downs of professional monopolies as their political opportunities have shifted. I take some of these rather far back into history because the organizational form of professional monopolies, in certain crucial cases, long predates their development of real technical skills. I also sketch some comparisons among the various forms in which the professions are organized in different modern industrial societies. This is important in order to show that there are alternative ways of organizing professions. All too often what a functional or structural universalist claims to be inevitable is merely the result of provinciality. It should also be apparent that the range of variations in professional organization, say, among the

United States, Britain, continental Europe, and the Soviet bloc *do not exhaust the range of possibilities.* But for theory-building purposes, some variation is crucial if we are to see the operating conditions producing these various types. Once we have grasped these principles, we should be in a better position to extend the range of actual types still further and design forms of organization yet untried. Finally, there are comparisons among the three main professions considered here; in particular, the fate of engineering as against law and medicine is instructive, for it tells us that the occupation nearest the core of modern productive technology nevertheless may lack the crucial resources of cultural group organization and formal credentialing to reach above the middle ranges of stratification.

The political process of monopolizing incomes from the practice of particular kinds of work is quite a general one. It goes on today on all levels where credentialing and licensing can be brought to bear upon an overcrowded labor market. It occurs not only in the traditional, high-status "professions," but also in the skilled trades where state contractors' licensing now proliferates, and in lucrative sales areas such as those now being monopolized through realtors' examinations. The details of economic stratification are increasingly modeled by this process.

THE MEDICAL MONOPOLY

Along with engineering, medicine is one of the few professions in which it is clear that there is an objective technical skill built upon general principles that can be taught. Medical education is often taken as the epitome of valid technical education, and the related professional monopoly over technical skill seems to be the clearest case of a functionally enforced restriction. If the social organization of power and status are found to be important in shaping the medical profession and medical education, they must *a fortiori* be so in other occupations and forms of education. That such social conditions are involved may be guessed from the fact that medical doctors have the highest social status and are consistently drawn from the highest social class backgrounds of any major occupation in industrial society. Reforms to raise the technical level of medical training have strengthened rather than weakened these patterns. Modern medicine is one of the most technically skilled of occupations, yet it shows the ambiguities of a purely technical explanation of its social positions and emphasizes the necessity of understanding technical skills and education within a larger context of stratification processes.

Traditional Pretensions

The early history of medicine is particularly revealing. Medicine was an honored profession in medieval Europe. It was one of the three subjects, along with theology and law, taught in the higher levels of the medieval university. Together with law, it attracted the wealthiest students (Schachner, 1962: 183, 373). The university degree conferred a monopoly on practice. In England, the universities of Oxford and Cambridge decayed during the sixteenth and seventeenth centuries, and their monopoly power was transferred to the Royal College of Physicians (founded in 1518). The latter enforced knowledge of the traditional medical texts, strictly limited membership, and maintained high social status (Carr-Saunders and Wilson, 1933: 66–75). Sharp distinctions were maintained among physicians, surgeons, and apothecaries. The latter two were looked down on because they involved manual labor and the life style of tradesmen. Physicians alone claimed genteel status because of their learning and their role as dignified consultants who stood above commercial pursuits. Similarly, in colonial America, the "better" doctors—those who could claim classical education and a disinterested outlook—were part of the upper classes, and backwoods practitioners had considerably lower status (Main, 1965: 144–146, 200–203).

What is striking about the traditionally high status of medicine is the fact that it was based on virtually no valid expertise at all.[6] The training on which physicians prided themselves consisted of ancient works like Galen, containing physiological theories whose practical application were not merely wrong but positively harmful. Prevailing theories of disease led to practices such as bleeding and purging as major cures. The most renowned physician of colonial America, the scholarly and genteel Philadelphian, Benjamin Rush, promulgated a theory whose recommendations for all ailments consisted of massive doses of enemas. In general, with the exception of Jenner's smallpox vaccination developed in 1798, there were no valid medical treatments at all until 1850. Then advances in science (largely in France and Germany) led to distinctions among different types of diseases, the understanding of infections and the development of antiseptics, and the recognition of the importance of public sanitation (rather than merely the old quarantine methods) in the control of epidemics. Only after 1880 did medical science begin to develop positive cures (Shryock, 1947: 129–204, 224–273; Mason, 1962: 517–519, 525–526).[7]

The monopoly position and high standing of physicians before the latter nineteenth century, insofar as it was based on claims to actually cure illness and alleviate suffering, was based on fraud. Indeed, whatever practical skill was available was more likely to be found among surgeons and apothecaries than among the elite physicians (Reader, 1966: 31–40). Yet the latter en-

---

[6]See Schachner (1962: 132–134, 152–155) on the state of medical knowledge in medieval Europe and on the corporate privileges of physicians.

[7]From ancient times there has been some knowledge of drugs, but this involved the most haphazard ideas as to their application.

joyed not only genteel status, but also lucrative incomes from wealthy patients. Doctors were rewarded for their ritual activities of making a show of power over unknown ills and therefore providing some psychological comfort to patients. The monopolistic organization and the classical learning of the medical profession were simply status-giving accouterments of a guild of priests. Since doctors appeared in emergency situations when patients were most fearful and in need of comfort, they found it crucial to allay fears about their benevolence by emphasizing an ideology of altruism. In England, this was done by such practices as prohibiting holders of medical licenses from suing to collect fees.

It was also desirable for doctors to appear as social equals of their most preferred—the wealthiest—clients. Hence they emphasized a genteel rather than a mercenary life-style, a classical education, and a monopoly organization designed to keep out the nongenteel. Because of these requirements, even medieval doctors were drawn from the wealthier classes; successful practice necessitated spending a great deal on living in a style that would attract the proper sort of patients. Once a practice was established, the returns might eventually be great, as physicians benefited from the gratitude of rich persons with whom they happened to be in attendance while spontaneously recovering from an illness. These conditions also explain why most doctors were concentrated in the big cities—in England, virtually all resided in London, and in the American colonies, the eminent doctors were in the major coastal cities—for it was here that the wealthy patients were found (Main, 1965: 99–101; Reader, 1966: 16–20).

When medicine finally acquired a valid skill base in the late nineteenth century, the prevailing social pattern was already set and reforms were absorbed within it. In England, the surgeons and apothecaries made efforts in the context of the general political mobilization of the middle class in the nineteenth century to acquire autonomous licensing powers giving them wider scope for practice and at the same time requiring stricter (and more practically oriented) training qualifications. Under these pressures, the physicians were forced to reform in 1858, with further modifications in subsequent years, raising their own technical qualifications and amalgamating their organization with that of the surgeons. Apothecaries, however, were placed in a position clearly subordinate to doctors. The medical profession was thus reorganized into high-status and low-status segments, drawn from upper and lower segments of the middle class, respectively (Carr-Saunders and Wilson, 1933: 75–89; Reader, 1966: 59–68).

In France, a more extensive revolution was carried out. The old university faculty of medicine was eliminated entirely in the aftermath of the 1789 Revolution and replaced by a medical profession based on training in public hospitals and oriented toward scientific research. It was this group that began to raise medicine into a science, followed by the research-oriented medical faculties of the German universities around mid-century. Their emphasis on technical validity rather than commercialism is shown by the rise of an ideology of "therapeutic nihilism" among them, stressing that their aim was to understand rather than to pretend to cure. The government-employed medical *scientist* thus acquired the highest esteem on the Continent, while the private practitioner was regarded for a considerable period during the nineteenth century to be a quack (Shryock, 1947: 129–176).

In the United States, yet another pattern appeared. The original English forms of organization were modified during the colonial period by the trend toward egalitarianism in politics and status relations. The distinction between physician and surgeon disappeared, and the medical practitioner came to be trained informally by an apprenticeship, usually lasting 6 years (Stookey, 1962: 3). Away from the coastal towns, the standard was more lax, and a large number of practitioners of varying degrees of certification eked out a living.

In the latter part of the eighteenth century, the upper-class American physicians gradually organized to regain something of the professional control found in England. Those who could afford it traveled to Europe, especially to Scotland or Holland, for the added status of university study. Under the leadership of such men, medical societies were formed that promulgated codes of ethics calling for restriction on advertising, forbade public criticism of others' practice, and secured licensing laws in most colonies and states between 1760 and 1830 (Shryock, 1947: 215, 219). These elite physicians also made efforts toward raising the status of the profession through medical training, albeit of the scientifically worthless classical sort. The first American medical school was established at the University of Pennsylvania in 1765, followed by King's College (later Columbia) in 1767, Harvard in 1783, and Dartmouth in 1798. On the eve of the Revolution, however, only approximately 400 of the 3500 American practitioners had attended medical school. Nevertheless, under the pressure of the elite medical societies, medical licensing came to be a prerogative of medical schools, and a fairly uniform requirement for the medical degree had come into existence by about 1820: apprenticeship to a practicing physician for 3 years, during the last 2 years of which one attended medical school (Shafer, 1936: 33–36; Carver, 1965: 100–101).

Democratization

The decline of the federalist aristocracy through the successive waves of Jeffersonian and Jacksonian democracy reversed the trend toward upper-class control on the English pattern. As early as 1810, the restrictive power of formal educational requirements was weakened by the founding of many new medical schools. In the course of the century, some 450 schools were established in the United States and Canada, of which 155 had survived in 1907 (Flexner, 1940: 77). Like the university-affiliated schools, they were generally proprietary—organized by a group of practitioners who augmented their incomes by sharing student fees. Since college charters generally contained unlimited powers and proprietary medical faculties were no expense, many colleges acquired nominally connected medical schools. The course of instruction usually lasted only a few months. The commercialism inherent in these arrangements offended the upper-class doctors, and periodic efforts were made to establish inspection by state boards of trustees. The American Medical Association (AMA), founded in 1847, attempted to further these purposes.

But popular resentment against upper-class control nullified these efforts. By 1845, restrictions on practice were repealed in 10 states and existing legislation was left unenforced in virtually all others (Shryock, 1947: 215–218). At the same time, the status of the traditional medical profession came under serious attack. In addition to American political changes, developments within medicine itself played a part in this decline. With the gradual rise of medical science in Europe and its attendant stance of "therapeutic nihilism"—an honest refusal to claim cures where none existed—a large number of pseudosystems and pseudoscientific remedies appeared. These ranged from patent medicine to systems of hygiene and mental techniques such as Mary Baker Eddy's Christian Science. Both the more scientifically oriented doctors and the more traditionalistic (both of which were found most heavily among those of highest class backgrounds) opposed the commercially oriented practitioners as "quacks." Yet at the same time, they could offer nothing better in their place. The effort of elite physicians to suppress commercialism, then, was popularly regarded as a selfish attempt to monopolize practice for themselves—as, in fact, it was.[8]

Reform

After 1870, a number of changes occurred that began to increase the resources of the medical elite. An effective medical science began to develop in Europe. Once again, it was the wealthier classes who were able to take advantage of the opportunities—by being able to travel abroad for training

---

[8]The outcry against "quackery" came almost entirely from doctors, not abused laymen. In fact, the Homeopaths, Eclectics, and other medical "sectarians" never amounted to more than 10% of the medical practitioners; the issue was primarily competition with the orthodox profession itself (Berlant, 1973: 284–286).

and by being able to devote themselves to public health activities that began to cut into the disease rate late in the century and simultaneously to reestablish the esteem of the profession as both effective and altruistic. With these developments, medical education was gradually transformed. Johns Hopkins Medical School was founded in 1893 as an explicit importation of the German clinical research-oriented university, and other German-trained faculties were developed at Harvard, Michigan, as well as a few other places. These faculties, in alliance with upper-class doctors in the AMA, began an effort to reform the rest of the educational system.

The improvement in technical resources—more precisely, their creation as effective tools for the first time—took place in a larger social situation that especially mobilized the higher-status doctors and gave them important outside allies. For the period after 1870 was also one of mass Catholic immigration and heightening ethnic consciousness. As in other spheres, the Anglo-Protestant medical elite enjoyed new political and ideological support and was able to use it to mobilize its members into a tighter organization and to ride with the prevailing mood of political "reform." The moralistic Protestant tradition invoked by reformers against Catholic vices and political power was nicely exemplified by the image of the altruistic, scientific doctor, struggling to free the world of disease and to rid his profession of quacks.

Yet a third structural change gave the medical elite the political resources it needed. The period after 1870 was also one of the consolidation of the national economy. Intense conflict was generated within the business community itself, between the new and threateningly monopolistic national corporations and their financial allies on the one hand, and the smaller local and agricultural businesses on the other. The turn of the century thus saw, among the other conflicts of the time, a movement by smaller business to limit the national monopolies. The more important side of the "antitrust" movement was less visible: On the local level, business interests mobilized to protect themselves, producing a burst of legislation at the state level favoring *local* combinations in restraint of trade (Cutler, 1939: 851—856; Wiebe, 1967; Berlant, 1973: 299–301). The associations of retailers and small producers that have controlled local business in twentieth-century America date from this period. Such laws restraining trade also favored professional associations, and the AMA rode this wave into its current monopolistic position.

Between 1875 and 1900, medical societies were able to have many states reestablish the examining and licensing boards that had existed early in the century. In 1891, the AMA helped organize the National Conference of State Medical Licensing Boards to push for uniform state licensing procedures. The existence of a large number of schools with openly commercial orientations posed a major obstacle, especially since their graduates could be found at many levels within the medical profession, even acting as a restraining influence within the AMA. In 1890, the Association of American Medical Colleges was formed, but it made little headway in limiting licensing powers to the more elite schools. In 1900, however, the reforming faction within the AMA was able to reorganize it on more elitist lines (Shryock, 1966: 30–32). The task of rating the various medical schools remained too touchy for decisive action by the organization. Outside aid was called in, in the form of the Carnegie Foundation for the Advancement of Teaching.

This organization was set up in 1905 under the leadership of Henry S. Pritchett, a genteel scientist and former president of the Massachusetts Institute of Technology (M.I.T.), who had persuaded Andrew Carnegie to make the endowment. Pritchett, in turn, called on a layman, Abraham Flexner, to make a report on medical schools as a disinterested outsider. Flexner was hardly disinterested, except in the commercial sense. Deriving from an upwardly mobile German-Jewish family, he had attended Johns Hopkins, Harvard, and Berlin, had run a private school preparing wealthy students for the Ivy League colleges, and was known for his writings recommending educational reforms in America along German lines. Flexner gained entree into the medical schools of America by giving the impression that he represented potential Carnegie endowments. In 1909, Flexner visited all 155 medical schools in the United States and Canada, usually spending a few hours at each (Flexner, 1940: 70–88).

His report, published by the Carnegie Foundation in 1910, described conditions in every school by name, showing that virtually all lacked laboratory facilities, were staffed by faculties with few academic qualifications, and accepted students with little previous education. Only 50 of the 155 required high school degrees or the equivalent for entrance, and even this requirement was often unenforced (Flexner, 1910: 29–36). Flexner recommended that 2 years of college training—then found in only 25 schools—become the prerequisite for medical school admission, with certain variations to fit regional conditions: In the South, where European-style university education was least developed, Flexner bypassed the universities and called for the establishment of medical school admission requirements equivalent to those of the state universities; and for admission to the leading medical schools, such as Hopkins and Harvard, he recommended 4 years of college. He further proposed the outright abolition of the weaker schools, reducing the total from 155 to 31, and the intervention of state medical boards in setting medical school admissions requirements, overseeing facilities, and licensing graduates.

By 1920, virtually all the schools on Flexner's blacklist had closed down. The medical schools that survived were almost all tied to universities and began to raise admission prerequisites toward a full college degree. Interstate licensing agreements became standardized, with the consolidation of previous boards into the Federation of State Medical Boards in 1912. The AMA's

Council on Education, established in 1904, took over Flexner's school rating work on a continuing basis, becoming a center of absolute authority over schools by 1920. The power of the AMA was firmly established. In 1916, specialty boards began to appear within it, which achieved great influence despite their legally voluntary status. Thus even its informal arrangements came to take on binding force (Shryock, 1966: 42).

The organization of American medical education had several effects. The raising of standards was accompanied by the reestablishment of the earlier guildlike elite. The aftermath of the Flexner report reduced the number of medical students in America from over 28,000 in 1904 to below 20,000 in 1907, with a long-run decrease in the proportion of doctors per capita: from 164 per 100,000 in 1910 to 125 in 1930, rising again to 142 in 1960; along with an alleged increase in the quality of training went a decrease in availability of doctors and a rise in their average incomes (Friedman and Kuznets, 1945; Shryock, 1947: 285; *Historical Statistics:* B181; Rayack, 1967). Unorthodox practitioners and quacks were greatly restricted; so were any other doctors who resisted the political and economic policies of the professional associations. Doctors' prestige, seriously sagging in the middle of the nineteenth century, was raised by 1925 to a position at the top of all occupational status polls (Hodge *et al.,* 1964: 289–302). Medical students have also reattained their top-ranking position among university-level students in social class background, if indeed they had lost that position during the efflorescence of schools in the nineteenth century (Davis, 1965: Table 2.19).

The same historical period saw a major shift in the location of medical practice, from almost exclusively home care in the late nineteenth century to a heavy reliance on hospitalization in the early twentieth.[9] The number of hospitals in the United States went from 149 in 1873 to 6762 in 1923. A movement for hospital organization, founded by the American College of Surgeons in 1913, was instrumental in this change. The political and economic effects upon the profession of this organizational shift were enormous. The displacement of home care was crucial in establishing effective control over individual practitioners since hospital committees not only came to influence career access through the new rules on internship and residency, but also exercised a permanent hold over all local members of the profession by controlling their hospital use privileges. At the same time, and above all during the decade of 1910–1920, hospitals shifted their economic policies from the traditional charity orientation to an emphasis on private, paying patients. In

---

[9]On the subject of hospitals see Shryock (1947: 283); Perrow (1963: 112–146; 1965: 948–949); Rosen (1963: 1–36); Glaser (1963: 37–72).

comparison with the more hierarchic and government-controlled European hospitals growing up in the same period, American hospitals became essentially adjuncts to the private practices of the local coalition of physicians; depending on these doctors for the medical services which they monopolized, and exercising no controls over their fees, the hospitals were forced to provide for them the free overhead of diagnostic and administrative services and professional assistance. From the point of view of professional power, status, and economic gain, the result for the American doctors was ideal.

In relation to the overall structure of American education, the new organization of the medical profession served especially to shore up the position of the university based on liberal arts. Nonuniversity medical schools were largely eliminated, doomed by their lack of high-status backing. The surviving medical schools came to require previous college training, thus eliminating any potential rivalry. Also avoided were the continental European pattern, whereby medical education was begun at the entering university level, and the English pattern of training in teaching hospitals. American medical studies became a purely postgraduate course, with hospital training postponed until after the medical degree. The lengthy and expensive contest mobility style of the American education system was thus further enhanced.

The contest mobility emphasis extended within the medical profession as well. Training in basic medical services and in specialties remained essentially informal, but became added on at the end of a unified medical school curriculum taken by everyone in the form of hospital internship and residence programs. The actual practical skills of medicine have thus been acquired on the job, as they are in most occupations (see Chapter 1); the elaborate educational requirements leading up to and including medical school have served primarily for screening, indoctrination into the group, and for an idealized facade. Separate statuses within the profession have been created by lengthening the period of training rather than by dividing it at an earlier point. One result has been to enhance the upper-class status of the profession by making its most prestigious positions require the most expensive training.

The pattern has also resisted expanding the availability of medical treatment by the provision of specialists of limited competence in areas of routine work. Obstetrics has become a specialty trained in postgraduate work, and the earlier occupation of midwifery has been eliminated by absorption into the area of physicians' practice rather than upgraded as a separate specialty. Similar processes have prevented nursing from taking over routine public health functions. The very existence of a closed, subordinate occupational hierarchy for women in medicine simply continues the traditional segregation of women into menial positions and their separate organization within religious and charitable activities (as if not to contaminate the office charisma of the dominant male roles in the spheres). Thus even with the token integration of women into the ranks of physicians in the twentieth century, the legacy of sexual stratification remains, with the existence of nursing careers as a separate enclave, differentiated from menial task workers at the bottom, essentially homogeneous by sex, and without promotion channels into the higher positions of medical authority. In America, nursing has become increasingly "professionalized" with educational requirements and internal status hierarchies, but the result of this closing in of the corporate barriers has been to reinforce its subordinate position. Ironically, comparative studies show that there is more delegation of medical power (such as in the areas of anesthesia, inoculations, and delivery in normal childbirths) to nurses in Europe (where specialized training programs are lacking) than to the more formally trained American nurses (Glaser, 1963: 61–62; Perrow, 1965: 960–965; Mechanic, 1968: 345, 357–358).

The organization of American medicine in the era of its first technological effectiveness has thus incorporated numerous aspects of traditional stratification. The newer structures have built upon the organizational advantages of the old for an elite that was lucky enough to find the right allies in the larger social conflicts of the early twentieth century. The history of the medical profession illustrates how efforts to raise the levels of technical expertise, displays of altruistic dedication, and the struggle for economic and status advantages are by no means mutually exclusive.

THE LEGAL GUILD

Like American government, the American legal profession had its roots in the history of English government organization. The profession of full-time specialist in laws and legal procedures began to appear in the twelfth and thirteenth centuries, initially as an officer of the king's court (Carr-Saunders and Wilson, 1933: 37–55; Harding, 1966: 167–190, 285–291, 351–354, 389–394). The first professional lawyers were judges who trained their successors by apprenticeship. The apprentices took on functions in the courtroom and gradually came to monopolize pleading before the royal judges. Training moved out of the courtroom and into the Inns of Court, which were the residences of the judges and practicing attorneys. The latter, after several reorganizations of their own ranks, finally became a group known as barristers. The members of the Inns became organized as a strong guild held together by a common aristocratic or gentry background and came to monopolize training in the law as well as its more fundamental resource: control of official business access to the government.

There were law professors at various times at Oxford and Cambridge, but the universities were never able to break the London monopoly on law training. Most clearly of any profession, monopoly over practice in the law is a matter of political power, and the conditions of power favored the London guilds. The universities, on the other hand, were agencies of the Church, and the civil law taught there was essentially codified Roman law, the instrument of bureaucratic centralization. The Common Law taught by the apprentice method, by contrast, consisted of procedural lore and historical precedent, which left greater power in the hands of the practitioner (Weber, 1968: 785–788). The nature of the skills that the professional group was to monopolize was thus shaped by its relative political power.

The relative weakness of the English kings and their centralized bureaucracy, and the eventual victory of the lesser aristocracy in the seventeenth-century revolutions, consolidated the power of the lawyers' guild. (In contrast, on the Continent the law was codified and taught monopolistically by the universities, and lawyers became administrators in government bureaucracies.) In England, a small, self-selecting elite of barristers, giving informal training in the Inns of Court, monopolized practice before the government courts of London as well as judgeships in those courts. Justices of the Peace throughout England, on the other hand, were usually amateurs drawn from the ranks of the local gentry. The barristers' monopoly of court functions helped create a second group within the legal profession: the solicitors, men who advised clients, prepared cases for trial, and handled matters outside of court. This group arose to meet the needs of clients, especially those outside of London; in effect, the barristers were too much officers of the court to be very responsive to outsiders. The barristers outranked solicitors, both by virtue of their monopoly over access to court and through control of training. Solicitors originally tended to be drawn from the ranks of those who attended the Inns of Court for some time short of the period (sometimes as long as 10 to 15 years) necessary to become a barrister. (This very long period of training necessitated considerable wealth on the part of aspirants, and thus served to severely monopolize the legal profession by class). Later solicitors came to be trained almost entirely by apprenticeship or through schools of their own. This formal ranking within the legal profession did not come about in America, due to its own peculiarities in the organization of political power.

Colonial Oligarchy and
Postrevolutionary Democratization

Colonial America was a transplant of English institutions, but with a bias toward even greater decentralization. The geographic remoteness of the colonies from England and of inland settlements from coastal centers, in a time of poor transportation and frontier expansion, contributed to this pattern. The practice of law, however, in the prerevolutionary period was virtually monopolized by the upper class of wealthy merchants and planters, who did their best to emulate the English pattern of the closed legal caste (Main, 1965: 101–103, 146–147, 203–206). In the South, wealthy planters tended to send their sons to the Inns of Court in London for legal training. In the northern colonies, bar associations developed in most of the populous places after 1750, beginning originally as social clubs, but gradually coming to control admission to practice. The colonial legislatures, following English precedent, delegated to the courts the power of admission to practice before them. In the late eighteenth century, the local bar associations, especially in Massachusetts and New York, had in turn been delegated responsibility for recommending lawyers for admittance, amounting to de facto control; their members comprised a powerful political elite.[10]

The Revolution reversed the trend toward legal oligarchy. Since lawyers were closely associated with the upper class in background and in practical interests, it was among this group that British sympathizers were most concentrated. Therefore a considerable proportion of lawyers emigrated during wartime persecutions of Tories. The prevailing custom of the bar to limit practice to a narrow social elite also contributed to lawyers' unpopularity, as did their prominence in efforts to collect wealthy creditors' claims in the period following the Revolution. The successful struggle to extend the franchise and the relative egalitarianism of the newer frontier states brought a shift in power to those hostile to a privileged legal caste. As a result, standards of admission to the bar became extremely loose, and bar associations crumbled and disappeared as their powers waned. The distinction between barristers and attorneys, which had grown up during the colonial period in imitation of the English system, disappeared with the democratization of the legal profession (Griswold, 1964: 10).

In the period between 1800 and 1870, power over admission to the bar devolved to the local courts, reinforced by rapid changes of settlement and the irregularities of communications. In its more extreme form, this meant that admission in one court conferred no right to practice before others, although it was more usual for the right to practice in one to carry admission before any other court in the same state. Centralized admissions (in theory but often not in practice) were found in 8 out of 30 states and territories in 1840 and in only 10 out of 39 in 1860.

The bar examination itself was usually oral and administered in a very casual fashion. Standards requiring preparation before admission to the exam were exceptional. Such requirements as were left over from the period of

---

[10]On the development of the American legal profession, see Hurst (1950: 249–311). Unless otherwise noted, sources for factual material on this topic are found therein.

colonial oligarchy were diminished by the movement for open access after the Revolution. In 1800, 14 out of 18 states and territories required a definite period of professional study, declining in 1830 to 11 out of 30, and in 1860 to 9 out of 39.

Throughout the nineteenth century, legal education was correspondingly informal. The chief method of education was apprenticeship in a lawyer's office, during which the student did small services, served papers, and copied legal documents (until the invention of the typewriter late in the century). In his spare time he read what law, history, and general books were available. In the offices of leading lawyers, the student was often charged fees for his apprenticeship. Given the expense of such training (since even if there were not fees, the student worked for free), many men prepared themselves for the profession by their own reading. Abraham Lincoln is the most famous example of the latter type of training, but it was also found among sons of the very wealthy, for whom it was merely an extension of prevailing patterns of home study or tutoring.[11]

There were a few university professorships of law, established as far back as 1779 at William and Mary and 1793 at Columbia, as well as at Harvard in 1817 and Yale in 1824. But attendance was so spotty that the Columbia chair was left vacant between 1798 and 1823, and an experiment begun in 1790 at the College of Philadelphia lasted only 2 years. Such courses as were given were short and informal, covering the same materials as apprenticeship programs and allowing students to drop in and out as suited their own convenience. Standards of passing the course were minimal; a single final oral exam was typical.

In addition to the universities, there were a number of private proprietary schools run by lawyers. The most famous was run by a judge at Litchfield, Connecticut from 1784 to 1833. It offered a 14-month course, and its students included many who were to rise to positions of political eminence, among them two vice presidents of the United States, three Supreme Court justices, as well as numerous justices of high state courts, cabinet officers, congressmen, and governors. Yet this school gave no diploma. At the time, university law degrees were of little worth. The system was not one of formal certification; the egalitarian cast of political power in nineteenth-century America extended to legal practice as well. A school like that at Litchfield appeared to have made its success primarily as an informal club of members of elite families. Even this school collapsed in the 1830s, as the tides of political power moved away from the New England federalist establishment

---

[11]Lincoln himself, despite many myths to the contrary, was hardly a poor man, and he had a prosperous career as, among other things, an attorney for the railroads, the wealthiest business of mid-nineteenth-century America.

and toward the West. In 1833, it was estimated that the total number of law students in any kind of school, proprietary or university, was below 150, and that the overwhelmingly dominant form of training was apprenticeship.

The Movement for Elite Control

From the 1870s onward, several interrelated changes took place which reestablished formalized stratification within the legal profession and brought university law schools to a commanding position. A nationally prominent group of lawyers developed, along with the consolidation of corporate control in the national economy. At the same time, university professors of law began to make claims for the scientific status of law. The combination of these events, along with an upper-class and upper-middle-class political movement in response to urban immigrant and working-class politics, led to the reestablishment of bar associations and efforts to restrict admission to the bar.

Before the Civil War, most legal business concerned land and commerce, especially representing speculative interests in the West. After mid-century, the most lucrative business came to center around the big corporations, beginning first with the railroads. After the Civil War, the position of general counsel for the railroads was the most highly esteemed legal position, and high-ranking judges were known to resign to take such positions during the 1880s and 1890s. During the same period, lawyers became closely involved with the major banks and began to sit on boards of directors. Lawyers were central in the growth of corporations, devising new forms of charters, helping companies and trusts to organize national business, while taking maximum advantage of variable state laws concerning incorporation and taxation. Their aid did much to enable major financial interests to gain control of manufacturing enterprises through stock manipulations and other devices, and details of the concentration of monopoly control in the post-Civil War economy were worked out by the legal profession (see Ripley, 1916; Chandler, 1968: 223–234; Berle and Means, 1968: 119–243).

It was through these activities that the large modern-style law firm came into existence. Prior to 1850, law practice was individual or carried on in two-man partnerships. After 1850, the most prominent partnerships—those dealing with corporate business interests—began to specialize internally, with one man handling the court appearances, the other becoming the "office man." At the same time, business clients began to solicit formal "opinions" from law firms on legal aspects of prospective policies, a practice that gradually led to the establishment of permanent relationships between firms and corporations. The size of major firms began to grow: The New York firm of Strong and Cadwalader grew from 6 lawyers and 4 staff assistants in 1878 to 23 lawyers and 20 staff assistants in 1913, and to 57 lawyers and 85 staff assistants in 1938. The currently prominent firm of Cravath, Swaine, and Moore, originating in the middle of the nineteenth century in the partnership of Treasury Secretary William H. Seward, had developed to 19 lawyers in 1906 and 94 lawyers in 1940.

To be sure, such large firms were the exception and remain so even today. The majority of lawyers in private practice (56% in 1964) continue to practice alone, usually in a particular ethnic community, and this has doubtless been the case throughout (Carlin, 1962; Ladinsky, 1963: 47–54; Griswold, 1964: 5). By far the largest concentration of big firms (20 of the 37 firms with more than 50 lawyers in 1959) was in New York City (Smigel, 1964: 29, 178). The prominence of the "Wall Street law firm," allied to the major corporations, originated in the later nineteenth century, growing along with the corporations whose economic dominance they helped make possible. What was occurring was not the raising of the economic status of lawyers as a whole, but the emergence of an elite within the profession tied to the newly consolidated business elite.

At about the same time, the teaching of law began to be reformed. In 1870, Harvard University began to teach law by the case method. Instead of using the older system of text reading and lectures, the instructor carried on a discussion of assigned cases designed to bring out their general principles. The advocates of the case method, notably Harvard Law Dean Christopher Columbus Langdell, held that law was a general science and that its principles could be experimentally induced from the examination of case materials. At the same time, Harvard introduced the practice of hiring instructors whose whole career was devoted to legal scholarship, rather than hiring former practitioners. Both innovations were supported by Harvard's new president, Charles W. Eliot, a former M.I.T. chemist, who was the first scientist to be appointed president of a major American university and the first leading advocate of the approach of the scientific researcher in university education. In this era of scientific advance, legal educators had to make their pretenses of sharing in these developments. Under this new emphasis, the lax oral examination for the law degree was replaced by a series of written exams with increasingly formal standards. In 1896, Harvard established the college degree as prerequisite for admission to law school (Griswold, 1964: 51–52).

The case method and the other Harvard reforms did not begin to take root elsewhere, except at other Ivy League schools, until after 1890, and became firmly established as a model to be emulated only after 1900. In the intervening period, a movement began that was to bring the Harvard method to the fore; the establishment of bar associations and their efforts to control admission to legal practice. The first bar association was established by a group of leading lawyers in New York City in 1878 as a response to a series of scandals involving the Tweed political machine. Wealthy Chicago lawyers founded a bar association in 1874, again motivated by the aim of bringing under control a group of nonelite lawyers involved in a local political machine. In all, 16 city and state bar associations were founded between 1870 and 1878, almost all in conjunction with efforts at municipal reform and the assertion of control over members of the bar active in corrupt local politics.

Even more explicitly than the AMA, the elite legal profession thus organized itself through the cultural and political mobilization of the late nineteenth-century ethnic crisis. The bar associations were Anglo-Protestant; the "corrupt" lawyers were largely ethnic or the representatives of ethnic enterprises. The concept of "corruption" itself is only the definition imposed on the situation by Anglo-Protestant values; the illegal or immoral activities protected by the political machines were the gambling, sports, prostitution, saloons, and riotous entertainment favored by immigrant and working-class culture.

The culmination of this wave of organization among upper-class lawyers came in August 1878, when the American Bar Association (ABA) was formed at Saratoga, New York. The organizer, and for many years the leader, of the ABA was Simeon E. Baldwin, a Yale law professor, judge, counsel to major financial organizations, and staunch political conservative. The upper-class nature of the ABA was evident. Saratoga Springs, where the ABA held its annual meetings until 1889, was a fashionable upper-class summer resort, and the nucleus of the ABA grew out of a group of wealthy lawyers who had habitually vacationed there. In keeping with its composition and aims, for many years the ABA made no effort to proselytize. Indeed, its admission policy was quite exclusive, and until a new phase occurred after 1912, membership never exceeded 3% of the lawyers in the United States. Even after the period of expansion, it included only 17% of American lawyers in 1940 and 40% in 1964, and its officers have always been drawn from high-status origins (Hurst, 1950: 289; Griswold, 1964: 23; Domhoff, 1967: 61).

This was in keeping with the aims of the ABA and of the leading local bar associations: to reassert upper-class and especially WASP control within the profession, and by extension, in politics as well. The ABA's political pronouncements from 1896 to 1937 were predominantly conservative, opposing capital gains taxes, favoring injunctions in labor disputes and the teachings of "Americanism" in the schools, and advocating softening of antitrust laws (Hurst, 1950: 363). Its main activities, however, were for reform within the legal profession, stressing higher educational requirements and attendant restrictions on admissions to practice.

The ABA took the lead in forming and financing the Conference of Commissioners on Uniform State Laws. Commissioners were formally appointed by state governments, but in practice were nominated by the ABA from among its own ranks. The local bar associations also played a part in raising standards of admission to practice. Centralized state boards of bar examiners, found in only 4 states in 1890, spread to almost all by 1914. Written exams, introduced by the leading university law schools, rapidly displaced oral exams after 1900. By 1937, 35 states had adopted the ABA standards for minimum qualifications at the bar. In 1860, only 9 out of 39 states and territories required any definite period of legal study; in 1890, 50%; in 1920, 75%; and in 1940, all states required professional study.

The change of standards meant, in practice, the adoption of the standards of the leading law schools. The informal oral exam was replaced by written exams patterned after school exams, and generally made up and graded by bar association members with close ties to the leading schools. The adoption of formal educational requirements for admission to bar exams further strengthened the schools, so that by 1940, 3 years of study was being required by 40 states. Once this was well under way, an effort was made to incorporate the standards of the leading and most exclusive law schools into the bar exam prerequisites by calling (in 1921) for the requirement of 2 years of college as preparation before law studies—a requirement adopted by 66% of the states by 1940. The leaders in the whole effort of reform included the group within the ABA made up of university law teachers—a group that included the founder of the association, Simeon Baldwin of Yale. In 1893 they organized the association's section on legal education, headed by a Harvard law professor. This group in turn organized the Association of American Law Schools in 1900 as an accrediting association. In 1923, the ABA's section on Legal Education and Admission to the Bar, headed by former Secretary of War Elihu Root, began formally to publish ratings of law schools according to their compliance with ABA's standards of educational prerequisites.

The process of tightening control went forward rather slowly, however. The decentralized state of the bar gave considerable power of resistance to the minor lawyer, and the patently upper-class and exclusionary policies of the ABA and leading Eastern bar associations provoked considerable hostility on the part of the less prosperous or less conservative lawyers, especially the ethnic and rural lawyers whom the bar association policies were designed to restrict. By the 1920s, bar associations in the West began to campaign for an "integrated bar." This was a euphemism for a bar association with compulsory membership, an official monopoly over practice, and legally enforceable powers of discipline over members. Such laws were in force in 20 states by 1940, mostly in the West and the South. Their geographic concentration reveals something of the dynamics of control within the legal profession, for it was in these states that the bar was more homogeneously drawn from upper-class and upper-middle-class backgrounds, and rival ethnic communities were less in evidence than in the East (Adams, 1957: 360–368).

In the East especially, as the upper-class lawyers increased pressure to require law school training for admission to bar exams, resistance to exclusionary tactics was manifested by the founding of new schools. Thus the number of degree-conferring law schools increased from 102 in 1900 to 124 in 1910, 146 in 1920, and 190 in 1936. In 1936, only 94 of the 190 schools were approved by the ABA, and only half a dozen states required study in an ABA-approved school. The unapproved schools were largely (88 out of 96) night schools or mixed day and night schools, whereas most approved schools (75 out of 94) were full-time schools attached to regular universities. It was the night schools that expanded in response to educational requirements for practice: In 1890 there were 59 "day" and 10 "night" schools; in 1900, 79 and 25, respectively; in 1910, 79 and 45; in 1920, 80 and 62.

A continual battle was carried on against these "unqualified" schools, especially through efforts to make the requirements of the leading law schools into the legal requirements for admission to practice. The leading schools, in turn, were moving to solidify their ties to high-status groups through college degree prerequisites for admission. This process moved slowly. In 1890, only 4 out of 61 leading law schools had entrance requirements equivalent to those necessary for admission to the liberal arts colleges of their universities. Only after 1890, led by Harvard, did the most elite law schools begin to require a college degree before admission. As late as 1931, the average American lawyer had about 1 year of college and 2.25 years of law school or office training, but by the latter date the pattern was confirmed, and in later decades law school had been increasingly tied to the standard sequence of American education. Some 66% of all law students in the 1960s were attending full-time schools, most of which had college degree prerequisites, and most of the rest were in part-time schools with prerequisites approved by the ABA. Social class background is an important determinant of access, with prospective law students well above average in social class background of other college students; and the average social background rises with the academic selectivity of the law school attended (Hurst, 1950: 268, 281; Griswold, 1964: 57–59).

Industrialization or Cultural Conflict?

The movement to raise educational standards and to tie law practice into the sequence of higher education was part of a more general movement of class and status group conflict occurring in America in the late nineteenth century. The law reform movement derived from several of the component currents of this movement. Thus the founding of bar associations and their efforts to centralize and raise requirements for legal practice were directly connected with the WASP counterattack on the political machines and patrimonial practices that were based on immigrants and the working class generally. At the same time, the involvement of some lawyers in these machines and the apparent influx of immigrants (or at least immigrant-oriented men) into the legal profession threatened the group's elite image. The influx of Jews in the major eastern cities was particularly feared. The campaign to raise entrance standards, and hence to make law practice more restrictive, was an effort to reassert traditionalistic upper-class and WASP monopoly over legal practice.

This interpretation is bolstered by an analysis of the recurrent outcries concerning "overcrowding in the bar" that have been heard from the late nineteenth century onward. Studies carried out in the 1930s indicated that lawyers' services were used almost entirely by the wealthiest 13% of the population, and that the lower groups had considerable occasion to use lawyers' services but could not afford them (Hurst, 1950: 311–316). Thus "overcrowding" could only be based on an upper-class or upper-middle-class perspective. Moreover, concentrations of large numbers of lawyers were found only in the large cities. It was here that the immigrant groups and their lawyers (often economically marginal) were found, but it was also the site of the most lucrative law practices—in the large firms allied to big business. Thus it appears that the "overcrowding" issue, raised constantly by elite lawyers throughout a lengthy period, primarily reflects efforts at status closure within the profession.

The efforts to raise requirements moved rather slowly, since it was held back by American political decentralization and by the democratic traditions, which had made the legal profession relatively accessible in the earlier part of the nineteenth century. That it did move forward nevertheless was owing to a number of resources available to the upper-class lawyers. The rise of the national corporation, and hence of the very wealthy and high-status law firm, gave them a base from which to claim professional leadership. At the same time, schools were available that were long identified with the WASP elite, notably Harvard and Yale. Such schools, facing economic problems of their own, were happy to enter into an alliance of interest with the upper-class lawyers; connecting individuals like Simeon Baldwin, who was both a law professor and a corporation lawyer, were the initiators of organizations to make the standards of the elite schools into the standards of the profession.

The reason the strategy took so long to pay off, and indeed failed in the effort to completely restrict nonelite lawyers, was because of a weakness of the American education system for exerting monopolistic control. In the decentralized conditions of American government, and against a long tradition of founding schools and other cultural organizations, it was too easy to respond to educational requirements by founding new schools, especially the night schools that proliferated after 1890. The structure favored credential inflation rather than an immediately effective monopolization. The bar associations were thus forced to take action a second time. Efforts to have state laws declare certain schools unqualified were not generally successful, but the less direct tactic of requiring college study as a prerequisite for law study made headway. This was designed to favor the schools attached to the elite colleges; one of its effects was to attach law study more and more firmly to the sequence of higher education, not as an alternative to it.

It might be argued that the rise of the modern corporation and of government regulation has made legal practice more complex, and hence the old apprenticeship training was no longer adequate, and increasingly formal study was a functional necessity. Comparative evidence does not lend much support to this view, however. On the continent, there are long-standing and highly rationalized legal systems based on university training and lacking the traditionalistic complexities of the Common Law, which have not produced any superiority in the rate of industrialization. In England, training that consisted of apprenticeship through the Inns of Court provided for legal "needs" throughout the complex changes of many centuries, on into the twentieth; we have noted that such "needs" are themselves the result of the power of lawyers to complicate the access of private citizens to government adjudication. For America, there are no studies available of the actual differences in skilled performance between those trained in schools versus those trained by on-the-job apprenticeship; the rise in educational requirement has made the latter group virtually unavailable for comparison, as well as probably attracting the more able persons into the more prestigious forms of preparation. Evidence from the 1920s shows that students trained in the more elite law schools are more likely to pass bar exams on their first try than those from schools with lower entrance requirements, who are in turn more likely to pass than those trained in offices. Nevertheless, a high proportion (87%) of all who attempt bar exams eventually pass (Hurst, 1950: 274). Moreover, there is no evidence that performance on bar exams is related to actual skill in practice; bar exams primarily reflect academic concerns and slight the practical skills that must be learned afterwards.

The history of corporation law suggests that innovations precede the education relating to the problem involved. The major role of lawyers in modern business history was in the modification of traditional restrictions on corporations and in the development of trusts and other legal instruments that advanced monopoly control in American industry. The first of these developments began in the 1830s and culminated in the 1889 New Jersey corporation law that permitted holding companies. The latter developed especially in the 1880s and 1890s. John D. Rockefeller's lawyer, Samuel C. T. Dodd, devised the "trust" instrument in 1880, bringing about great monopolization during the decade and provoking the Sherman Anti-Trust Act in 1890.[12] The lawyers involved, generally educated at high-status liberal arts colleges, were legally trained in fairly traditionalistic methods and did their innovating based on practical experience. Moreover, the case method introduced by the reforming law schools was not particularly suited to the needs of modern business or government. In its effort to extract "scientific" principles, it concentrated on the appellate level to the exclusion of the actual working with legal cases, and until well into the twentieth century it concentrated on the most traditionalistic sectors of the law, ignoring newer developments, especially in the fields of administrative law (Hurst, 1950: 269–271; Harno, 1953: 137–140). Certainly much innovative legal work has been done during the institutional changes of modern society, but it appears to have been made possible largely through on-the-job experience, with schools lagging behind in teaching it. Thus the most important figure on the American bench during the period of industrialization, Justice Stephen Field of the California and United States Supreme Courts, devised the modern codes and principles of business law on the basis of a legal education that consisted entirely of apprenticeship in his brother's law firm (McCurdy, 1976).[13]

The link between the educationally innovating Ivy League law schools and the elite Wall Street law firms, and the tie of both of these to positions of national government power in the cabinet and judiciary, appears to be primarily the result of their common status group composition. This link, strongly in evidence during the twentieth century, has roots reaching back at least to mid-nineteenth century when lawyers for emerging national business, like William H. Seward, were prominent as cabinet officers (Smigel, 1964: 4–12, 37–42, 72–74; Domhoff, 1967: 58–62, 84–114). The social linkage between the most elite schools and the powerful legal positions was crucial for the growth of educational requirements. It meant that success within the legal profession was associated with elite education, thus giving leverage for the raising of educational requirements, as well as setting a status ideal for lesser lawyers to emulate.

The effect of these processes was not to reestablish complete upper-class monopoly over law; the flexibility of the American educational system was too

---

[12]For an account extolling the creative role of the corporation lawyer, see Levy (1961: 43–106).

[13]Weber (1968: 890), although stressing the importance of some form of rule-following judiciary as a structural background for capitalism, concluded that a highly academic system was not at all necessary.

> Once everything is said and done about these differences in historical developments, modern capitalism prospers equally and manifests essentially identical economic traits under legal systems containing rules and institutions which considerably differ from each other, at least from the juridical point of view. . . . Indeed, we may say that the legal systems under which modern capitalism has been prospering differ profoundly from each other even in their ultimate principles of formal structure.

strong a defense against this. Nevertheless, enough pressure was exerted, both through legal requirements and through standards of elite law practice, to bring a steady rise in educational requirements, both in years of law school and in prior college preparation. The status struggle among lawyers thus contributed to the vertical extension of the American educational system. It also tended to keep the legal profession from splitting into high- and low-status segments, as in the barrister—solicitor split in England. However much informal distinction there might be among firms (or between firm lawyers and solo lawyers), or between high-status and low-status law schools, the profession stayed united, with differences based essentially on the total amount of schooling the individual received, both in and before law school. In law, as in other areas, American structure has fostered a school-oriented contest mobility system.

THE FAILURE OF THE ENGINEERS

Engineers are the biggest group of professionals in modern societies, and the one professional group whose services are clearly required by industrialism. This is particularly so when we recognize that there is no sharp dividing line between engineers, technicians, and mechanics; it is this group, as a whole, that makes industrialism work. By comparison, doctors, dentists, and nurses simply provide consumption services that a wealthier populace can increasingly afford; lawyers, as a group, monopolize dispute settlement and administrative functions to the degree that their power permits; and teachers are in demand to the degree that the educational system itself is extensive. The call for these professions can vary considerably in different industrial societies; the need for a considerable body of engineers, however, is found in all.

Given the clear-cut importance of engineers above all other professions in industrial society, we might expect that engineering training would dominate the educational system. Indeed, it is plausible that an industrial society could operate with an educational system devoted almost entirely to engineering. This tends to be the case in the USSR, China, and other communist countries; in a less exclusive fashion, the French educational system gives special prominence to engineers. Moreover, there was a period in mid-nineteenth-century America when the existing educational system in America was under attack as vocationally useless, and its ability to provide nonvocational certification was weakened by the proliferation of colleges. Vocationally oriented educational programs centering on engineering were offered as an alternative, both at the high school and college levels. If purely technical demands had dominated, such schools should have become the center of the educational system, outranking other forms of education in prestige and attracting the bulk of the financial support and the most elite students. If Calvin Woodward's high school version of engineering training (see Chapter 5) had been given strong support in the nineteenth-century—as it might have on grounds of sheer vocational efficiency, since it eliminated nontechnical preparatory training and provided the quickest path to technical skills—the entire edifice of higher education would likely have crumbled and the total length of high-level training in America greatly shortened.

But these consequences did not occur, as testimony to the importance of nontechnical factors in explaining the place of education in stratification. The vocationally irrelevant but high-status classical education system was not destroyed, but modified to permit the passage of large numbers of students from increasingly wider class origins. Threats to this system of cultural certification, especially in the form of vocationally relevant education of which engineering is the best example, were eventually incorporated into the sequence, thus becoming supports to it rather than rivals. The organization of professional engineering is as much a social phenomenon as a purely technical one, and status interests and conflicts among engineers have been the main forces that kept engineering from making a serious challenge to the nontechnical educational system and to the larger system of stratification by status group membership and financial and political resources.

Comparative Perspectives: French and English Models of Engineering

Historically, the occupation of engineer emerges from a variety of roles.[14] At one level, predecessors included skilled artisans such as millwrights, stonemasons, blacksmiths, and clockmakers. At the opposite extreme were the high-status roles of the military officer or the government official, as found for example in the Roman Empire, who directed large numbers of men in building roads, bridges, and fortifications. In between these levels of power and status could be found the artist–architect and the master builder–construction gang boss. The man with technical skills relevant to large-scale operations thus occupied an ambiguous status between gentry and laborer, combining elements of master and servant. His actual status depended on historical conditions that determined the distribution of power, and hence the dividing lines between classes. The highest status of the technician–engineer in premodern society was probably in the merchant-dominated cities of Renaissance Italy; in this situation, the dividing line between skilled worker and boss was most ambiguous.

---

[14]There is no adequate history of the social role of the engineer; for historical material, see Finch (1960) and Armytage (1961); the Armytage work is marred by its technocratic ideology.

    With the rise of industrialism, the value of the techniques at the disposal
of the engineering expert was increased, and his claims for status among the
higher ranks of society—among the order-givers rather than among the
order-takers—became secure. But just how much power could be won on the
basis of expertise remained a variable. In France, the engineer acquired an
early foothold in the royal government in the seventeenth century: first as
artillery officer and specialist in fortifications, later as builder of roads and
public works in the civil administration. The first organized group of engineers
and the first school of engineering anywhere in the world were thus established in France: the *Corps Imperial du Génie* (Military Engineering Corps) in
1672 and the *Ecole des Ponts et Chaussées* (School of Bridges and Roads) in
1747. To be sure, the engineering officers were looked down upon by the
aristocrats of the army and the legal guilds because they smacked too much of
the status of workmen. Thus engineering posts were filled by commoners or
by impoverished provincial aristocrats like Napoleon Bonaparte.
    During the eighteenth century, the royal bureaucracy came increasingly
to take over the actual administration of France from the aristocracy, and the
characteristically French centralization was established. The Revolution of
1789 eliminated the hereditary aristocracy and the king and elevated the
bureaucracy to preeminence. The process was further advanced by the ac-
cession to power of Napoleon in 1799. The major result was to abolish the
classical, church-based university and replace it by a central engineering
school, the *Ecole Polytechnique,* to train the administrators of France. Subsequent counterrevolutions and revolutions revived alternative forms of
French education, including the law schools, but overall the position of engineers in French society has remained extremely high. Government posts are
centrally controlled and largely filled at their higher levels by graduates of the
Polytechnique and the other *Grandes Ecoles:* the *Centrale* and the *Ecole des
Mines* (School of Mines). High positions in large-scale industry, itself organized in cartels with semiofficial status, are also the province of the technical
elite. Thus technical education in France has come to virtually monopolize
major command posts (Granick, 1960: 60–72; Crozier, 1964: 238–244,
252–258; Artz, 1966; Ben-David, 1971: 88–107).
    A very different pattern developed in England. There the centralized
government bureaucracy was relatively weak until well after the Industrial
Revolution; the universities provided classical culture for a genteel elite. Until
the nineteenth century, science was carried out largely by gentlemen-
amateurs. In this context, engineers were essentially self-trained craftsmen.
Brindley, Metcalf, Telford, Watt, Stephenson, and other leading engineers
were men with little formal education. Engineering schools gradually developed by the twentieth century, but as low-prestige sectors of the educational system; even in 1961, only 22% of mechanical engineers were

graduates (Gerstl and Hutton, 1966: 42, see also 6–13; Reader, 1966: 69–71, 118–126, 142–145). Throughout the nineteenth century, the pattern was one of relatively informal, self-acquired or apprenticeship-style engineering training for middle-stage careers in construction and industry; whereas the high-status educational institutions, pointedly stressing nonvocational education for gentlemen, fed into the positions of government power.

The centralized French model of a political–industrial engineering elite and the British model of informally trained engineers of modest status represent the polar types of the social organization of engineering in modern societies. Both of them are workable; neither can be called "functionally necessary." Most other societies have adopted one or the other of these models—the French system most strongly imitated by the communist countries and the English system by its former colonies. Germany, whose model was imitated especially by Japan, represents a mixed form of engineering education. The German universities had already monopolized employment in the ranks of government officials by the late eighteenth century, but they trained only doctors, lawyers, clergymen, and teachers. A separate system of secondary and higher schools was set up for engineers to meet the demands of industry in the nineteenth century. These were of lower status than the universities, which looked down on them; hence the engineering schools recruited from a lower-class milieu and filled less elite positions in society. The German system thus came to represent a bifurcated educational system, with technical training as the lower branch in terms of power and prestige (Ben-David and Zloczower, 1962; Armytage, 1965: 76–93).

The position of American engineers has come to constitute a pattern all its own. In mid-nineteenth century, the possibility of dominating the school system in the French style, if in more massive numbers (perhaps like the modern Russian system), might have seemed a likely possibility. The widespread popular attack on the vocational irrelevance of traditional education lent support in this direction. Instead, it has tended to become part of a greatly democratized version of the classical British system, following from a nonspecialized, nonvocationalized secondary education, and then taking higher education that has consistently moved closer to the status aims of traditional liberal arts schools. Among the leading engineering schools there has been a continual effort to avoid the low-status connotations of the purely technical education reflected in the status composition of its students. In recent years this has taken the form of moving elite engineering training toward the postgraduate level and introducing greater nonvocational elements at the undergraduate level. The American pattern, for all the talk of its vocational emphasis, is still the most massively nonvocational system of education in the modern world.

Origins of American Engineering

The first American engineers to emerge in the late eighteenth and early nineteenth centuries were builders of roads, bridges, canals, and other works of transport construction. They were a mixed group in origin. Some were artisans, trained as carpenters, blacksmiths, or clockmakers; others were merchants engaged in profitable new ventures in the first wave of American economic expansion; others were literate gentry, often lawyers or judges, who took an interest in publicly useful works and admired the accomplishments of the French and English builders of the time (Struik, 1962: 135–174). Virtually all acquired their skills informally. The early bridge and canal builders operated by trial and error, initially creating structures that were quite wasteful of materials. Unlike the artisans, the gentlemen engineers were classically educated, some of them in the colonial colleges, but they learned their engineering skills as a second form of education by their own practice or by the passing on of lore from other practitioners. Such skills as surveying were known among landowners of the period, in the same fashion as a craft passed on from one person to another, often within a family. For the more complex projects, such as the building of canals with systems of locks, American organizers made use of European skills, either by taking trips to visit the English practitioners or sometimes by hiring them to oversee American projects and to pass on advice.

The organization and financing of large projects fell to the wealthier classes, and they alone could afford travel abroad to acquire advanced techniques. It appears that once construction projects had become a thriving business and practical knowledge had begun to accumulate at a more advanced level than the original trial-and-error techniques, civil engineering began to be consolidated as an occupation of the upper rather than of the artisan classes. This trend was accentuated by the establishment of the U.S. Military Academy at West Point in 1802. West Point was to train an elite of engineers; it was modeled on the French *Ecole Polytechnique,* founded a few years earlier in 1797. Thomas Jefferson, then president, regarded it as the beginning of a national university system to train a rationally organized, scientifically educated elite on the French model.

The effort to create a centralized system of elite selection failed under American conditions. Political decentralization, heightened by expansion westward, militated against the dominance of a single elite throughout American government, and the strong position of private education prevented the flow of federal funds to a single national institution, although West Point had an important effect on the American engineering profession (Struik, 1962: 311–316). After 1817, it was headed by Sylvanus Thayer, a gentleman officer who had been sent by President Madison to study at the *Ecole Polytechnique.* Thayer brought the original plan for the academy into full operation, introducing the French engineering curriculum and importing French instructors. Members of the Army Engineering Corps became the basis of the civil engineering profession in America. The government freely detached them to work for the railroads, which expanded in the decade after 1830, and it appears that virtually all railroads were built with the aid of engineers trained at West Point. In 1824, Rensselaer Polytechnical Institute (RPI) was founded by a wealthy New York landowner in direct imitation of the West Point model for producing the scientifically trained, elite engineer.

For many years, these two institutions were the only organized schools of civil engineering training. Founded in the tradition of the *Polytechnique,* they emphasized the ideal of engineering as an elite profession and resisted identification with other technicians who might lower their status. Even those civil engineers who were not graduates of these schools held the elitist view: They emphasized their gentry status and avoided anything smacking of manual labor and, to a degree, of commercialism as well. The nonmilitary engineer thus moved increasingly to an occupational stance of independent consultation or government employment (Calhoun, 1960). Their model for engineering looked back essentially to the eighteenth-century French official rather than forward to the commercial organizations of emerging American industry.

Mechanical engineering originated similarly. Its early practitioners comprised two groups: (a) carpenters, clockmakers, and other artisans, who developed their skill by experimenting with new forms of machinery; and (b) wealthy gentlemen, frequently possessing classical education, who ventured into promising new areas of business enterprise, such as the building of steam engines or the mass production of firearms and textiles, while acquiring the necessary technical skills in the process. For the early period, American industry depended heavily on European borrowing. The railroad locomotive was introduced by buying an English model, which was studied and used as a prototype for further developments. English mechanics were also imported directly; somewhat more frequently, American gentlemen would travel to England to meet the English inventors, and sometimes to France as well to visit the *Polytechnique* (Struik, 1962: 175–200, 303–334).

The latter forms of training were available exclusively to wealthy men, thus giving them an edge over the artisan engineers. Moreover, the importance of financial backing for engineering enterprises grew with their expansion of size during the early nineteenth century, and the wealthy gentlemen came to dominate the mechanical engineering field. Within this group, training came to take place by a sort of apprenticeship system of working in a shop where machines were made and improved. On the surface, it appeared that considerable equality prevailed in such shops, with sons of wealthy gentry working alongside sons of uncultivated mechanics; in the later controversy over engineering education, the leading mechanical engineers were to make much of egalitarianism and free opportunities for mobility in the early shops (Calvert, 1967: 3–27, 63–85).

But chances for mobility were not equal; the gentry moved much more rapidly into business partnership or into superintendent positions elsewhere, having learned their practical know-how from the mechanics, who were more likely to stay behind. The split between the mechanic and the engineer thus began to appear at an early date, based essentially on class background. That it did not grow sharp until the late nineteenth century was owing to a number of factors, including some real possibilities for upward mobility among mechanics into such positions as superintendents (if not as plant owners), and by an effort of engineer–businessmen to maintain an informal, paternalistic system of control over their valuable laborers.

The Struggle over Engineering Education

Status issues were crucial in determining the form of education and of professional organization that would come to prevail among professional engineers. The fact that engineering in America has not attained a strong professional organization even today can be traced to the multiple lines of status conflict among engineers and potential engineers in the nineteenth century. Five separate models of engineering education were put forward by competing factions:

1. The first half of the nineteenth century saw a vigorous movement of **mechanics institutes** (Struik, 1962: 266–271; Calvert, 1967: 29–40). Some commercial, others supported by wealthy benefactors, these institutes were designed for the artisan or workingman to acquire a more formal background in science and mathematics in order to advance as an engineer. Their emphasis was on upward mobility, and their clientele—at times a very large one—was drawn from the nongenteel classes. These institutes were a phenomenon of the period when working-class mechanics still had fair chances to rise to positions of command, and the close association with gentlemen who were learning their skills in the shops raised the mechanics' hopes of higher status. After the Civil War, however, the hopes of mechanics to freely enter the engineering profession diminished. Trade union forms of organization, designed to ensure job security, began to gain popularity, and the mechanics institutes went into decline. Part of the failure of mechanics institutes may be attributed to the indifference or hostility of the genteel engineers for whom the status connotations of such training were detrimental to their own positions. Some such training schools survive even today in highly commercial forms;

these have been quite ineffective in providing mobility opportunities, however, in competition with modern engineering schools styled on university lines.[15]

2. Another highly democratic effort in engineering education was the **training school movement** in the public high schools prominent in the late nineteenth century. As we have seen in the previous chapter, this movement drew its strength through a reaction to the practical uselessness of the classical education. The promise was to make high school—at the time not greatly distinguished in content from college—into the real center of the educational system as the place for the training of engineers. Indeed, the positions held by graduates of the St. Louis Training School around 1900 were very comparable to those held by graduates of the university-level engineering schools; both comprised an assortment of manufacturers, superintendents, and engineers on the one hand, and of assistants, draftsmen, and middle white-collar and technical employees on the other (Calvert, 1967: 149–150; Fisher, 1967: 77). Nevertheless, the high school level training schools never took hold against the hostility of nontechnical high school administrators and of the gentry engineers. As in the case of mechanics institutes, public training schools, despite their technical feasibility for nineteenth-century engineering requirements and their efficiency in eliminating extraneous teaching materials, were regarded primarily as a threat to the genteel status of the profession.

3. The high-status model of engineering education was the French **Ecole Polytechnique,** producing an elite of military officers and government officials. This was the model favored by the civil engineers and attempted at West Point and RPI. But the status aim embodied in the *Polytechnique* was too high to be attained under American conditions. American government, with its emphasis on autonomous local jurisdictions, was virtually the opposite of the centralized French government bureaucracy, and the close link between government and industry that made French engineers an elite of industrial managers as well as government officials was missing in America. Nevertheless, the civil engineers, as the earliest and best-educated section of engineering, had opportunities to take over the leadership of the entire engineering profession. The precedent established by the free assignment of West-Point-trained army engineers to the railroads could conceivably be extended to industry as well.

But far from attempting to gain dominance over the emerging industrial society, American civil engineers resisted any such ties. Secure in their own genteel status and oriented toward an idealized European image of themselves, the civil engineers scorned commercial employment and mechanical

---

[15]For a modern description, see Clark and Sloan (1966).

engineering as well. West Point, Rensselaer, and other schools of engineering long slighted the teaching of mechanical engineering, forcing such education to be established elsewhere (Calvert, 1967: 44– 45, 197–224). As late as 1903, civil engineers refused to join with the professional organizations of mechanical, mining, and electrical engineers in a common engineering association building in New York. The *Polytechnique* model, instead of being extended, was sharply constricted to the civil engineering profession.

4. The leading mechanical engineers had their own version of high-status education: the **informal system of apprenticeship** in the shops of machine manufacturers. This "shop culture," as Calvert has termed it, emphasized a career of gentlemanly ideals: personal relationships rather than formal or bureaucratic procedures, labor paternalism, and an unspecialized role combining capacities for creative innovation with the independence of the business owner. If the civil engineers invoked the ideal of the Napoleonic officer, mechanical engineers invoked the ideal of the gentleman of the Thomas Jefferson type—a man of knowledge and affairs, capable of any task.

The leading mechanical engineers were wealthy businessmen. When the profession finally formalized itself in 1880 as the American Society of Mechanical Engineers (ASME), manufacturers were its leading segment. As a professional organization, they were remarkably free from the usual interest of such organizations, opposing the development of engineering schools, licensing requirements, and the establishment of legal standards of performance (Calvert, 1967: 63–85, 107–139). The ASME operated essentially as a club for the wealthy leaders of the "shop culture." It made little effort to include the increasing numbers of engineers, especially those employed in lower positions of large bureaucracies. Its opposition to licensing and legal standards reflected the commercial interests of its members as well as its concern with keeping the profession informal. Since most were involved in the sale of machinery, they felt no need for external regulations. Their resistance to licensing was part of their battle against formal engineering schools, for licensing procedures eventually take on the tone of school exams and tend to move toward formal educational requirements. The slow rise of schools of mechanical engineering was, in large part, a result of the opposition of this group.

5. Finally, there were the **university-level schools of mechanical engineering.** Initial efforts to train engineers for industrial employment foundered because of a variety of opposition: the refusal of the civil engineering schools to include mechanical engineering in the curriculum; the denial of its importance by the high-status group of mechanical engineers; and the hostility of the traditional colleges to a practical curriculum (Calvert, 1967: 43–62, 87–105). The last fear was particularly acute because of the enormous failure rate among colleges and the growing tone of criticism in mid-nineteenth century of the uselessness of the classical curriculum. Only after

the passage of the federal Morrill Act in 1862 (i.e., during the period of patriotic enthusiasm of the early period of the Civil War) did mechanical engineering schools begin to appear. The land-grant aids of the Morrill Act went primarily for setting up state universities. In the East, some of this was acquired by new private schools such as Cornell (founded in 1871) and M.I.T. (1865). Yet even the land-grant colleges, provisioned under the ideology of providing practical training in mechanical engineering and agriculture, were under constant pressure to evolve into imitations of the high-status universities, emphasizing traditional studies and scholarship (Jencks and Riesman, 1968: 224−230). Training in scientific agriculture, although important for gaining political support, was scarcely implemented until well into the twentieth century. Engineering as well tended to be neglected by university administrators eager to raise the social and scholarly status of their institutions.

Against these obstacles, mechanical engineering education grew slowly. The major source of teachers was former navy engineers. Such men were available in part because of declining military opportunities after the Civil War, in part because of antagonism toward them on the part of the aristocratic, regular navy officers, who looked down upon an occupation that included a great many mechanics recruited during the wartime needs for boiler experts (Calvert, 1967: 245−261). These teachers represented a bureaucratic rather than an entrepreneurial or genteel image of the engineering profession. The nature of the university engineering training as well, and the antagonism of the small engineering shops to such education, fitted its graduates for employment primarily in the emerging business corporations. The traditional mechanical engineering elite, defending their own version of informal training, pointedly called attention to the nonelite nature of many graduate careers. Many became draftsmen, with typical careers within the middle ranges of bureaucratic hierarchy. Electrical engineers, in particular, were likely to be hired by two major corporations—Westinghouse and General Electric. Relatively fewer of the university-trained engineers became entrepreneurs or executives, although engineering was to become an important new path upward within new corporations during the twentieth century.[16]

Modern American Engineering

Throughout the nineteenth century, then, American engineering failed to achieve either a united profession or a widely accepted system of education.

---

[16]Calvert (1967: 217). Gooding (1971: 72−75, 142−146) reports that the pattern has continued in recent years; although some engineers reach top management, a much larger proportion experiences the vicissitudes of the more open labor market, including periodic unemployment; about 40% of engineers surveyed indicated they would choose another profession if they could; currently popular demands among engineers are for the development of job security and promotional opportunities on nonmanagement job ladders.

These failures did not prevent the United States from experiencing tremendous economic growth, attaining a position of world leadership by World War I. What it did prevent was the dominance of an engineering elite over American industry or over the American educational system. Just as ethnic conflicts have split the American working class, analogous conflicts among rival status groups within engineering (some based on class origins, others perhaps on ethnicity) have kept a strong occupational community from emerging to monopolize practice and control the routes to organizational power. As bureaucratic organizations came to dominate American industry, the "shop culture" and its genteel upholders gradually disappeared or became transformed into bureaucrats themselves. The more popularly oriented forms of engineering education—the mechanics institute and the training schools—failed from their fatal trait of low-status connotations. But the *Polytechnique* ideal, the dominance of the pure technical culture and its carriers, was not to prevail either.

By 1910, the university-level engineering schools were firmly established, feeding their graduates to the bureaucratic sectors of industry. This education, however, never achieved elite status, nor did it uphold the ideal of a purely scientific and technical education as a substitute for the genteel but vocationally useless liberal arts curriculum. Its students tended to be recruited from among the lower middle class and ethnic minorities, and to represent a type of culture—the nongenteel, nonsociable, technical specialists (in undergraduate parlance, "the greasy grind")—that could not compete with the traditionally high-status professions (medicine, law, and liberal arts teaching) and their upper-middle-class students.[17] Well aware of their status problems, the engineering teachers made an effort to tie themselves to the status of the traditional education system. From the early period, with the exception of occasional experiments with acceleration movements, leading engineering schools moved to model themselves on the classical colleges in all external particulars, including numbers of years of study and admissions requirements, stressing graduation from a liberal arts high school, with preparation in English and history rather than strictly in science (Calvert, 1967: 76–77; Jencks and Riesman, 1968: 229).

Engineering thus moved into the twentieth century, no longer a threat to the main body of American education: the unitary system of preparation in a modified liberal arts curriculum and branching off from the traditional liberal arts college. Indeed, there have been constant efforts by leaders of the engineering profession to upgrade its status, not by emphasizing its technical qualities but by attempting to incorporate more of the high-status culture of liberal arts. In 1890, the president of the ASME, a representative of the

---

[17]Calvert (1967: 70–71); for more modern data, see Perrucci and Gerstl (1969: 29–32, 41–52).

wealthy business engineering group, argued against purely vocational education on the grounds that engineers should be able to "meet wealthy and
cultivated clients upon their own levels; to excel them, if anything, in the
intelligent appreciation of their mutual affairs and in the amenities of social
intercourse [Calvert, 1967: 83]."

A Carnegie Foundation report in 1918 criticized the quality of engineering schools (Mann, 1918). In 1929, a group of professional leaders centered
in the high-status engineering schools published the Wickenden Report, yet
another effort to do for engineering what the Flexner Report had done to raise
the status of the medical profession.[18] The Wickenden Report again criticized
the narrow vocationalism of much of engineering education and argued for
greater inclusion of liberal arts preparation in the curriculum, with the ideal of
translating education into an exclusively postgraduate training as in the more
prominent schools of medicine and law. (Unlike medical reform, status and
technical interests here pushed in opposite directions.) This was followed by
the organization of foundations to enforce these standards through state
licensing laws and accreditation of engineering schools.

Implementation of such proposals has been slow. The leading engineering schools, especially those attached to the high-status liberal arts colleges,
have gradually introduced more nonengineering courses into the curriculum.
Graduate degrees in engineering have indeed risen. As compared with the
engineers of 1900, virtually none of whom had M.A.s or Ph.D.s, of the cohort
graduating during the 1950s, 13% had M.A.s and 1.7% had Ph.D.s; of the
1965 cohort, 24% had M.A.s and 4% Ph.D.s.[19] Nevertheless, engineering has
continued to recruit most heavily from among the upwardly mobile, ethnic
minority working class and lower middle class for whom a narrow vocational
emphasis rather than a training in high culture was the primary aim. For those
of lower social origin, a position as a technical specialist in the middle ranks of
a bureaucratic organization is an acceptable goal, although it may not be for
the upper-middle-class person seeking elite status.

The engineering profession and its related educational system thus remain full of strain. Elite status pretensions still act to push educational requirements up and to make them less narrowly technical. This process has

---

[18]Wickenden (1930; 1934). See also Selden (1960), Soderberg (1967: 213–218, 227–
228), and Perrucci and Gerstl (1969: 77) for more recent efforts by leading engineering
educators to raise engineering into a postgraduate course.

[19]These figures are calculated from Soderberg (1967: 216) and Perrucci and Gerstl (1969:
58). Most engineers in 1900 lacked engineering degrees entirely: the U.S. census listed 43,000
engineers in that year, while engineering schools (after a period of expansion) awarded approximately 1000 degrees. In 1950, it was estimated that 57% of all engineers held college degrees,
and the percentage is no doubt higher now (Soderberg, 1967: 213, 216; Perrucci and Gerstl,
1969: 58–59).

been aided, at least in part, by the rapid rise in the number of students in the twentieth century, which has gradually pushed up educational requirements for employment in engineering and made a graduate degree useful for staying one step above the mass. Nevertheless, advanced degrees—especially Ph.D.s—are training primarily in research, and their holders tend to advance in research jobs rather than in the command hierarchy of organizations (Perrucci and Gerstl, 1969: 131, 135). Engineering students from lower economic backgrounds, less able to afford lengthier education and less attracted to the cultural status values of education for its own sake, are a strong counterforce, especially at the lower-status engineering schools.

Employers are a third element in the struggle over requirements. They have resisted the tendency to upgrade all engineers through lengthening training and periodically have called for separate programs to train technicians who do not pose the promotion and status pressures of the engineers (Perrucci and Gerstl, 1969: 281–284). Engineers generally have resisted such proposals, perhaps from a consciousness of their relatively weak professional organization independent of business employment, and from reluctance to have many of their employment opportunities frozen at lower levels. Technicians do not always constitute a clearly separate group, however, but are often drawn from engineering students who have not yet finished their degrees.[20] Thus, not only has engineering failed to create a major challenge or split in the unified status hierarchy of American education, but even within the profession, technicians tend to be distinguished from engineers through quantitative differences in achievement within the school system, not through differences in kind of training. In engineering, as elsewhere in the American occupational structure, the credential market pushes for the continued elaboration of vertical distinctions.

CONCLUSION: CULTURAL COMMUNITIES AND OCCUPATIONAL MONOPOLIES

From a theoretical viewpoint, the formation of professions is determined by the same general principles that govern the formation of any kind of consciousness community. The strong professions are merely a particular

---

[20]This was indicated by employer comments in the 1967 California survey, reported in Chapter 2. A high proportion of students among technicians is reflected in the relative ages of male engineers and technicians: In 1960, engineers' median age was 38.0, compared to 31.1 for electronics and electrical technicians; the latter figure contrasts with a median age of 40.6 for the entire male labor force and is one of the youngest of all occupational groups (*Statistical Abstract*, 1966: Table No. 328).

kind of occupation, one that has an especially distinctive culture and self-conscious organization. And occupations in general exhibit the same range of variation in cohesiveness and power as the cultural communities that are more conventionally studied as leisure status groups made up of friends, families, and religious and ethnic memberships. A truly general theory of group formation would apply to both the occupational and status group realms (and indeed would show a good deal of their interpenetration). Such a theory would give us the conditions determining how many groups would be formed, how strongly organized each would be, whether they would be local or extensive, with strong or weak boundaries, and—in large part as the result of the preceding—what relationships of domination and subordination would exist among them.

We do not have such a full-fledged theory at present. But it seems clear that a major determinant of the numbers and characteristics of groups is the form of cultural production that exists. It is culture—the symbolic reflections upon and communications about the conditions of daily life, and the more abstract transformations and distortions of these experiences that can be symbolically created—that is the medium for conversations and other personal exchanges, and it is out of such exchanges that groups are formed and various identities and states of self-consciousness are generated. Thus culture is the crucial vehicle for the organization of the struggle over economic goods (as well as any other goods), and for the division of productive labor into distinctive occupations. As argued in Chapter 3, cultural organization shapes the class struggle at one of its most crucial points: the formation of various degrees of property in the form of occupational "positions."

The history of the professions, then, is especially revealing because it shows us the conditions that have produced some of the most striking variations in the formation of occupational groups and positional property. The conditions are very much like those that produce ethnic groups.[21] That is to say, the conditions of everyday life in a particular historical time and place generate a distinctive culture, and hence the basis for interacting as a group or set of groups. In the case of ethnic groups, a crucial point occurs when the group moves to a new situation; it will maintain a group identity only if there

---

[21]There is no well-developed theory of ethnic groups either; even the special subcases of a theory of group formation are not filled in as yet. Analytically, the subtheories of professionalization and ethnicity have focused on opposite ends of the same continuum: In ethnicity, the interest has been on the conditions for maximal assimilation; in professionalization, on the conditions for maximal distinctiveness. It should be noted that the opposite of professionalization would be class solidarity among larger occupational groups with an ideal extreme (nowhere realized) of solidarity among all occupations. Thus professionalization theory has been analytically (and generally speaking, politically) the obverse of Marxist sociology.

are means of encapsulating its historical culture, by enforcing group boundaries (whether from within or without), and often by the explicit, formal
reproduction of its culture by specialized agencies. In the case of occupational
groups, similarly, the deliberate encapsulation of a historical identity is crucial
for a strong and self-conscious organization. Thus we may expect that not
only will the strongest occupational communities be the most culturally traditional ones, but also that these occupations will place the strongest reliance
on the formal and specialized reproduction of culture.

It is not surprising, from a theoretical viewpoint, that the history of the
professions is so much entwined with the history of education, or that both of
these are entwined with the history of ethnic conflicts and with the shifting
patterns of politics. The difference between centralized and decentralized
states plays a large part in the volatility of cultural markets, thus having an
indirect effect upon the formation of occupational communities, as well as a
direct effect through state intervention in legally shaping positional property.
And the transformation of the United States from a near monoethnic to a
highly multiethnic society has had crucial effects on its occupational structure,
both indirectly and directly. In overviewing the factors that have shaped the
professions into their distinctive forms in modern America, we are summariz-
ing the conditions that have given this society its distinctive form of economic
domination.

The historical process by which medicine, law, and engineering have
acquired their identities is very revealing in this respect. Medicine has always
emphasized its ritual procedures and its self-idealization. Behind the modern
"bedside manner" stands a long tradition, not only of making oneself culturally acceptable to the dignified upper class, but also of taking a priestly role
toward clients. During the long majority of medical history when no practical
cures existed, ritual manipulation and its attendant secrecy and mystification
were the *sine qua non* of the occupation's existence. Western medicine
branched off from the religious studies of the medieval university, and for a
long period doctors were a special type of clergyman.[22] Pursuing the medical
tradition back to antiquity, we find the religious cult of the followers of the
demigod, Hippocrates; behind this is the tradition of the shaman, a role from
which medicine, divination, and priestcraft all developed. Physicians thus
have an unbroken tradition of emphasizing ritual exclusion for the purposes of
occupational impressiveness. Lawyers come from a more secular tradition,
although the monopoly of the church over medieval education gave Euro-

---

[22]The medical licensing act passed by the English Parliament in 1523 gave nonclergy the
right for the first time to practice medicine. In the early American colonies, where the medieval
pattern persisted longer than in Europe, clergymen routinely practiced medicine as well (Berlant,
1973: 171, 110).

pean lawyers their first resources toward a powerful group status. Medicine and law both acquired their core occupational cultures in the Middle Ages, based on the experience of literate groups with access to traditional texts, in a society in which the ruling aristocracy was illiterate. The modern organization of elite doctors emerged as the university-trained group that specialized in ritually treating the wealthy aristocrats in times of illness; lawyers emerged as the group that specialized in oral arguments and written texts surrounding government administration, first of all in the area of justice.

These occupations emerged with high-status cultures, both by virtue of their original access to the sacred books and institutional charisma of religious education and by virtue of their association with an upper-class clientele. In contrast, engineers have a dual occupational origin: the all-around skills of the gentleman–entrepreneur or administrator, and the technical lore of skilled laborers. Neither had any religious sanction, although the former was connected with the gentry class (nevertheless, in the prevailing tone of aristocratic society, engineering was not considered to be a very honored side of its activities). The skilled laborer side of engineering proved an even more serious embarrassment. Medicine actually has had a parallel plebeian group, that is, pharmacists, midwives, and barber-surgeons—indeed, all those who had some actual practical skills rather than mere Galenic theory. But the very capacity of the book-trained elite to define themselves as *alone* "practicing medicine" is an indication of the power of their ritual resources, above all in its influence upon the licensing power of the state. By comparison, engineers' cultural heritage has always contained an ambiguity based on the difficulty in separating its two internal components, and hence their ability to act as a cohesive group in support of their interests was much lower. Engineers thus turn out to be the most occupationally assimilative of any profession: Its higher-level segment tends to merge with that of managers in general, its lower group into the class of skilled workmen.

Moreover, engineers have an ironic weakness in comparison with doctors and lawyers. The strongest cultural resources for the formation of a dominant group are those that involve a great deal of ritual impressiveness, especially in situations of high emotional stress. Engineers, however, deal with relatively uncontroversial and unemotional tasks, and hence lack a culture that is politically and morally impressive. Even more ironically, engineers and technicians suffer from the very successfulness of their techniques. The outcomes of their work are quite reliable, and hence even though outsiders may not always be able to judge the processes by which they work, they can control such technical employees by fairly simple judgments of work completed. The strength of doctors and lawyers vis-à-vis their clients, on the other hand, is precisely in the fact that their cures or legal maneuvers are not necessarily efficacious, and hence they are held much less accountable for their failures. Engineers' and technicians' work is productive labor; that of doctors and lawyers is primarily political labor. The one produces real outcomes; the other tends to manipulate appearances and beliefs.[23] It is the very reliability of the productive realm that makes it relatively unrewarding, even for its most skilled practitioners, compared to the unpredictability and mystification of the political realm.

For medicine, the old cultural resources have remained salient throughout most of its history. Technically efficacious cures (in some but not all areas) emerging in the late nineteenth century have not eliminated the advantages of the older status idealization and monopolistic community closure; the older resources have been used to claim a monopoly on the new technical skills themselves. There was a crisis period in the American medical profession, however, during the early nineteenth century, when political decentralization through western expansion removed its political support for enforcing monopolization, and the rise of a new class of consumers began to call forth a diverse and uncontrolled market for medical services. We have seen how a number of auxiliary resources and alliances came to the rescue of the traditional medical organization, but it was nip and tuck for awhile, and one might well imagine that without the cultural conflicts of the later immigration period, medicine in America might have evolved into a much more economically modest and market-responsive occupational sector, little differentiated from the sale of other services.

Politics is crucial for the survival and prosperity of professions, above all through the power of the state in licensing their monopolies. Lawyers are in a particularly good position, since they are tied to the state more intimately than any other occupation except government employees and politicians. But the power of these latter groups is mediated by other interest groups outside the state, whereas lawyers claim to be esoteric specialists in the mediation process itself. Lawyers have the resources to perpetuate their distinctive culture, their apparently intrinsic skills; in the medieval tradition, this has meant to keep the

---

[23]This is not to say that doctors do not have any real technical tools today. They do, largely in the form of drugs. These could be dispensed in a much simpler (and cheaper) fashion on a public market for pharmaceuticals, without the extra taxation of the medical doctors' monopoly over prescriptions. This control over the technically efficacious part of medicine, by forcing clients to go through the ritual of a medical consultation, exemplifies very nicely the power of a strong occupational culture. The doctors' monopoly over drugs is justified by their long-standing cultivation of an altruistic self-image, which simultaneously defines those who are not doctors (sufferers from ills) as incompetent to judge or even hold the proper moral perspective toward their symptoms. This also serves the economic advantage of doctors, making them far and away the highest paid of all occupational groups, and the pharmaceutical industry the most profitable of all industry groups (Thurow, 1975: 8, 144).

procedures of legal argument and decision so complex and esoteric as to monopolize the channels of communication with judicial powers.[24]

By the same token, the strength of the legal guild is immediately affected by changes in the structure of political power. In medieval Europe, decentralized conditions favoring and institutionalizing the powers of the independent aristocracy vis-à-vis the king—including the archaic institution of the collegial courts themselves—made the lawyers a self-perpetuating status group. In contrast, the profession did not emerge at all in the long-centralized state of China, where laws remained part of the diffuse culture of all educated officials. Similarly, the rise of strong centralized bureaucracies to administer the continental European states tended to assimilate lawyers to the category of governmental administrators in general. In England, on the other hand, the balanced struggle between aristocracy and crown gave the lawyers, as intermediaries, many opportunities to elaborate the distinctiveness of their occupational culture (the Common Law) and the scope of their powers. The decentralization of government in America favored the continuation of this structure, although westward expansion in the nineteenth century and political democratization for a time diluted the occupational culture and threatened to assimilate the occupation to the larger politically mobilized populace generally. But the struggle against alien immigrant groups and the rise of the large, nationally centralized corporations toward the end of the century began to turn back this tide, giving elite lawyers other power resources and helping reestablish the balance between centralized and decentralized authority that most favors the power of lawyers.

With regard to the status of engineers, the increased economic significance of their skills in contributing to industrialization has continued to be offset by the split between the managerial and skilled labor aspects of the profession. Where political conditions have favored the former, the result has been an elite profession, as in the successful opposition of technically trained French administrators to the nonpractical aristocrats of the Old Regime. An even more extreme case is the Soviet Union, where political ideology has given engineers (along with specialists in political ideology, the equivalent of political priests trained in the ideological school system) special political significance, displacing all other professional competitors (and reducing lawyers to virtual insignificance). In England and America, however, the two sides of the occupational culture have remained in uneasy symbiosis, leaving engineering the least unified, and hence least powerful, of the major modern professions. The conflict between the subgroups of American engineering

---

[24]Technically, American attorneys are officials of the court, serving without remuneration from the government and with almost complete delegation of certain aspects of authority.

ruined its apparent opportunity to displace the traditional university culture when the latter came under severe attack in the middle of the nineteenth century. With the bureaucratization of employment in the early twentieth century, the gentry ideal of the nineteenth-century engineer virtually disappeared, hastened by the influx of alien ethnic groups into engineering. At the same time, the last-ditch effort to tie engineering to elite culture, via incorporation in the standard educational sequence, tended to cut its earlier direct ties to the culture and personal circles of workingmen. The result was to produce a more diffuse engineering culture, held together primarily by educational credentials of moderate status value. The split between higher-status engineers (management-oriented) and lower-status engineers (technicians) has continued, but in a more graduated form, based on how far one has gone in the educational sequence.

The larger historical process whereby earlier organizational and cultural resources are carried over and help mold new situations is well illustrated by the professions. The shape of modern American medicine, law, and engineering clearly shows the marks of their origins and of the successive transformations along the way. Above all, in their embeddedness in a lengthy educational sequence (which essentially precedes the actual learning of practical skills, especially in the cases of medicine and law), we find that the ontogeny of the modern individual's professional career recapitulates the phylogeny of its monopolistic status.

The main effects of a decentralized situation of status group stratification have been in the relative salience and spread of cultural distinctions. Multiethnic societies usually have a history of cultural conflict and emulation, with a tendency to extend cultural distinctions once marking off the elite into a lengthy hierarchy of cultural steps throughout society. Monoethnic societies are culturally stratified in terms of a simpler distinction between the elite and the masses; without an elaborate culture hierarchy throughout, class domination operates much more transparently.

The occupational equivalent of a multiethnic society is one containing strong autonomous professional communities. The analogy to diffuse cultural emulation and cultural hierarchy is an emphasis on education, especially in the lengthy hierarchic form that has been referred to as a "contest mobility" system. This is what we find in the United States of the twentieth century, following upon the consolidation of the professions around the turn of the century. We find the elaboration of a gradually lengthening educational sequence, with no sharp dividing point between elite and nonelite credentials, but a constant tendency to upgrade requirements relative to those of occupations below and to the numbers of aspirants. Professions have attached themselves vertically to the end of this sequence, requiring general cultural respectability for entrance into their training (rather than specific technical preparation). Internally, the professions add on further specialized requirements at the end of the common professional training period, thus extending the contest mobility system within their own ranks.

The model of professional organization has been widely emulated outside of the traditional professional occupations. In America this is found to an extent not experienced elsewhere in the industrial world. The elaboration of educational credentials, licensing procedures, and other formally monopolistic structures is found not only among dentists, librarians, and teachers, but also spreads to accountants, medical technicians, morticians, social workers, and business administrators, and into the traditional skilled crafts of the construction and household repairs occupations. The extension of monopolistic controls through government licensing is often justified by the same "altruistic" ideals as in the case of the traditional professions; thus campaigns to protect the consumer in such areas as auto repairs result in licensing requirements that decrease competition and monopolize entry to the occupation.

The same conditions that favored the elite professions—decentralized politics and multiple ethnic competition—may be seen operating here in the mobilization of occupational communities of all sorts to secure licensing and other monopolistic advantages from the state legislatures in the early years of the twentieth century. Labor unions did not initially share in this, above all because of their conflict with the interest groups closer to political power; since finally receiving government sanction in the 1930s, however, unions have not tended to act as pan-working-class—"assimilative"—organizations; the tendency has been to break up more and more into protective associations for the incumbents (often ethnic enclaves) of particular occupations. Through this process, occupational structures come more and more to resemble the closed guilds of medieval Europe, themselves the products of a situation of political decentralization and ethnic multiplicity.

America is surely the most capitalistic society in the world today, and has been so since at least the end of the last century. This feature is not accidental. For capitalism is above all the predominance of the private business enterprise over centralized state economic control and the elaboration of mechanisms for establishing and controlling a market in the hands of private interests. In numerous ways, the ethnic conflicts and political decentralization of America have contributed to this pattern to a degree not found elsewhere in the industrial world.

Organized labor, which elsewhere has lent its political weight toward some version of socialism (often in alliance with traditionalistic statist interests), has not had this effect in America. During the initial period of industrialization and its accompanying class conflicts, American labor was ideologically socialist but also heavily identified with immigrant ethnic blocs. The class conflicts of the time became shaped by a crusade for ethnic cultural domination as Anglo-Protestant America mobilized its resources to crush alien ethnic organization. Although by no means all of the Protestants were a single economic interest bloc, the central position of business interests in their cultural alliance meant that these were the interests most favored; henceforth, an antisocialist stance and "American" cultural identity became virtually synonymous. The same period saw the consolidation of professional associations as part of these ethnic conflicts; with their delegated state powers for self-regulation, they became little private governments, controlling their own sources of economic privilege and thus splitting up (and making more invisible) the targets for any reform of the economic order and bolstering a privileged, upper middle class alongside the national upper class. The elaboration of the school system, under the impetus of this conflict, and the establishment of educational credentials for employment, especially in the wealthiest corporations, has further disguised the means of domination and turned the class struggle into efforts of innumerable small occupational groups to gain control over their own positional property.

In the 1930s, when unions finally achieved political recognition and support, they did so in a situation in which the prevailing pattern was private bargaining against particular industrial enclaves rather than politically oriented class action. Unions became the local preserves of particular ethnic groups— especially the crafts unions, borrowing their legal structure from the same legislation that favored autonomous professions—and hence interethnic conflict within the working class has fragmented European-style class unity. Late-mobilizing ethnic groups, such as blacks and Latin Americans, have found their economic interests blocked by other ethnic working-class groups and have thus fought for their own economic enclaves, especially within government employment.

The growth of governmental regulatory agencies since the New Deal has not shifted the overall balance of power greatly. It has produced no shift toward a European-style confrontation between a unified, working-class party pushing for socialist-style controls and a united party of big business. American parties remain primarily ethnic coalitions, loosely organizing a mass of private group interests; their main legislative achievements involve setting aside protected economic enclaves for their groups. One should not be deceived by the rhetoric of laissez faire used by many conservatives and the rhetoric of regulation in the "public interest" by many liberals. Both sides fight for government support of particular monopolies and privileges, with the conservatives seeking these for business groups, the liberals for particular (usually ethnic) labor groups, government employees, and professions. It is not surprising, then, that liberals and conservatives find it so easy to compromise on particular pieces of legislation, since both favor the same pattern: government charters for the protection of private economic enclaves.

Most American government activity toward business has consisted of granting various rights for private self-regulation and appropriation of opportunities. On the local level, this takes the form of granting licenses and franchises to operate liquor stores or taverns, legal, medical and quasi-medical services, repair services, construction, crafts, insurance, real estate brokerages, banks, and other financial institutions. Although much of this has not been investigated in detail, we can surmise from studies of professions that the rhetoric of "protecting the public interest" that has justified this regulatory activity is mainly a dissimulative ideology, and that the activity serves the economic interests of the groups involved. For the "regulated" group (which usually is delegated the power of self-regulation by its most formally organized sector), this means monopolization of a particular area of business, reduction of competition, and often a form of price fixing. For the politicians who pass such legislation, there are payoffs in the form of having created an area of patronage under their disposal, often involving quasi-legal or illegal contributions (or at least political support) to procure licenses. Insofar as such regulative activities are sponsored more heavily by liberal politicians, it seems primarily because these are the types of small monopolies that can be sought by the ethnic minorities they represent.

The same activities may be seen on a more grand scale at the federal level: not only the licensing of radio and television stations, airlines, drug sales (usually under prodding from interested medical lobbies), and international trade, but especially indirect protection of favored industries (through taxation and tariffs) and direct protection in the form of government purchases (in military expenditures, in "foreign aid" purchased from American producers, and in price supports for large agricultural businesses). The rhetoric of "public interest" involved in such regulatory activities does not mirror the actual pattern of monopolization, patronage bargaining, and market controls involved.

From a more sociological viewpoint, however, there is a certain appropriateness in this terminology. It is no accident that professions, the most privileged and monopolistic of occupations, should define themselves in altruistic terms, and that at least a certain aspect of this should be convincing. For moral categories refer to the preeminence of the community over the individual, and professions are above all occupational communities. Their ideology reflects reality in the sense that individual practitioners are supposed to subordinate all self-seeking that conflicts with the general interests of other practitioners. Since we commonly miss the difference between private communities and the larger community of the whole populace, it is easy for the rhetoric of altruistic dedication to the former to slide over into an appearance of altruism toward the latter. The same conceptual trick is played by the rhetoric of justifying governmental regulation, and in a double sense.

Monopolies are generally given to groups rather than to individuals; thus the very fact that it is the government—which seems to represent the entire community—that grants the monopoly, seems to indicate that the whole population is acting to enforce altruistic standards on one of its parts. But the governments of America do not represent the community as a whole; rather they represent the most mobilized interest communities within it, and the political representatives bargain among themselves to transfer certain governmental powers to private groups to make their private community structure even stronger. The ongoing process of reform in America, as different private groups enter the bargaining, only serves to make private property interests ever more strongly entrenched. American capitalism permeates not only the upper reaches of the corporate economy, but much of the occupational structure as well.

7

The Politics of a Sinecure Society

What effects has credentialism had on the overall shape of stratification?
In some areas, it appears to have had no effects at all. Rates of intergenerational social mobility, for example, have been constant from decade to decade as far back as the 1920s (Rogoff, 1953; Jackson and Crockett, 1964; Blau and Duncan, 1967: 110). Indeed, the rates have been virtually constant back to the early nineteenth century as far as we can tell from more limited information on economic and political elites (Taussig and Joslyn, 1932: 97; Warner and Abegglen, 1955: 37–68; Newcomer, 1955: 53; Bendix, 1956: 198–253; Mills, 1963: 110–139) and on particular communities (Thernstrom, 1964). The nineteenth century, in other words, was no golden age of opportunity, but neither was it an inferior situation to the modern one. The implication of this for the rise of educational stratification has gone unnoticed. The enormous expansion of education since the mid-nineteenth century *has had no effects at all* for increasing opportunities for social mobility. There is no alleged shift from "ascription" to "achievement." On the face of it, there has been the same level of correlation between fathers' and sons' occupations with a large educational system, a moderate-sized one, or virtually no educational system at all.

In one respect, this is not surprising. If education does not provide occupational skills, one should not expect that making education more widely available should have any effects on occupational careers. Yet educational credentials have become the currency for employment, so that a greater abundance of even this artificial good might be expected to make a difference. But perhaps precisely because of this artificiality, the order of groups' access to credentials has not changed their relative stratification. As education has become more available, the children of the higher social classes have increased their schooling in the same proportions as children of the lower social classes have increased theirs; hence the ratios of relative educational attainment by social classes has remained constant throughout the last 50 years (Spady, 1967) and probably before.[1]

A comparative finding from central Africa shows the basic pattern even more sharply: Kelley and Perlman (1971) calculated mobility rates for an older generation whose careers had started before the introduction of a formalized school system and the rates for a younger generation whose careers began afterwards. The mobility rate *declined,* and in approximately the proportion that education now played in careers. Cultural goods, it appears, are even more readily passed on from parents to children than are economic and political resources.[2]

THE EARLY TWENTIETH-CENTURY INCOME REVOLUTION

Nevertheless, there has been one major shift in the socioeconomic structure. The distribution of income and of property did change between approximately 1930 and 1950, and in a more egalitarian direction. We find this shift

---

[1]This consistency of mobility rates does not mean that particular ethnic groups have not changed their average occupational levels, or even, in some cases, their levels relative to each other. As of the 1960s, Jews held the highest occupational level of any ethnic group, and Catholics as a whole had passed white Protestants as a whole. The latter result, though, was due primarily to the fact that the white Protestant population is much more rural than the Catholic population, whereas occupational opportunities are better in the cities. The white Protestant population, in fact, seems to be split into two segments: an urban group that dominates the upper class and much of the upper middle class, and a rural–small town group of below-average occupational level. See Glenn and Hyland (1967), Duncan and Duncan (1968), Jackson *et al.* (1970), Featherman (1971).

[2]Given this pattern, in fact, we should have expected that mobility rates would *decline* in the twentieth-century United States as education expanded. That rates have stayed constant may indicate some offsetting force in the noneducational realm, or it may indicate only that mobility rates are higher in a mixed horticultural society than in an industrial one.

in Gini coefficients, describing the overall shape of income distribution: averaging .433 during 1920–1929 and .421 during 1949–1958 (Stack, 1976: Table 3.2);[3] and in the declining share of the upper 1% of the property owners, from 36% of the wealth in 1929 to 23% in 1945, and fluctuating between 20 and 26% since then (*Statistical Abstract*, 1976: Table 693).

This shift coincides with the New Deal period of government and with a period of significant expansion of the educational system. Here, at least, one might find one egalitarian promise of educational liberalism paying off.

If we examine the twentieth-century income revolution, however, it appears that the redistribution has been to specific groups rather than across the board. Summary measures like Gini coefficients hide which portion of the income curve has shifted. Examination of the shares going to each decile of the income-receiving population shows that the bottom tenths have not improved their positions: the lowest 10%, in fact, was best off in 1910, when it received 3.4% of total income; but this group declined to 1.0% in 1937 and has fluctuated very slightly around that figure every since. The ninth decile has fluctuated at 2–3% for 60 years, the eighth decile at 4–5%, the seventh decile at 6%, the sixth decile at 7–8%, the fifth decile at 8–9%, and the fourth decile at 10–11%. The major shift has been from the top decile to the second and third deciles. The top decile *fell* from its height of 39% of the income in 1929 to 29% in 1945 and has fluctuated around that figure ever since. The second decile was the major gainer, rising from 12% in 1929 to 16% in 1945, while the third decile rose from 10% in 1929 to 13% in 1945, both groups holding constant since then.[4] And within the top decile, it appears that the holdings of the top few percent have declined in favor of those just below them.

The pattern looks like a shift from the upper class to the upper middle class. But is it correct to describe the second and third deciles or even the portion of the top decile below the top few percentages as "upper middle class" in terms of occupation? Pilcher (1976: 216–244), in analyzing British data, found that this was not so, and the American data presented in Table 7.1 show a similar pattern.

The top 10% of American income earners in 1972 breaks down into: 34% managers and administrators, most of them salaried; 30% professional and technical, again most of them salaried; and 9% salesmen. I say *salesmen* explicitly because all the groups cited here are male; female workers in all

---

[3]Another source of data (Pilcher, 1976: 297) gives Gini coefficients from 1949 to 1969 as fluctuating from .383 to .406. Such differences in Gini values can be produced by calculations based on different categorizations of the same data (deciles, quintiles, etc.) or by different data sources.

[4]Data from various sources for 1910 through 1969 are presented in Pilcher (1976: 57–59).

categories make up only 3.4% of the top income decile. The managers, administrators, and professionals are readily enough described as upper middle class; given their high proportions of salaried employees, it appears that most of them work for the large corporations and government bureaucracies. Salesmen fit the label less obviously. Although most of these are not in retail sales, and hence are likely to be employed in these same corporate structures, they represent a more entrepreneurial component of it. The most striking finding, though, is that 18% of the top decile is working class or upper working class: 11% craftsmen, 3% foremen, and 4% operatives.

Similarly for the second and third deciles. The second decile is almost equally composed of (male) salaried professionals (20%), salaried managers (18%), and craftsmen (18%), with a large representation of operatives (11%); self-employed professionals and owners make up a very small proportion, and the total female representation in this favored decile is 8.0%. The third decile is dominated by (male) craftsmen (20%) and operatives (15%), while salaried professionals make up 14% and salaried managers 12%. Male craftsmen and operatives also dominate the middle deciles (fourth through sixth). The lower deciles (seventh through ninth) are dominated by *female* clerical workers, while the lowest two deciles are heavily composed of female service workers, operatives, clerical workers, and male farmers.

The entire upper half of the income distribution is heavily male, urban, and (surmising from other data, e.g., in Thurow, 1975: 6; and Pilcher, 1976), full-time employed. The lower half consists of female workers, agricultural workers, and—extrapolating from Pilcher's data (1976: 216–221, 44)—those who are part-time employed, unemployed and underemployed, and those living on welfare payments. Thus the most crucial dividing lines turn out *not* to be occupational class divisions per se, but: (*a*) the segregation between higher-paying male occupations; and (*b*) admission into full-time and relatively secure jobs within the urban labor force. The big distinctions are essentially ones of "positional property." Getting into and holding onto a male-designated position, especially within the wealthy corporations and within governmental bureaucracies, by itself is enough to ensure an above-average income.

More specific occupations show the same pattern. The highest paying of all occupations is that of the physician, especially self-employed ones (of which latter group 68% were in the top 3.5% of all income earners), and this is the occupation with the strongest monopolistic controls over their own numbers. Similarly, other self-employed professionals such as lawyers are also very likely to be in the most favored income levels (41% in the top 3.5% of income earners), while salaried professionals such as engineers (5.9%) and teachers (1.9%), with much less control over their own positions, are much less likely to be in this group (all figures from Thurow, 1975: Table 6). And at

Table 7.1

Occupational Composition of Decile Shares, 1972[a]

Type of occupation	Tenth decile (lowest)	Ninth decile ($3706—)	Eighth decile ($5078—)	Seventh decile ($6282—)	Sixth decile ($7176—)	Fifth decile ($8686—)	Fourth decile ($9274—)	Third decile ($11,940—)	Second decile ($13,940—)	First decile ($19,200—highest)	Top 3.5% (income $25,000+)
Male											
Self-employed professional and technical (556)[b]	.5	.1	.2	.3	.3	.3	.6	.5	1.3	6.2	13.5
Salaried professional and technical (5217)	2.6	1.7	2.6	5.0	6.6	8.0	14.0	13.9	19.6	23.6	19.0
Self-employed managers and administrators (1153)	3.8	1.3	1.4	1.7	1.6	1.6	1.9	1.8	2.4	4.0	5.7
Salaried managers and administrators (5071)	1.7	1.5	2.2	4.4	5.7	6.7	11.9	11.8	18.0	30.3	39.7
Farmers and farm managers (1333)	10.0	2.5	2.1	1.8	1.6	1.4	1.3	1.3	1.3	1.4	1.5
Clerical (2673)	2.1	2.9	3.4	4.7	6.0	7.1	7.7	7.6	5.7	2.6	.8
Sales (2251)	1.9	2.1	2.4	3.4	3.4	3.4	5.1	5.0	6.3	8.8	10.8
Foremen (1228)	.3	.6	.9	1.7	2.2	2.6	1.7	4.0	3.9	2.6	.6
Craftsmen (7127)	5.7	6.6	6.3	4.7	11.0	16.3	20.3	19.9	17.7	11.0	3.0
Operatives (6748)	6.7	10.6	12.1	15.3	17.0	18.2	15.7	15.2	10.6	4.0	1.4
Service except private household (2507)	4.8	5.2	5.6	6.7	5.7	4.8	4.4	4.2	3.3	1.8	.8
Farm laborers and foremen (442)	3.0	1.4	1.1	.8	.7	.5	.2	.1	.2	.2	.1
Laborers (1870)	3.0	4.6	4.5	4.3	4.5	4.8	2.9	2.8	1.7	.2	.4

Female

Occupation (number)											Total
Self-employed professional and technical (48)	.3	.1	.1	.1	—	—	.1	.1	.1	.2	.2
Salaried professional and technical (2993)	3.0	3.3	4.4	7.9	8.8	9.6	6.7	6.4	4.3	1.5	.8
Self-employed managers and administrators (211)	1.6	.4	.3	.3	.2	.2	.2	.2	.2	.2	.2
Salaried managers and administrators (900)	1.4	2.1	2.3	2.6	2.1	1.7	1.4	1.4	1.1	.7	.4
Farmers and farm managers (115)	1.1	.3	.2	.1	.1	—	—	—	—	—	—
Clerical (6349)	11.7	25.5	25.9	22.9	15.4	8.8	2.9	2.6	1.6	.6	.7
Sales (684)	4.4	3.2	2.4	.1	.7	.4	.2	.1	.2	.2	.1
Craftsmen and foremen (276)	1.0	1.0	1.0	.9	.4	.2	.1	.1	.1	—	—
Operatives (2306)	9.7	11.3	9.7	5.3	3.5	2.0	.5	.5	.2	—	—
Private household workers (305)	4.0	.7	.4	.1	.1	—	—	—	—	—	—
Service except private household (2308)	15.4	10.4	8.1	3.8	2.2	1.4	.4	.3	.2	.1	.1
Laborers (114)	.7	.5	.4	.2	.1	.1	—	—	—	—	—
Total	100.4	99.9	100.0	99.1	100.0	100.1	100.2	99.8	100.1	100.1	99.8

Source: Calculated from U.S. Bureau of the Census (1972: 136–138). Percentage totals vary from 100% due to rounding.

[a] Full-time employed income earners, civilian labor force.

[b] Total numbers in parentheses in thousands; other figures in this table represent percentages of each decile share.

a lower occupational level, it is the craftsmen rather than the foremen who make up the significant working-class representation in the top income decile; it is the former, with their strong unions, amounting to guildlike control over the numbers in their own ranks, who achieve the high incomes rather than the latter, whose positions are subject to an external organizational control. And equally significant is the shaping of positions in the artificial distinction between male and female jobs, resulting in a form of positional property with major economic consequences.

What do these data imply about the twentieth-century income revolution? Lacking a comparable occupational breakdown for an earlier point in the century, we cannot be sure. But we do know that personal shares of the total incomes became less concentrated in the top $1-2\%$ of the population, and have shifted from the top decile generally to the next two deciles. In terms of the current occupational composition of those deciles, the groups that have lost out *relatively* have been the big business executives, entrepreneurs, elite (especially self-employed) professionals, and the leading salesmen; those who have gained have been the salaried professionals, the craftsmen, and to a smaller degree, bureaucratic managers and administrators below the highest level, and further down, male clerical and manual workers generally in the urban and bureaucratic sectors of employment.[5]

The height of the income shift came during the New Deal period when government employment substantially took off. This was a period of liberal reform as well as of consciously Keynesian employment policies. Substantial bureaucratization occurred in that period, but not only within government: This is the period of the massive bureaucratization of the private corporations as well. This bureaucratization, I would suggest, was responsible for the income revolution. But notice: It was not a shift from the top to the bottom, despite the liberal and egalitarian rhetoric within the government at the time.

---

[5]What if the occupational composition of the deciles has shifted since before the income revolution? Whatever their composition, we know that the relative proportions of money going to each decile (and within the top decile) have shifted, and we know what occupations are *now* the beneficiaries of this shift. It is conceivable that some occupations have both lost *relative* preponderance of incomes and have also moved out of the top income groups; the latter is not *necessary* for the known shift in decile shares (and hence in Gini coefficients) to have occurred. Conversely, some occupations may have both gained relative income and even moved up into a higher decile of the population; again, the latter is not *necessary*, unless the shift in relative absolute incomes is sufficiently great. Lacking direct information on the occupational composition of income deciles in the 1920s or earlier, we can only estimate that the amount of income shifting that has occurred seems compatible with either considerable stability in occupational composition of the decile shares or some change. I would estimate that the formerly highest-paying occupations are still the highest paying, but that their distance from the next highest-paying occupations has narrowed; and that the presence of the upper working class in the top two deciles is a new development.

The welfare system developed at that point has done nothing to improve the position of the lowest decile groups, unless one assumes that transfer payments keep them out of even direr poverty. Rather, the beneficiaries of the income revolution have been the bureaucratic middle class themselves and particularly favored craft-union enclaves of the upper working class.

At the same time, one notable bureaucratic group did *not* benefit from the expansion of their employment sector: women workers. For bureaucratic position shaping meant an improvement in the male-defined managerial and professional positions, but an actual decline in the relative income position of secretaries, typists, and other positions segregated into a sex-defined, subordinate enclave (Pilcher, 1976: 90).

How has the expansion of educational credentials figured in this income revolution? It has been by the use of educational credentials that the lucrative professions have closed their ranks and upgraded their salaries, and it has been in imitation of their methods that other occupations have "professionalized." The expansion of bureaucracy, especially in the tertiary sector, has been accompanied by the most prominent emphasis on educational requirements of anywhere in the economy (as Table 2.2 indicates). Educational credentials in such organizations go along with spending large proportions of time—and money—on administration and control rather than on production; credentials have been a principal vehicle by which the sinecure sector has been built. The rhetoric of professionalization, of liberal reform, and of educational expansion has been all of a piece; these calls for reforms have gone together as a single mode of argumentation that underlay the transfer of some of the income flow from the upper to the middle class.[6]

Not all of the income shift may be directly explained in this manner. The upper working class—especially the craftsmen who make up a sizable fraction of the top income decile, as well as some of the operatives and foremen—has made gains especially by means of strong craft unions and by advantageous seniority pay systems within the wealthy corporations. But even these mechanisms bear a relation to the shift to a highly credentialized society. That shift has been building up since the late nineteenth century in response to the pressures of a multiethnic version of the economic class struggle and in response to the problems of overproduction and insufficient aggregate demand. Both issues came to a head simultaneously in the New Deal period when ethnic minorities achieved substantial concessions in the national political

---

[6]Why hasn't the creation of these new middle-class jobs brought about increased upward mobility? It has, in a sense. But our measures of mobility are constructed to capture "pure mobility," independent of shifts in the occupational structure. "Pure mobility" rates have not changed because the credential system and bureaucratic employment are no more meritocratic with respect to family background than the organizational forms they replaced.

arena, including governmental legitimation of labor unions, and when the huge credentialized bureaucracies made their largest strides. The same underlying conditions that produced the credential system, with its most prominent effects on the middle class, also produced the powerful forms of labor organization that have benefited the upper working classes. The upper working class does not rely particularly upon formal school credentials to control admission to its ranks (though many craft unions now use high school degree requirements); they use instead the mechanisms of lengthy apprenticeship programs, state licensing procedures, and in many unions, outright nepotism (Greer, 1959). But these (except for the last) are the types of occupational monopolization pioneered by the formally credentialed professions. The same background conditions have operated in each case, and the atmosphere of credentialism has both advertised the path for the upper working class to follow and made it easy to secure acceptance from employers and from the state for restrictive practices of their own educational (apprenticeship) and licensing requirements.

The income revolution of the first half of the twentieth century is all of a piece. It has been carried out under the rhetoric of liberal reform that has simultaneously built up the school system, the highly protected trade unions, massive government employment, and bureaucracy generally. None of these institutions has actually done what it officially claims to be doing. There has been no wholesale revamping of the class structure, nor a shift to widespread equality of opportunity or of distribution. The bureaucratic middle class has gained at the expense of the upper class, but not all bureaucratic workers have gained as a whole: Only the male-designated jobs have benefited, whereas female-designated jobs, although expanding equally rapidly, have not. The upper segment of the working class has achieved a comfortable and well-protected position, while the less-protected mass of the manual labor force has made only modest gains (in the case of urban males), and the lower section—female workers, rural labor, the chronically unemployed, and others living on transfer payments—have gained nothing at all (Pilcher, 1976: 57–59).

The income revolution represents the outcomes of class conflicts. It illustrates once again that these conflicts are not between two large, broadly defined classes, but between a much larger number of contenders. Within the white-collar and blue-collar sectors alike, some classes have won and others have lost.

This is in keeping with the hypothesized effects of a multiethnic and decentralized society. Indeed, the ethnic nature of these multiple class divisions has not disappeared. Particular enclaves continue to be heavily populated by particular ethnic groups. White Protestants tend to be disproportionately in the professions and in entrepreneurial businesses, Catholics heavily in government and bureaucracy generally.[7] Particular craft unions have their own ethnic stamp and set their boundaries against ethnic outsiders (Greer, 1959). Blacks are disproportionately in lower-working-class positions and in specialized sectors of the white-collar world, especially government employment.[8] Thus the lines of class struggle are doubly fragmented, with ethnic bonds continuing to subdivide the interest groups contending over economic spoils.

Given this fragmentation, there are severe restraints upon large-scale, Marxian-style confrontations between class blocs. The multiclass structure and the related credential system shape conflict into other channels. But it is still possible for general, society-wide crises to appear. The focus of such crises is likely to be the market for credentials.

THE LATE TWENTIETH-CENTURY CREDENTIAL CRISIS

As of the 1960s, the credential system went into a state of explicit crisis. The rising credential price of jobs had been going on for many decades, but at this point the change began to be consciously seen as inflationary. With near-universal high school completion and one-half the youth cohort attending college, these formerly valued goals lost much of their appeal. They no longer guaranteed a respectable job, at the high school level, or an elite one, at the college level. At the same time, there was tremendous pressure from subordinated ethnic groups, especially blacks and Latin Americans, for integration into the dominant educational and occupational institutions. The result has been a multifaceted crisis in confidence in the system and a variety of reactions and criticisms.

Initially, in the context of a militant civil rights movement for minority integration, mass student rebellions broke out within the universities. The rebellions took advantage of the state of growing delegitimation of credentials to demand revision of traditional curricular requirements. Such demands were usually put in the form of a shift to greater "relevance," or toward the cultures of the ethnic minorities themselves. But in fact, the alternatives lacked substance; their principal appeal was negative, a reaction against the tra-

---

[7]See sources in footnote 1 to this chapter.

[8]In 1975, 56.5% of black workers were operatives, laborers, or service workers, as compared to 32.8% of whites (*Statistical Abstract*, 1976: Table 601). In the same year, 21% of government employees were minorities, as opposed to 16% of private employees (U.S. Civil Service Commission, 1976; U.S. Economic Opportunity Commission, 1977). It seems especially likely that minority white-collar employees are disproportionately in government jobs.

ditional requirements that were now recognized as purely procedural formalities of the process of gaining a credential. More recently, the idealistic
rhetoric of curricular alternatives has been replaced by a manipulative cynicism. Students electing to remain within the system have adopted the goal of
high grades, irrespective of content and by any means whatsoever, producing
an inflation in college grades, while at the same time achievement levels have
been steadily dropping.

Similarly, educators have reacted to their increasingly uncomfortable
position of attempting to control masses of students in a situation in which
previous legitimating ideals were no longer accepted. Most of the reformers'
schemes—those of Holt, (1964), Kozol (1972), even one of the most radical,
Ivan Illich (1970)—assumed that the real problem was to make education
more relevant, less structured by academic status systems, closer to everyday
concerns, and less regimented by bureaucratic requirements and compulsion.
In these respects, they reflected the rhetoric of student activists. None of them
came to grips with the underlying issue: the fact that education is part of a
system of cultural stratification and that the reason most students are in school
is that they (or their parents on their behalf) want a decent job. This means
that the reasons for going to school are extraneous to whatever goes on in the
classroom. Reformers expecting that intellectual curiosity can be rearoused by
curricular reforms or by changes in the school authority structure were projecting their own intellectual interests onto a mass of students for whom education is merely a means to a nonintellectual end. This even applies to radical
proposals like that of Illich that schools should be taken completely out of the
classroom and into factories, offices, shipyards, or wherever else students
want to learn. This overlooks the fact that most skills are—or can be—learned
on the job; if the idea is that persons should have a chance to try any job they
want, then schools are not what is needed, but rather some device to provide
high interjob mobility.

Most of the "deschooling" talk was another version of Progressive education. It contained the same ideals, many of the same slogans, and it arose
among school teachers at times in which schools have undergone crises of
credential devaluation that destroy belief in their old functions. "Deschooling" is not so much a way of abolishing schools because they are proven
useless, but of revising them internally in order to retain students. The influence on this of teachers' interests in maintaining jobs for themselves is obvious; less obvious is the way in which the proposed curricular and authority
changes—like those of Progressive education half a century earlier—help
reestablish rapport between teachers and students, giving them a common
rhetoric and de-emphasizing the authority relations that have been the focus
of so much rebellion. In all this, "deschooling" simply carries the Progressive
innovations one step further. Indeed, there are many proposals—generally

ncial support, and seem likely to cut it still further in the future. In the
ate sector (especially in higher education), rising operating costs and de-
ng enrollments are likely to force the closing of a considerable number of
tutions.

The underlying source of pressure is the condition of credential inflation.
cation is both more costly and promises less of a payoff for given levels of
lentials than previously; hence students and those who pay their bills are
tively less willing to make the investment (Freeman, 1976: 9–50). Thus
historical peak in the proportion of the youth group attending both high
ool and college was reached in the early 1970s. Since 1972, high school
npletion rates actually fell (*Statistical Abstract,* 1976: Tables 230 and 231).
endance rates at colleges and universities fell off for male students from
% of the 18–19-year-old group, and 29% of the 20–24-year old group in
70, to 50% and 26% for those age groups in 1975. Only an increased
endance rate for females—from 42% of the 18–19-year-olds and 15% of
 20–24-year-olds in 1950, to 44% and 19% respectively in 1975—offset
s trend (*Statistical Abstract,* 1976: Table 191). The survival of the tra-
onal educational credential, then, seems to be increasingly tied to the
orts of women to break out of their subordinate occupational position,
ile male employment may well be shifting into a separate set of trades-
d-business-controlled credentialing institutions.

The credential system, severely challenged at one point, seems to be
haping itself in new directions. From a long-term viewpoint, it may be the
se that the crisis of the 1960s and 1970s is a temporary one, and that
edentialing sequences may extend indefinitely into the future. Once tempor-
y periods of imbalance are past and the numbers of students return to a
el at which inflation in the credential price of jobs is kept at an acceptably
idual rate, it may be that the finances of schools will stabilize. Possibly even
 some point in the future, the system could begin to grow again.

Of course, the growth of the credential system has not occurred simply
 its own dynamics, but in interaction with the struggle for economic position
d with the level of economic productivity. The accumulation of highly
icient capital has steadily decreased the labor needs of the economy. The
nerican industrial plant operates at only about half of full capacity, and a
ntinual problem has been unemployment and underemployment and the
ated problem of maintaining aggregate consumer demand. It is here that
 can see the economic importance of our educational system—not because
the technical skills that it might provide, but rather as a counterbalance to
cess industrial capacity. This works in two ways: Both because education is
major area of government spending (7.5% of the GNP in 1975; *Statistical
bstract,* 1976: Table 183) and because it absorbs a considerable portion of
e labor force as students. The 9.7 million college and university students

made by those who consider themselves educational "li
even advocated by adherents of "deschooling" plans–
pulsory education requirements to age 18 or beyond.

Outside the schools, there has been a heightened c
as insufficiently relevant to jobs and a revival of the techr
oric that was so prominent in the mid-nineteenth-centur
education. As in the previous crisis, we see the reemerg
among different types of educational institutions. The con
and higher educational sequence has been challenged
commercial trade schools, business-operated training
crowding of professional and paraprofessional school
schools.

Nevertheless, given the evidence that job skills of a
acquired in the work situation rather than in a formal trai
apparent that the technical training rhetoric is a response
credential market rather than a substantively significant ch
content. New types of credentials are proposed because
confidence in the value of the old types. Hence the infla
credentials seems to be building up in new directions. V
previously unprecedented use of Ph.D.s in accounting a
quire business jobs; we also hear of a massive expansi
external credentialing in the business school sector. Skill
tors, and realtors continually establish more restrictive l
usually based on their own formal training requirements.
tions have established their own training programs.

The effect of these sorts of shifts is not to open up
channels, but to increasingly monopolize and control t
example, major automobile companies and chain stores a
ing auto repair jobs for graduates of their own training p
only replaces the current—and technically effective—pat
acquiring skills through their own experience, but also r
control of procedures (so-called "preventive maintenanc
replacement rather than repair of parts) that tighten their
consumers. In general, the emerging pattern is to build up
tialing in new sectors where the traditional school credent
trated.

The shift to private credentialing is the counterpart of tl
the public, formal school credentialing system. Apart from cc
claims, the crisis has a material aspect. The public schools a
are facing difficulties from two directions. In the context of
affecting all prices in the material economy, schools have t
luxuries. In the public sector, taxpayers' reactions are cu

alone would add 10% to the labor force. Adding any sizable portion of the 15.7 million high school students would, of course, increase the problem proportionately (*Statistical Abstract,* 1976: Tables 185 and 571). Cutting back on education to any considerable degree would tend to have disastrous economic consequences.

Thus the credential system of occupational placement is caught between opposing forces. On one side the system has become central to propping up an economy of excess productive capacity and surplus labor. On the other side the system has become extremely expensive and relatively unrewarding for many individual investors and for its political supporters, Although a rough balance continues to be possible, the potential for crisis exists in either direction. Too rapid growth in the credential market brings disillusionment and withdrawal of material investment in it; too little investment, on the other hand, feeds economic depression.

VARIETIES OF SINECURE POLITICS

A number of different political positions have been taken regarding the credential market. Few of them explicitly recognize the arbitrary currency nature of the educational system; most operate within some more familiar legitimating rhetoric. Nevertheless, they might be named:

Credential capitalism is the traditional laissez faire attitude toward individual competition in the credential marketplace. It naively assumes that one should get as much education as possible in order to cash in on as much career advancement as possible. As individualistic advice, it ignores aggregate effects on the value of the credential currency, or simply proposes to override them by outcompeting others, at whatever level it takes.

Credential socialism is the program of government intervention to equalize the distribution of educational opportunities. Like traditional political socialism, it has failed to have much effect on the underlying system producing the inequalities and instead has added on to it a superstructure that has mainly been successful in redistributing some of the wealth to itself. Like political socialism (including that which has gone under such American labels as "liberalism"), credential socialism is a popular position among employees of the alleged redistribution system itself: in the one case government bureaucrats, in the other case, teachers and administrators.

These have been the traditionally dominant ideologies about American education. More recently, there has been an upsurge of demands by particular ethnic groups for more opportunities for themselves to acquire credentials. Sometimes this has been demanded with socialist–egalitarian rhetoric, sometimes in the name of ethnic cultural nationalism. In either case, its actual material goals are entrée on easier terms into the credential system, a demand entirely analogous to the traditional pattern in American politics of ethnic groups demanding a share of political patronage. This might simply be called **ethnic-patrimonial credentialism** or **patronage-credentialism.**

In reaction to such pressures from subordinated minorities, some members of dominant ethnic groups have created what might be called **credential fascism:** the effort to exclude particular minorities on principle. Earlier versions of racial ideologies have been updated for this purpose in the form of genetic arguments for inherited IQ differences. That this is a highly ideological stance is apparent from the evidence (cited in Chapters 1 and 2) that IQ predicts success only *within* the school system, and that the link between school success and occupational success is an entirely artificial one. Thus credential fascism attempts to shore up an arbitrary system of domination as the exclusive possession of its own ethnic group.

In a different direction, we find an upsurge of **credential radicalism:** the advocates of "free schools" or "deschooling" mentioned earlier. Their politics of liberating the schools by giving control to a communal group of students (and sometimes teachers) is rather like an extreme version of "communism in one country." For local communal control of the credential-producing institution does nothing to affect the larger credential market within which they exist. If, as such schools usually attempt, their policy is to make credentials easy for students to attain, perhaps even automatically awarded (whether giving all "A" grades or automatically conferred degrees), they simply contribute to galloping credential inflation. In the larger context, such regimes tend to destroy their own economic base.

In my opinion, there are only two honest and realistic positions in regard to credentialism. One might be called **credential Keynesianism.** This would explicitly recognize that education creates an artificial credential currency and that this is economically useful to offset deficiencies of aggregate demand. Thus both investment in the school system and the credentialing of occupations would be encouraged, not in order to promote work efficiency or equal opportunity, but simply in the interest of keeping the economy running. The danger of this kind of policy, like that of ordinary economic Keynesianism, is inflation, but this can be taken as a side effect of the system to be accepted and managed by quantitative manipulation of whatever variables are under government control. In other words, one could decide to work openly within the sinecure system, to recognize the migration of leisure into the interior of jobs, and to deliberately set out to enhance such sinecures.

Such a policy, of course, has implicitly been in force for some time. Schools have often been supported for reasons of employment policy, and there has been a long-standing liberalization within the system that has affected the ethos of many jobs, making them more casual and less subject to ritual acknowledgments that nothing but productive work is going on. An open, unhypocritical recognition of the sinecure component in our society would certainly constitute a cultural revolution in public honesty and would make it easier to assess and control the effects of the factors affecting sinecures.

My own preference, however, is for an opposite policy: **credential abolitionism.**[9] The prospects of continuing to expand the credential system indefinitely, to let job requirements inflate to the point where 4 years of college is needed for a manual laborer or 20 years of postdoctoral study is required for a technical profession, would be exceedingly alienating to all concerned. Moreover, it would not affect the rate of mobility, if past precedent is any indication, nor change the order of stratification among ethnic groups; it would simply reproduce their order at higher and higher levels of education. The alternative, to freeze the credential system at some point by allowing only given numbers of students to reach given levels, would be to freeze the existing system of stratification and to keep credential barriers in place that segregate the labor force into noncompeting sectors. Existing advantages of monopolization of lucrative job sectors would be maintained. Either way, letting the credential system expand, or holding it at its present level, would maintain existing stratification and would have culturally debilitating effects as well.

A serious change would depend upon abolishing the credential system. This does not mean abolishing the schools, but it does mean returning them

---

[9]The various forms of "credential politics" might be labeled more generally as factions in "sinecure politics." This generates some interesting historical parallels. "Sinecure capitalism," in fact, existed in the late Middle Ages in Europe, and in many other agrarian societies, where sinecures (prebends) could actually be bought and sold. The very mention of this is taboo for our society, though, and "sinecure capitalists" are doomed to operate under a misleading ideology. "Sinecure socialism," on the other hand, is rather close to the goal of Marxists, who could share out equally the fruits of superproductive technology if they would propose to do this by distributing occupational positions instead of incomes. "Sinecure ethnic-patrimonialism" or "sinecure patronage" is familiar already: It is what ethnic patronage politics always was. "Sinecure fascism" would be the equivalent to returning to the medieval principle reserving nonwork positions for a hereditary aristocracy. "Sinecure radicalism" would be making work relations highly egalitarian; current movements for participatory democracy are quite close to this, but without yet recognizing that most of what is being shared is not work responsibilities but on-the-job leisure and on-the-job politicking. "Sinecure Keynesianism" means a radical extension of WPA-style make-work hiring; some short-lived revolutions such as the Paris Commune of 1871 carried this out fairly widely. "Sinecure abolitionism" has its religious precedents, notably the Protestant Reformation, which led to the elimination of monasteries and many other church prebends. In that case, the result was government confiscation of these properties, greatly enriching the new absolutist state—the real economic significance of the Reformation. Whether there would be analogous consequences of a modern-day "sinecure Reformation" is worth careful consideration.

to a situation where they must support themselves by their own intrinsic products rather than by the currency value of their degrees. Legally, this would mean abolishing compulsory school requirements and making formal credential requirements for employment illegal. Within the framework of civil rights legislation, such legal challenge to credential requirements has already established precedents (White and Francis, 1976). Since the evidence strongly shows that credentials do not provide work skills that cannot be acquired on the job, and that access to credentials is inherently biased toward particular groups, the case for discrimination is easy to make.

The main advantages of legal decredentialing would be two. It would improve the level of culture within those schools that continue to exist, and it would provide the opening wedge of a serious effort to overcome economic inequality.

The expansion of the credential-producing school system to mammoth proportions has made intellectual culture into a short-term obstacle for students to pass through on their way to their credentials. Thus it is hardly surprising that high school achievement test scores have fallen precipitously in the period since 1963 (Advisory Panel on the Scholastic Aptitude Test Score Decline, 1977), when school promotion became not only perfunctory but near universal. The pressures to get high college grades in order to enter graduate schools has had a similar effect upon substantive intellectual concerns. Humanistic culture has become very nearly the exclusive province of professional teachers of the humanities, and they themselves have turned their subjects from cultural ends to be created and enjoyed in themselves into the mere basis of a currency of numbers of publications on a professional *vitae* by which their careers in academic bureaucracies are made.

In science as well, it is likely that smaller would be better. Despite the self-serving rhetoric of university lobbyists, it is not at all necessary to have an extremely large component of university research to support the national economy or national security. Most practical inventions, in fact, are made in applied settings, and the basic science that they may draw upon tends to come from relatively small sectors of research carried out decades earlier (Sherwin and Isenson, 1967; Price, 1969). Moreover, the massive size of current American science is not *proportionately* efficient; the much smaller but proportionately more creative and better integrated organization of British science shows the superiority of a more elitist structure (see figures presented in Collins, 1975: 578). In the very large system, on the contrary, a kind of bureaucratization of scientific ideas takes place so that specialties are minute, mutually remote, and hard to integrate; information retrieval problems are serious; and the huge numbers of researchers enforces a *lingua franca* of the most rigidly operational and quantifiable concepts, to the denigration of more powerful theoretical ideas. The latter sort of problem especially afflicts the American social sciences, making them prematurely specialized around quantitative techniques while ignoring theoretical issues that give meaning to research. One might well claim that American social science—and natural science as well—has been living off of theoretical ideas that it has itself been unable to produce, either by importing the ideas from Europe or actually importing European theorists (as in the case of the refugees of the 1930s and 1940s, who have led American sciences in the last generation).

In sum, existing levels of mass credential production are unfavorable to American science and especially to humanistic culture. Further expansion of the credential system would be even more debilitating. Probably the initial building up of the educational system in the early twentieth century encouraged high-level scientific production, but the scale of operations has long passed the level of diminishing returns.

The other major argument for decredentialing is that only in this way can we move toward overcoming income inequality. Educational requirements have become a major basis of separating work into distinct positions and career lines, and hence in keeping labor markets fragmented. The gap between blue-collar and white-collar jobs constitutes a barrier to direct promotion in almost all organizations and is upheld by the disparity in educational requirements for each. These requirements are not necessary for the learning of work skills of these different sorts, but operate precisely to prevent members of one group from having the on-job opportunities to learn the skills of the other. Similarly, specialized "professional" and "technical" activities are reserved for separate labor pools by the same means. Thus it is not only ethnic and sexual segregation that produces "dual labor markets" (Edwards *et al.,* 1975), but above all educational requirements that have become built into the definitions of "positions" themselves. Moreover, as direct ethnic and sexual discrimination becomes increasingly illegitimate and subject to legal challenge, educational discrimination becomes increasingly relied upon as a surrogate means of group domination.[10]

Hypothetically, income equality would occur if there were no barriers to movement among occupations. Hence positions that paid less than others, or whose work is especially dirty or unpleasant, would have to raise their wages to attract labor; positions that paid more than the average, or that had especially attractive work (such as planning and giving orders), would attract a surplus of applicants and could lower their wages. It has been proposed that

---

[10]Educational requirements were highest in those organizations making the strongest efforts to racially integrate employment, according to the 1967 San Francisco Bay Area Employer survey reported in Chapter 2.

educational barriers are the principal impediment to this income-equalizing tendency of a free labor market (Thomas, 1956). This is correct as far as it goes. But eliminating credential requirements would be only the opening wedge of the necessary restructuring. Under existing conditions, a large surplus of qualified applicants for managerial positions would not likely lower their salaries (Thurow, 1975); the number of positions would remain limited, and those few who did hold such positions would act to appropriate high salaries in any case.

This is clear from a realistic model of organizational behavior that sees power (i.e., "political labor") rather than productivity as the key to income and advancement. Hence organizations themselves are the obstacle to a freely operating labor market. Similarly, although the elimination of credential requirements might increase competition within the professions, this would not necessarily eliminate stratification within any particular profession. Lawyers and engineers with links to wealthy organizational clients would still get large fees, and only the most decentralized and small-scale aspects of legal services would be subject to competitive price reductions.

Nevertheless, elimination of educational requirements for jobs would be a necessary step in any overall restructuring of the occupational world to produce greater income equality. The key would be to break down *current forms of positional property*. Managerial work could be brought back into responsiveness to labor market pressures if it did not constitute a distinctive, long-term "position" but was one activity to be shared among workers who carried out immediate production as well. By job rotation across the existing lines of authority and specialization, all types of work would become subject to a common labor pool and respond to the same wage conditions. This would mean that opportunities for learning *various* kinds of work on the job, including technical and managerial work, would have to be rotated or otherwise widely shared, possibly by rotating apprenticeship of "assistant-to" assignments. To do so would require eliminating current definitions of jobs as allegedly based upon prior, external preparation by specialized education.

Educational credentials, then, are not the only basis of barriers to a free labor market, but they are a crucial component of the system of barriers that would have to be removed. Secretaries, for example, are in a perfect situation for on-job learning of managerial skills. At present, the sex-caste barrier defines their positions as a separate enclave, however, so that virtually no secretary is ever promoted to take her boss's position. Nevertheless, this is not only technically feasible, but once was the standard promotion line, before the late nineteenth century, when secretaries were males acting as apprentices for later administrative responsibility.

The current feminist movement has by and large ignored this form of positional discrimination; its emphasis has been on getting into the elite professions and managerial positions by following existing career channels—hence female college enrollments have gone up rapidly even as male enrollments have tended to decline. Desirable as this may be, it is an elitist reform that will have little effect on the economic prospects of the majority of women, especially in the vast clerical sector of bureaucracies. Indeed, applicants bringing more educational credentials to the professional and managerial labor markets will further raise, and in turn specialize, the credential requirements of those positions, making them even less accessible to promotion from within from the secretarial ghetto.

In this sense, a better long-term strategy for overcoming sexual stratification in employment would be to press for job reshaping instead of educational credentials, to explicitly substitute on-job apprenticeship as a means of managerial recruitment.

How might the credential restructuring of a strong profession such as medicine take place? As it stands, American medical training is attached at the end of a very long and expensive education that keeps the supply of physicians low and their incomes and social backgrounds very high. This formal education appears to have little real practical relevance; most actual training is done on the job in the most informal circumstances, through the few years of internship and residency. The existing medical structure is not only highly expensive, inefficient, and inegalitarian in terms of career access; but it is also tied to a system of job segregation in which the menial tasks are shunted off onto a separate medical hierarchy of women with the assistance of low-paid ethnic minorities in service jobs with no career possibilities.

It is likely that far greater quality and efficiency could be attained by eliminating the distinction between nurses and doctors and combining their career sequences with that of hospital orderlies. (No doubt this would offend the status concerns of doctors, but it would at least challenge them to take their altruistic claims seriously.) All medical careers would begin with a position as orderly, which would be transformed into the first stage of a possible apprenticeship for physicians. After a given number of years, successful candidates could leave for a few years of medical school (2 years seems sufficient background for most practitioners, and this could be done equally well at an undergraduate or postgraduate level, with the option being left open) and then return to the hospital for advanced apprenticeship training of the sort now given in internship and residency programs. The motivation of orderlies would be enhanced, and the implicit opportunities for apprenticeship-type training could simply be brought into the foreground. Advanced specialties could continue to be taught as they now are—through further on-job training; only medical researchers would be involved in lengthy schooling. The overall effect would certainly be less expensive and would provide better medical care from all personnel; there is no evidence to make one believe that the technical quality of treatment would suffer.[11]

Similarly, even an explicitly education-based hierarchy, such as a university department, could open up its career channels to secretaries on an apprenticeship basis. If one regards it as important that department and higher-level supervisers should be academic professionals, it still would be possible to merge the various training sequences or rotate the positional duties themselves. Students could be required to do secretarial duties as part of their training, and secretaries could be given the opportunity to acquire academic training as part of their work. This would make for changes in the structure of power, to be sure, that might not be palatable to incumbents of currently dominant positions, but such power differences are the crux of the obstacle to greater income equality.

Fundamental changes in the structure of inequality, then, and in the quality of modern culture, imply the abolition of credentialing. A thorough-going program of this sort would eliminate approximately half of existing inequality. It would not directly touch the other source of inequality, the distribution of physical and financial capital. But socialist programs for overcoming this inequality attack only half the problem; Gini coefficients in socialist countries are approximately one-half of those in capitalist countries, averaging around .240 in the former and .440 in the latter (Stack, 1976). But even these lower Gini coefficients indicate a structure of *occupational* inequality than remains when capital is socialized. The socialist countries as well as the capitalist ones still need a second revolution.

I have argued that decredentialing of this order would have momentous, even revolutionary consequences. It could not be carried out without a thorough restructuring of organizational forms. This would be especially necessary because the currently existing credential system helps counteract the problem of excess capacity, and some other means of keeping up em-

---

[11]To repeat the relevant points cited in Chapters 1 and 6: Medical school requirements are essentially arbitrary screening devices, as virtually no one ever flunks out of medical school; subsequent performance bears no relation to school grades; and the *actual* practical training of doctors is of the most casual sort—orderlies probably could acquire as much over the course of their work experience, especially if they are at all motivated (contrary to the enforced expectations of their current roles) to acquire it. Moreover, a reformed medical system ought to be more technically efficacious than the one that exists now. American medical care, despite the haze of national glorification in its own pronouncements and in the mass media, is a good deal less effective than that provided in the less professionally autonomous medical systems of Europe. This is illustrated by the higher infant mortality rate and lower longevity in the United States than in almost every European country, despite the superiority of the United States in GNP per capita of from 50 to 300% (Taylor and Hudson 1972: 253, 314).

ployment would have to be found. In the context of a thorough-going reform, such measures would not necessarily be difficult, by institutionalizing a shorter work week and/or by giving longer vacations. Under current conditions, of course, such measures are much more difficult to implement because of the income redistribution they imply; instead, spending on education has been a politically cheap way of practicing Keynesian economics in America.

The issue of credential stratification points us at the central feature of occupational stratification today: property in positions. To restructure these would be a more fundamental economic revolution than any we have yet seen. For that very reason, we cannot expect this reform to be easily made. It is possible that organizational and professional career hierarchies could be restructured piecemeal by local action. But local resistance would be hard to overcome without a widespread atmosphere of reform and a highly mobilized movement in this direction. It is far easier for allegedly liberal or even radical movements to continue the long-standing tradition of expanding access to the credential system. These efforts will only extend the inflationary nature of that system. In that direction, one can foresee that current issues around educational costs, discrimination, and integration will go on unresolved into the indefinite future.

To be realistic, one should bet on an expansion of current credentialism, even though this brings reformers no closer to their avowed goals than a donkey chasing a carrot held over its nose. This means, though, that crises of the class struggle continually threaten, not only within the material economy, but within the cultural economy as well. And using the educational system as a basis for an arbitrary currency of domination means that it suffers a continually increasing internal contradiction in the consciousness of its inhabitants. For all its claims to be raising the level of rationality of its students, education itself operates as part of a larger system that denigrates its own contents and ignores any insights it might provide into the nature of that system.

Hence although it would be unrealistic to expect a decredentialing revolution in the short run, it would be equally unrealistic to rule it out in the long run. Given the trend of credential expansion toward potentially absurd levels, it seems more than likely that credential abolitionism will come to the fore whenever any very sharp imbalance occurs between the size of the school population and the distributional processes of the material economy.

In effect, we are very much more like a tribal society than we like to admit. Despite our self-image of rational control, our institutions are no more reflectively chosen than the tribal initiation rites, secret societies, and implacable gods that our educational and occupational procedures resemble so much. Or to shift the analogy to more large-scale societies, we are subject to the same forces that transformed India over the centuries into a series of closed occupational castes, or that made medieval Europe a network of monopolistic guilds. Such societies undergo convulsions from forces beyond their control, as in the Reformation, which destroyed the religious currency upon which the medieval monopolies were legitimated. In the long run, unless we raise our own level of rational control over our institutions, we can expect that such forces will be waiting for us.

References

Adams, S.
    1957 Origins of American occupational elites, 1900–1955. *American Journal of Sociology*
    62: 360–368.
Advisory Panel on the Scholastic Aptitude Test Score Decline
    1977 On further examination: Report of the Advisory Panel on the Scholastic Aptitude
    Test Score Decline. New York: The College Board.
Althusser, L.
    1971 Ideology and ideological state apparatus. In *Lenin and philosophy and other essays.*
    London: New Left Books.
Anastasi, A.
    1967 Psychology, psychologists, and psychological testing. *American Psychologist* **22:**
    297–306.
Arensberg, C. C., and S. T. Kimball
    1948 *Family and community in Ireland.* Cambridge, Massachusetts: Harvard Univ. Press.
Aries, P.
    1962 *Centuries of childhood.* New York: Knopf.
Armytage, W. H. G.
    1961 *A social history of engineering.* London: Faber and Faber.
    1965 *The rise of the technocrats.* London: Routledge and Kegan Paul.
Artz, F. B.
    1966 *The development of higher technical education in France.* Cambridge, Massachusetts:
    M.I.T. Press.

Bailyn, B.
  1960 *Education in the forming of American society.* New York: Random House.
Bajema, C. J.
  1968 Interrelations among intellectual ability, educational attainment, and occupational achievement. *Sociology of Education* **41**: 317–319.
Baller, W. R., D. C. Charles, and E. L. Miller
  1967 Midlife attainment of the mentally retarded. *Genetic Psychology Monographs* **42**: 235–327.
Baltzell, E. D.
  1958 *An American business aristocracy.* New York: Macmillan.
Banfield, E. C.
  1958 *The moral basis of a backward society.* New York: Free Press.
Banfield, E. C., and J. Q. Wilson
  1963 *City politics.* Cambridge, Massachusetts: Harvard Univ. Press.
Barnard, C. I.
  1938 *The functions of the executive.* Cambridge, Massachusetts: Harvard Univ. Press.
Bartholomew, J.
  1954 *Physical world atlas.* New York: American Map Company.
Becker, H. S.
  1961 Schools and systems of stratification. In *Education, economy, and society,* edited by A. H. Halsey, J. Floud, and C. A. Anderson. New York: Free Press.
Becker, H. S., B. Geer, and E. C. Hughes
  1968 *Making the grade.* New York: Wiley.
Bell, D.
  1973 *The coming of post-industrial society.* New York: Basic Books.
Bell, H. M.
  1940 Matching youth and jobs. Washington: American Council on Education.
Ben-David, J.
  1971 *The scientist's role in society.* Englewood Cliffs, New Jersey: Prentice-Hall.
Ben-David, J., and A. Zloczower
  1962 Universities and academic systems in modern societies. *European Journal of Sociology* **3**: 44–85.
  1963–1964. Professions in the class systems of present-day societies. *Current Sociology* 12: 247–330.
Bendix, R.
  1956 *Work and authority in industry.* New York: Wiley.
Bensman, J., and A. Vidich
  1971 *The new American society.* New York: Quadrangle Books.
Bereday, G. Z. F., ed.
  1969 *Essays on world education.* New York: Oxford Univ. Press.
Berg, I.
  1970 *Education and jobs.* New York: Praeger.
Berlant, J. L.
  1973 *Medical professionalism and monopolistic institutionalization in the United States and Britain.* Unpublished Ph.D. thesis, Univ. of California, Berkeley.
Berle, A. A., and G. C. Means
  1968 *The modern corporation and private property.* New York: Harcourt.
Bernstein, B.
  1971, 1973, 1975 *Class, codes, and control.* 3 volumes. London: Routledge and Kegan Paul.

Bidwell, C. E.
1965 The school as a formal organization. In *Handbook of organizations,* edited by J. G. March. Chicago: Rand McNally.
Billington, R.
1938 *The protestant crusade.* New York: Rinehart.
Blau, P. M.
1955 *The dynamics of bureaucracy.* Chicago: Univ. of Chicago Press.
Blau, P. M., and O. D. Duncan
1967 *The American occupational structure.* New York: Wiley.
Blewett, J. E., ed.
1965 *Higher education in postwar Japan.* Tokyo: Sophia Univ. Press.
Bloch, M.
1964 *Feudal society.* Chicago: Univ. of Chicago Press.
Block, N. J., and G. Dworkin, eds.
1976 *The IQ controversy.* New York: Pantheon Books.
Boudon, R.
1973 *Education, opportunity, and social inequality.* New York: Wiley.
Bourdieu, P., L. Boltanski, and M. de Saint Martin
1974 Les stratégies de reconversion: Les classes sociales et le système d'enseignement. *Social Science Information* **12:** 61–113.
Bourdieu, P., and J. C. Passeron
1964 *Les héritiers.* Paris: Les Editions de Minuit.
1977 *Reproduction.* Beverly Hills, California: Sage Publications.
Bowles, S., and H. Gintis
1976 *Schooling in capitalist America.* New York: Basic Books.
Boyle, R. P.
1969 Functional dilemmas in the development of learning. *Sociology of Education* **42:** 71–90.
Braverman, H.
1974 *Labor and monopoly capital.* New York: Monthly Review Press.
Bright, J. R.
1958 Does automation raise skill requirements? *Harvard Business Review* **36:** 85–97.
Brunschwig, H.
1947 *La crise d'état Prussien.* Paris: Presses Universitaires de France.
Calhoun, D.
1960 *The American civil engineer, origins and conflict.* Cambridge, Massachusetts: Harvard Univ. Press.
Callahan, R.
1962 *Education and the cult of efficiency.* Chicago: Univ. of Chicago Press.
Calvert, M. A.
1967 *The mechanical engineer in America, 1830–1910.* Baltimore: Johns Hopkins Press.
Carlin, J. E.
1962 *Lawyers on their own.* New Brunswick: Rutgers Univ. Press.
Carnoy, M.
1974 *Education as cultural imperialism.* New York: David McKay.
Carr-Saunders, A. M., and P. A. Wilson
1933 *The professions.* London: Oxford Univ. Press.
Carver, G. W.
1965 *Two centuries of medicine: A history of the school of medicine, university of Pennsylvania.* Philadelphia: Lippincott.

Chadwick, O.
    1972 *The reformation.* Baltimore: Penguin Books.
Chandler, A. D.
    1959 The beginnings of "big business" in American industry. *Business History Review*
    33: 1–31.
    1962 *Strategy and structure, chapters in the history of American business enterprise.*
    Cambridge, Massachusetts; M.I.T. Press.
    1968 The coming of big business. In *The comparative approach to American history,*
    edited by C. V. Woodward. New York: Basic Books.
Cicourel, A. V., K. H. Jennings, S. H. M. Jennings, K. C. W. Leiter, R. MacKay, H. Olehan, and
D. R. Roth
    1974 *Language use and school performance.* New York: Academic Press.
Clark, B. R.
    1960 The "cooling-out" function in higher education. *American Journal of Sociology* **65:**
    569–576.
    1962 *Educating the expert society.* San Francisco: Chandler.
Clark, H. F., and H. S. Sloan
    1966 *Classrooms on main street.* New York: Teachers College Press.
Coates, C. H., and R. J. Pelligrin
    1957 Executives and supervisors: Informal factors in differential bureaucratic promotion.
    Administrative Science Quarterly **2:** 200–215.
Cochran, T. C., and W. Miller
    1961 *The age of enterprise.* New York: Harper and Row.
Coleman, J. S.
    1961 *The adolescent society.* New York: Free Press.
    1966 *Equality of educational opportunity.* U. S. Office of Education. Washington, D.C.:
    U.S. Government Printing Office.
Collins, O., M. Dalton, and D. Roy
    1946 Restriction of output and social cleavage in industry. *Applied Anthropology* **5:** 1–14.
Collins, R.
    1969 *Education and employment.* Unpublished Ph.D. thesis, Univ. of California, Berkeley.
    1971 A conflict theory of sexual stratification. *Social Problems* **19:** 1–21.
    1974 Where are educational requirements for employment highest? *Sociology of Education*
    47: 419–442.
    1975 *Conflict sociology: Toward an explanatory science.* New York: Academic Press.
    1977 Some comparative principles of educational stratification. *Harvard Educational Re-
    view* **47:** 1–27.
    1978 Some principles of long-term social change: The territorial power of states. In *Re-
    search in social movements, conflicts, and change,* volume 1, edited by L. Kriesberg.
    Greenwich, Connecticut: JAI Press.
Cox, S. G.
    1968 *Relationships between student scores on various predictor measures and-vocational
    success.* Iowa City: Unpublished Ph.D. thesis, Univ. of Iowa.
Cremin, L. A.
    1961 *The transformation of the school.* New York: Knopf.
Crozier, M.
    1964 *The bureaucratic phenomenon.* Chicago: Univ. of Chicago Press.
Curoe, P. R. V.
    1926 *Educational attitudes and policies of organized labor in the United States.* New York:
    Teachers College Press, No. 201.

Curti, M.
  1935 *The social ideas of American educators.* New York: Scribner's.
Cutler, L. N.
  1939 The legislative monopolies achieved by small business. *Yale Law Journal* **48:** 851–856.
Dalton, M.
  1951 Informal factors in career achievement. *American Journal of Sociology* **56:** 407–415.
  1959 *Men who manage.* New York: Wiley.
Davis, J. A.
  1965 *Undergraduate career decisions.* Chicago: Aldine.
De Charms, R., and G. H. Moeller
  1962 Values expressed in American children's readers. *Journal of Abnormal and Social Psychology* **64:** 136–142.
Denison, E. F.
  1965 Education and economic productivity. In *Education and public policy,* edited by S. Harris. Berkeley: McCutchen.
Dill, W. R., T. L. Hilton, and W. R. Reitman
  1962 *The new managers.* Englewood Cliffs, New Jersey: Prentice-Hall.
Domhoff, G. W.
  1967 *Who rules America?* Englewood Cliffs, New Jersey: Prentice-Hall.
Drake, L. R., H. R. Kaplan, and R. A. Stone
  1972 How do employers value the interview? *Journal of College Placement* **33:** 47–51.
Duncan, B.
  1964 Dropouts and the unemployed. *Journal of Political Economy* **73:** 121–134.
  1967 Education and social background. *American Journal of Sociology* **72:** 263–372.
Duncan, B., and O. D. Duncan
  1968 Minorities and the process of stratification. *American Sociological Review* **33:** 356–364.
Duncan, O. D.
  1965 The trend of occupational mobility in the United States. *American Sociological Review* **30:** 491–498.
  1966a Intelligence and achievement: Preliminary results. *Eugenics Quarterly* 13: April.
  1966b Intelligence and achievement: Further calculations. *Eugenics Quarterly.* 13: July.
  1968 Ability and achievement. *Eugenics Quarterly* 15: 1–11.
Duncan, O. D., and R. W. Hodge
  1963 Education and occupational mobility: A regression analysis. *American Journal of Sociology* **68:** 629–644.
Eckland, B. K.
  1964 Social class and college graduation: Some misconceptions corrected. *American Journal of Sociology* **70:** 36–50.
  1965 Academic ability, higher education, and occupational mobility. *American Sociological Review* **30:** 735–746.
Edwards, R., M. Reich, and D. Gordon
  1975 *Labor market segmentation.* Lexington, Massachusetts: D. C. Heath.
Emmanuel, A.
  1972 *Unequal exchange.* New York: Monthly Review Press.
Ensign, F. C.
  1921 *Compulsory school attendance and child labor.* Iowa City: Athens Press.
Epstein, C. F.
  1970 *Woman's Place.* Berkeley: Univ. of California Press.

Etzioni, A.
1961 *A comparative analysis of complex organizations.* New York: Free Press.
Farley, R., and A. I. Hermalin
1971 Family stability: A comparison of trends between blacks and whites. *American Sociological Review* **36:** 1–17.
Featherman, D. L.
1971 The socioeconomic achievement of white religio-ethnic subgroups: Social and psychological explanations. *American Sociological Review* **36:** 207–222.
Finch, J. K.
1960 *The story of engineering.* New York: Doubleday.
Fisher, B. M.
1967 *Industrial education.* Madison: Univ. of Wisconsin Press.
Flexner, A.
1910 *Medical education in the United States and Canada.* Bulletin No. 4: 29–36. New York: Carnegie Foundation for the Advancement of Teaching.
1940 *An autobiography.* New York: Simon and Schuster.
Folger, J. K., and C. B. Nam
1964 Trends in education in relation to the occupational structure. *Sociology of Education* **38:** 19–33.
1967 *Education of the American population.* U. S. Bureau of the Census, Washington, D.C.: U.S. Government Printing Office.
Franke, W.
1960 *The reform and abolition of the traditional Chinese examination system.* Cambridge, Massachusetts: Harvard Univ. Press.
Freeman, R. B.
1976 *The over-educated American.* New York: Academic Press.
Friedman, M., and S. S. Kuznets
1945 *Income from independent professional practice.* New York: National Bureau of Economic Research.
Galbraith, J. K.
1967 *The new industrial state.* Boston: Houghton Mifflin.
Gans, H. J.
1962 *The urban villages.* New York: Free Press.
Gates, P. W.
1960 *The farmer's age.* New York: Holt, Rinehart and Winston.
Gerstl, J. E., and S. P. Hutton
1966 *Engineers: The anatomy of a profession.* London: Tavistock.
Getzels, J. W., and P. W. Jackson
1962 *Creativity and intelligence.* New York: Wiley.
Giddens, A.
1973 *The class structure of advanced societies.* New York: Barnes and Noble.
Gilb, C. L.
1966 *Hidden hierarchies: The professions and government.* New York: Harper and Row.
Glaser, B. G., ed.
1968 *Organizational careers: A source book for theory.* Chicago: Aldine.
Glaser, W. A.
1963 American and foreign hospitals: Some sociological comparisons. In *The hospital in modern society,* edited by Eliot Friedson. New York: Free Press.
Glenn, N., and R. Hyland
1967 Religious preference and worldly success. *American Sociological Review* **32:** 73–85.

Goode, W. J.
1957 Community within a community: The professions. *American Sociological Review* **22:** 194–200.
Gooding, J.
1971 The engineers are redesigning their own profession. *Fortune* **83:** 72–75, 142–146.
Gordon, M. M.
1964 *Assimilation in American life.* New York: Oxford Univ. Press.
Gordon, M. S., and M. Thal-Larsen
1969 *Employer policies in a changing labor market.* Berkeley: Institute of Industrial Relations, Univ. of California.
Gordon, R. A., and J. E. Howell
1959 *Higher education for business.* New York: Columbia Univ. Press.
Goslin, D. A.
1966 *The search for ability.* New York: Russell Sage.
Gouldner, A. W.
1976 *The dialectic of ideology and technology.* New York: Seabury Press.
Granick, D.
1960 *The European executive.* New York: Doubleday.
Greeley, A. H.
1970 Religious intermarriage in a denominational society. *American Journal of Sociology* **75:** 949–952.
1974 Political participation among ethnic groups in the United States. *American Journal of Sociology* **80:** 170–204.
Greer, C.
1972 *The great school legend: A revisionist interpretation of American public education.* New York: Basic Books.
Greer, S. A.
1959 *Last man in: Racial access to union power.* New York: Free Press.
Griswold, E. N.
1964 *Law and lawyers in the United States.* London: Stevens.
Gusfield, J. R.
1958 Equalitarianism and bureaucratic recruitment. *Administrative Science Quarterly* **2:** 521–541.
1963 *Symbolic crusade: Status politics and American temperance movement.* Urbana: Univ. of Illinois Press.
Habermas, J.
1970 Technology and science as "ideology." In *Toward a rational society.* Boston: Beacon Press.
Hall, O.
1946 The informal organization of the medical profession. *Canadian Journal of Economic and Political Science* **12:** 3–44.
Hamilton, R., and J. Wright
1975 Coming of age—a comparison of the United States and the Federal Republic of Germany. *Zeitscriff für Soziologie* **4,** 4: 335–349.
Harbison, F., and C. A. Myers
1964 *Education, manpower, and economic growth.* New York: McGraw-Hill.
Harding, Alan
1966 *A social history of English law.* Baltimore: Penguin Books.
Hargens, L., and W. O. Hagstrom
1967 Sponsored and contest mobility of American academic scientists. *Sociology of Education* **40:** 24–38.

Harno, A. J.
   1953 *Legal education in the United States.* San Francisco: Bancroft-Whitney.
Hartz, L.
   1964 *The founding of new societies.* New York: Harcourt.
Havemann, E., and P. S. West
   1952 *They went to college.* New York: Harcourt.
Havighurst, R. J., ed.
   1968 *Comparative perspectives on education.* Boston: Little, Brown.
Hechter, M.
   1974 The political economy of ethnic change. *American Journal of Sociology* **79:** 1151–1178.
Hess, R. D., and J. Torney
   1967 *The development of political attitudes in children.* Chicago: Aldine.
Hirsh, P. M.
   1972 Processing fads and fashions: An organization-set analysis of cultural industry systems. *American Journal of Sociology* **77:** 639–659.
Historical Statistics of the United States
   Washington, D.C.: U.S. Government Printing Office.
Hodge, R. W., P. M. Siegel, and P. Rossi
   1964 Occupational prestige in the United States, 1925–1963. *American Journal of Sociology* **70:** 289–302.
Hofstadter, R.
   1948 *The American political tradition.* New York: Knopf.
   1963 *Anti-intellectualism in American life.* New York: Random House.
Hofstadter, R., and W. Metzger
   1955 *The development of academic freedom in the United States.* New York: Columbia Univ. Press.
Holland, J. L., and R. Nichols
   1964 Prediction of academic and extra-curricular achievement in college. *Journal of Educational Psychology* **55:** 55–65.
Hollingshead, A. B.
   1949 *Elmtown's youth.* New York: Wiley.
Holt, J.
   1964 *How children fail.* New York: Dell.
Hoselitz, B. F.
   1965 Investment in education and its political impact. In *Education and political development,* edited by J. S. Coleman. Princeton, New Jersey: Princeton Univ. Press.
Hughes, E. C.
   1949 Queries concerning industry and society growing out of the study of ethnic relations in industry. *American Sociological Review* **14:** 211–220.
   1958 *Men and their work.* New York: Free Press.
Huntington, S. P.
   1966 Political modernization: America vs. Europe. *World Politics* **18:** 378–414.
Hurst, W.
   1950 *The growth of American law.* Boston: Little, Brown.
Husband, R. W.
   1957 What do college grades predict? *Fortune* **55:** 157–158.
Husen, T., ed.
   1967 *International study of achievement in mathematics.* New York: Wiley.

Illich, I.

1970 *Deschooling society.* New York: Harper and Row.

Jackson, E. F., and H. J. Crockett, Jr.

1964 Occupational mobility in the United States: A point estimate and a trend comparison. *American Sociological Review* **29:** 5–15.

Jackson, E. F., W. S. Fox, and H. J. Crockett, Jr.

1970 Religion and occupational achievement. *American Sociological Review* **35:** 48–63.

Jacob, P. E.

1957 *Changing values in college.* New York: Harper.

Janowitz, M.

1960 *The professional soldier.* New York: Free Press.

1968 Military tactics of promotion. In *Organizational careers,* edited by B. G. Glaser. Chicago: Aldine.

Jencks, C., and D. Riesman

1968 *The academic revolution.* New York: Doubleday.

Jencks, C. M. Smith, H. Acland, M. J. Bane, D. Cohen, H. Gintis, B. Heyns, and S. Michelson

1972 *Inequality: A reassessment of the effects of family and schooling in America.* New York: Basic Books.

Jepsen, V. L.

1951 Scholastic proficiency and vocational success. *Education and Psychological Measurement* **11:** 616–628.

Johnson, B. C.

1968 The democratic mirage: Notes toward a theory of American politics. *Berkeley Journal of Sociology* **13:** 104–143.

1976 Taking care of labor: The police in American politics. *Theory and Society* **3.**

Jones, M.

1960 *Immigration.* Chicago: Univ. of Chicago Press.

Karabel, J.

1972 Community colleges and social stratification. *Harvard Educational Review* **42:** 521–562.

Katz, M. B.

1968 *The irony of early school reform.* Boston: Beacon Press.

1971 *Class, bureaucracy, and schools.* New York: Praeger.

Kehoe, M.

1949 International cooperation as a human problem. *Human Relations* **2:** 375–380.

Kelley, J. L., and M. L. Perlman

1971 Social mobility in Toro. *Economic Development and Cultural Change* **19:** 204–221.

Kennedy, R. J. R.

1952 Single or triple melting pot? Intermarriage in New Haven, 1870–1950. *American Journal of Sociology* **58:** 56–59.

Kerr, C., J. T. Dunlop, F. H. Harbison, and C. A. Myers

1960 *Industrialism and industrial man.* Cambridge, Massachusetts: Harvard Univ. Press.

Kornhauser, W.

1962 *Scientists in industry: Conflict and accommodation.* Berkeley: Univ. of California Press.

Kotschnig, W. M.

1937 *Unemployment in the learned professions.* London: Oxford Univ. Press.

Kozol, J.

1972 *Free schools.* New York: Bantam.

Ladinsky, J.
    1963 Careers of lawyers, law practice, and legal institutions. *American Sociological Review*
    28: 47–54.
    1967 Higher education and work achievement among lawyers. *Sociological Quarterly* **8:**
    222–232.
Laumann, E. O.
    1969 The social structure of religious and ethno-religious groups in a metropolitan commu-
    nity. *American Sociological Review* **34:** 182–197.
    1973 *The bonds of pluralism.* New York: Wiley.
Learned, W. S., and B. D. Wood
    1938 *The student and his knowledge.* New York: Carnegie Foundation for the Advance-
    ment of Teaching.
Lenski, G. E.
    1958 Trends in intergenerational occupational mobility in the United States. *American
    Sociological Review* **23:** 514–523.
    1963 *The religious factor.* New York: Doubleday.
    1966 *Power and privilege.* New York: McGraw-Hill.
    1971 The religious factor: Revisited. *American Sociological Review* **36:** 48–50.
Levy, B. H.
    1961 *Corporation lawyer: Saint or sinner?* Philadelphia: Chilton.
Liebow, E.
    1967 *Tally's Corner.* Boston: Little, Brown.
Lipset, S. M., and R. Bendix
    1959 *Social mobility in industrial society.* Berkeley: Univ. of California Press.
Lombard, G. F.
    1955 *Behavior in a selling group.* Cambridge, Massachusetts: Harvard Univ. Press.
Lukacs, G.
    1971 *History and class consciousness.* Cambridge, Massachusetts: M.I.T. Press.
Lyman, S. M.
    1972 *The black American in sociological thought.* New York: Putnam.
Lynd, R.S., and H. M. Lynd
    1929 *Middletown.* New York: Harcourt.
Main, J. T.
    1965 *The social structure of revolutionary America.* Princeton, New Jersey: Princeton Univ.
    Press.
Mann, C. R.
    1918 *A study of engineering education,* Bulletin 11. New York: Carnegie Foundation for the
    Advancement of Teaching.
March, J. G., and H. A. Simon
    1958 *Organizations.* New York: Wiley
Marrou, H. I.
    1964 *A history of education in antiquity.* New York: New American Library.
Marsh, R. M.
    1963 Values, demand, and social mobility. *American Sociological Review* **28:** 567–575.
Martin, N. H., and A. L. Strauss
    1968 Patterns of mobility within industrial organizations. In *Organizational careers,* edited by
    B. G. Glaser. Chicago: Aldine.
Mason, S. F.
    1962 *A history of the sciences.* New York: Collier.

McCarthey, J. D., and W. L. Yancey
1971 Uncle Tom and Mr. Charlie: Metaphysical pathos in the study of racism and personal disorganization. *American Journal of Sociology* **76**: 648–672.

McCauly, S.
1966 *Law and the balance of power: The automobile manufacturers and their dealers.* New York: Russell Sage Foundation.

McCurdy, C.
1976 *Stephen Field and judicial conservatism.* Unpublished Ph.D. thesis, Univ. of California, San Diego.

McEvedy, C.
1972 *The Penguin atlas of modern history.* Baltimore: Penguin Books.

Mechanic, D.
1968 *Medical sociology.* New York: Free Press.

Merton, R. K. A. P. Gray, B. Hockey, and H. Selvin, eds.
1952 *Reader in bureaucracy.* New York: Free Press.

Metzger, L. P.
1971 American sociology and black assimilation. *American Journal of Sociology* **76**: 627–647.

Michels, R.
1949 *Political parties.* New York: Free Press.

Miller, G. A.
1967 Professionals in bureaucracy: Alienation among industrial scientists and engineers. *American Sociological Review* **32**: 755–767.

Mills, C. W.
1963 *Power, politics, and people.* New York: Oxford Univ. Press.

More, D. M.
1968 Demotion. In *Organizational careers,* edited by B. G. Glaser. Chicago: Aldine.

Morgan, Edmund S.
1966 *The puritan family.* New York: Harper and Row.

Murdock, G. P.
1959 *Africa: Its peoples and their culture history.* New York: McGraw-Hill.

National Assessment of Educational Progress.
1975 *National assessment and the teaching of English.* Urbana, Illinois: National Council of Teachers of Education.

Newcomer, M.
1955 *The big business executive.* New York: Columbia Univ. Press.

Noland, E. W., and E. W. Bakke
1949 *Workers wanted.* New York: Harper.

North, D.
1961 *The economic growth of the west, 1790–1860.* Englewood Cliffs, New Jersey: Prentice-Hall.

Nosow, S.
1956 Labor distribution and the normative system. *Social Forces* **30**: 25–33.

O'Connor, J.
1973 *The fiscal crisis of the state.* New York: St. Martin's Press.

Oliver, R., and J. D. Fage
1962 *A short history of Africa.* New York: New York Univ. Press.

Olsen, M. E.
1970 Social and political participation of blacks. *American Sociological Review* **35**: 682–697.

Orum, A. M.
    1966 A reappraisal of the social and political participation of Negroes. *American Journal of Sociology* **72:** 32–46.
Parsons, T.
    1939 The professions and social structure. *Social Forces* **17:** 457–467.
    1966 *Societies: Comparative and evolutionary perspectives.* Englewood Cliffs, New Jersey: Prentice-Hall.
Peaslee, A. L.
    1969 Education's role in development. *Economic Development and Cultural Change* **17:** 293–318.
Perrow, C.
    1963 Goals and power structure: A historical case study. In *The Hospital in Modern Society,* edited by E. Friedson. New York: Free Press.
    1965 Hospitals: Technology, structure, and goals. In *Handbook of Organizations,* edited by J. G. March. Chicago: Rand McNally.
Perrucci, C., and R. Perrucci
    1970 Social origins, educational contexts, and career mobility. *American Sociological Review* **35:** 451–463.
Perrucci, R., and J. Gerstl
    1969 *Profession without community: Engineers in American society.* New York: Random House.
Pierson, F. C.
    1959 *The education of American businessmen.* New York: McGraw-Hill.
Pilcher, D. M.
    1976 *The sociology of income distribution.* Unpublished Ph.D. thesis, Univ. of California, San Diego.
Platt, A. M.
    1969 *The child savers: The invention of delinquency.* Chicago: Univ. of Chicago Press.
Plunkett, M.
    1960 School and early work experience of youth, 1952–1957. *Occupational Outlook Quarterly* **4:** 22–27.
Potts, D. B.
    1977 "College enthusiasm!" as public response, 1800—1860. *Harvard Educational Review* **47:** 28–42.
Price, D. K. de S.
    1969 The structure of publication in science and technology. In *Factors in the transfer of technology,* edited by W. H. Gruber and D. R. Marquis. Cambridge, Massachusetts: M.I.T. Press.
Price, P. B., J. M. Richards, C. W. Taylor, and T. L. Jacobsen
    1963 Measurement of physician performance. Report presented at American Association of Medical Colleges, Second Annual Conference on Research in Medical Education.
Rashdall, H.
    1936 *The universities of Europe in the middle ages,* revised edition. London: Oxford Univ. Press.
Rayack, E.
    1967 *Professional power and American medicine: The economics of the American Medical Association.* Cleveland: World Publishing Company.
Reader, W. J.
    1966 *Professional men, the rise of the professional classes in nineteenth-century England.* New York: Basic Books.

Rehberg, R. A., W. E. Schafer, and J. Sinclair
1970 Toward a temporal sequence of adolescent achievement variables. *American Sociological Review* **35:** 34–48.

Riesman, D.
1958 *Constraint and variety in American education.* New York: Doubleday.

Ripley, W. Z., ed.
1916 *Trusts, pools, and corporations.* Boston: Ginn.

Rogoff, N.
1953 *Recent trends in occupational mobility.* Glencoe: Free Press.

Rosen, G.
1963 The hospital: Historical sociology of a community institution. In *The hospital in modern society,* edited by E. Friedson. New York: Free Press.

Rosenbaum, J. E.
1976 *Making inequality: The hidden curriculum of high school tracking.* New York: Wiley.

Rosenberg, H.
1958 *Bureaucracy, aristocracy, and autocracy.* Cambridge, Massachusetts: Harvard Univ. Press.

Roy, D.
1952 Quota restriction and goldbricking in a machine shop. *American Journal of Sociology* **57:** 427–442.

Rudolph, F.
1962 *The American college and university.* New York: Knopf.
1978 *Curriculum.* San Francisco: Jossey-Bass.

Schachner, N.
1962 *Medieval universities.* New York: A. S. Barnes.

Schnabel, F.
1959 *Deutsche geschichte im neunzenhnten jahrhundert,* volume 1. Freiburg: Verlag Herder.

Schultz, T. W.
1961 Investment in human capital. *American Economic Review* **51:** 1–16.

Schuman, H.
1971 The religious factor in Detroit: Review, replication, and reanalysis. *American Sociological Review* **36:** 30–48.

Scott, J. F.
1965 The American college sorority: Its role in class and ethnic endogamy. *American Sociological Review* **30:** 514–527.

Selden, W. K.
1960 *Accreditation.* New York: Harper.

Sewell, W. H., A. O. Haller, and G. W. Ohlendorf
1970 The educational and early occupational status attainment process: Replication and revision. *American Sociological Review* **35:** 1014–1027.

Sewell, W. H., and R. M. Hauser
1975 *Education, occupation, and earnings.* New York: Academic Press.

Sexton, P. C.
1961 *Education and income.* New York: Viking Press.

Shafer, H. B.
1936 *The American medical profession, 1783 to 1850.* New York: Columbia Univ. Press.

Sharp, L. M.
1970 *Education and employment.* Baltimore: Johns Hopkins Press.

Sherwin, C. W., and R. S. Isenson
1967 Project hindsight. *Science* **156:** 1571–1577.

Shryock, R. A.
    1947 *The development of modern medicine.* New York: Knopf.
    1966 *Medicine in America: Historical essays.* Baltimore: Johns Hopkins Press.
Simon, H. A., H. Guetzkow, G. Kozmetsky, and G. Tyndall
    1954 *Centralization versus decentralization in organizing the controller's department.* New York: Controllership Foundation.
Skolnick, J. H.
    1966 *Justice without trial.* New York: Wiley.
Smigel, E. O
    1964 *The Wall Street lawyer.* New York: Free Press.
Soderberg, C. R.
    1967 The American engineer. In *The professions in America,* edited by K. S. Lynn. Boston: Beacon Press.
Solomon, B.
    1956 *Ancestors and immigrants.* New York: Wiley.
Southern, R. W.
    1970 *Western society and the church in the Middle Ages.* Baltimore: Penguin Books.
Spady, W. G.
    1967 Educational mobility and access: Growth and paradoxes. *American Journal of Sociology* **72:** 273–286.
Srinivas, M. N.
    1955 Sanskritization. In *Social change in modern India.* Berkeley: Univ. of California Press.
Stack, S.
    1976 *Inequality in industrial societies: Income distribution in capitalist and socialist nations.* Storrs, Connecticut: Unpublished Ph.D. thesis, Univ. of Connecticut.
Statistical Abstract of the United States
    1966, 1971, 1972, 1976 Washington, D.C.: U.S. Government Printing Office.
Stone, K.
    1975 The origins of job structure in the steel industry. In *Labor market segmentation,* edited by R. Edwards, M. Reich, and D. Gordon. Lexington, Massachusetts: D. C. Heath.
Stookey, B. R.
    1962 *A history of colonial medical education.* Springfield, Illinois: Thomas.
Strauss, G., and L. R. Sayles
    1960 *Personnel.* Englewood Cliffs, New Jersey: Prentice-Hall.
Struik, D. J.
    1962 *Yankee science in the making.* New York: Collier Books.
Swift, D. W.
    1971 *Ideology and change in the public schools: Latent functions of progressive education.* Columbus, Ohio: Charles E. Merrill.
Taussig, F. W., and C. S. Joslyn
    1932 *American business leaders.* New York: Macmillan.
Taylor, C. L., and M. Hudson
    1972 *World handbook of political and social indicators.* New Haven, Connecticut: Yale Univ. Press.
Tewksbury, D. G.
    1932 *The founding of American colleges and universities before the Civil War.* New York: Teachers College Press.
Thapar, R.
    1966 *A history of India.* Baltimore: Penguin Books.

Thernstrom, S.
1964 *Poverty and progress: Social mobility in a nineteenth-century city.* Cambridge, Massachusetts: Harvard Univ. Press.
Thomas, L.
1956 *The occupational structure and education.* Englewood Cliffs, New Jersey: Prentice-Hall.
Thomas, W. I., and F. Znaniecki
1918 *The Polish peasant in Europe and America.* Chicago: Univ. of Chicago Press.
Thurow, L. C.
1975 *Generating inequality.* New York: Basic Books.
Torrance, E. P.
1964 Education and creativity. In *Creativity,* ed. by C. W. Taylor. New York: McGraw-Hill.
Trow, M.
1966 The second transformation of American secondary education. In *Class, status, and power,* second edition, edited by R. Bendix and S. M. Lipset. New York: Free Press.
Turner, R. H.
1960 Sponsored and contest mobility and the school system. *American Sociological Review* **25:** 855–867.
1964 *The social context of ambition.* San Francisco: Chandler.
U.S. Bureau of the Census
1972 *Current population reports: Consumer income 1972.* Washington, D.C.: U.S. Government Printing Office.
United States Civil Service Commission
1976 Annual report of federal civilian employment.
U.S. Department of Labor
1967 Special Labor Force Report No. 83: Educational Attainment of Workers, March 1966.
United States Equal Employment Opportunity Commission
1977 Equal employment opportunity report.
Useem, M., and S. M. Miller
1975 Privilege and domination: The role of the upper class in American higher education. *Social Science Information* **14:** 115–145.
Valentine, C. A.
1971 Deficit, difference, and bicultural models of Afro-American behavior. *Harvard Educational Review* **41:** 137–157.
Vesey, L. R.
1965 *The emergence of the American university.* Chicago: Univ. of Chicago Press.
Waller, W.
1932 *The sociology of teaching.* New York: Russell and Russell.
Warner, W. L., and J. C. Abegglen
1955 *Occupational mobility in American business and industry 1928–1952.* Minneapolis: Univ. of Minnesota Press.
Weber, M.
1946 The protestant sects and the spirit of capitalism. In *From Max Weber: Essays in sociology,* edited by H. Gerth and C. W. Mills. New York: Oxford Univ. Press.
1951 *The religion of China.* New York: Free Press.
1952 *Ancient Judaism.* New York: Free Press.
1958 *The religion of India.* New York: Free Press
1961 *General economic history.* New York: Collier.
1968 *Economy and society.* New York: Bedminster Press.

Wechsler, H.
    1977 *The qualified student: A history of selective college admission.* New York: Wiley.
Wegner, E. L.
    1969 Some factors in obtaining postgraduate education. *Sociology of Education* **42:** 154–169.
Weinstein, A.
    1943 *Pharmacy as a profession in Wisconsin.* Unpublished M.A. thesis, Univ. of Chicago.
Wesman, A. G.
    1968 Intelligent testing. *American Psychologist* **23:** 267–274.
White, D. M., and R. L. Francis
    1976 Title VII and the masters of reality: Eliminating credentialism in the American labor market. *Georgetown Law Journal* **64:** 1213–1244.
White, H. C.
    1970 *Chains of opportunity: System models of mobility in organization.* Cambridge, Massachusetts: Harvard Univ. Press.
Whyte, W. F.
    1943 *Street corner society.* Chicago: Univ. of Chicago Press.
Wickenden, W. E.
    1930 Report of the investigation of engineering education, 1923–1929, Volume I. *Journal of the Society for Promotion of Engineering Education.*
    1934 Report of the investigation of engineering education, 1923–1929, Volume II. *Journal of the Society for Promotion of Engineering Education.*
Wiebe, R. H.
    1967 *The search for order: 1877–1920.* New York: Hill and Wang.
Wilensky, H. L.
    1956 *Intellectuals in labor unions.* Glencoe, Illinois: Free Press.
    1961 The uneven distribution of leisure. *Social Problems* **9:** 32–56.
    1964 The professionalization of everyone? *American Journal of Sociology* **70:** 137–158.
    1968 *Organizational intelligence.* New York: Basic Books.
Wilensky, H. L., and J. Ladinsky
    1967 From religious community to occupational group: Structural assimilation among professors, lawyers, and engineers. *American Sociological Review* **32:** 541–561.
Wolfle, D.
    1954 *America's resources of specialized talent.* New York: Harper.
Wolfle, D., and J. G. Smith
    1956 The occupational value of education for superior high-school graduates. *Journal of Higher Education* **27:** 201–232.
Woodward, J.
    1965 *Industrial organization.* London: Oxford Univ. Press.
Zbrowski, M.
    1969 *People in pain.* San Francisco: Jossey-Bass.
Zilboorg, G.
    1941 *A history of medical psychology.* New York: Norton.
Zola, I. K.
    1966 Culture and symptoms: An analysis of patients presenting complaints. *American Sociological Review* **31:** 615–630.

Index

221